The Golden Collection 2

WORLD YOGA CONVENTION 2013

GANGA DARSHAN, MUNGER, BIHAR, INDIA

23rd–27th October 2013

The Golden Collection 2

A collection of original publications from the Bihar Yoga Tradition

Yoga Publications Trust, Munger, Bihar, India

First published as *Satyam Speaks* 1961 by Satyananda Publication Society; *Words of Satyam* 1962 and *Satyam Speaks Part II* 1963 by International Yoga Fellowship; *Discussions on Yoga* 1974 by Bihar School of Yoga.

Published by Yoga Publications Trust
First edition 2013

ISBN: 978-93-81620-51-9

Publisher and distributor: Yoga Publications Trust, Ganga Darshan, Munger, Bihar, India.

Website: www.biharyoga.net
www.rikhiapeeth.net

Printed at Aegean Offset Printers, Greater Noida

Dedication

In humility we offer this dedication to
Swami Sivananda Saraswati, who initiated
Swami Satyananda Saraswati into the secrets of yoga
and to our guru Sri Swami Satyananda Saraswati
who continues to inspire and guide us
on our spiritual journey.

Swami Niranjan

Contents

Preface

In the early 1970s and 1980s, the devotees of Sri Swami Satyananda carefully printed and published his lectures, discourses and class transcripts in small booklets, preserving and disseminating these important teachings. The booklets were their first contribution to their guru's mission of 'spreading yoga from door to door and shore to shore'. For many years these gems from the past have been out of print and unavailable. On the occasion of the Bihar School of Yoga's Golden Jubilee 2013 celebrations, these lost works have been compiled into a set of volumes aptly named *The Golden Collection*, so that once again the classic words which launched a yoga movement can inspire spiritual aspirants around the world.

In reproducing the booklets the original language has been kept intact, conveying the flavour of the time. The language shows the care that Sri Swami Satyananda took to make his teachings clear to his audience, never compromising clarity for fashion or style. His ability to present and adjust any topic to any audience is proof of the versatility which enabled him to convey his deep understanding of the potential of yoga to meet the needs of all.

A pioneer of his time, Sri Swami Satyananda gave a new dimension to the practice of asana, stating clearly that it can take the practitioner far beyond physical wellbeing. He often guided his disciples through letters brimming with snippets of wisdom, which are as valuable and pertinent today as they were almost fifty years ago. *The Golden Collection* also includes a systematic introduction to the various meditation practices expounded by Sri Swami Satyananda. No step is missed and no precaution left out, allowing the aspirant to safely travel the journey of yoga and spiritual life. For each practice, whether antar mouna, ajapa japa or nada yoga, precision and clarity are the key. The branches of yoga are concisely elucidated, making them relevant to the daily life of each yoga aspirant.

Much that is taken for granted today was unknown or misunderstood at that time: it is the great achievement of Sri Swami Satyananda to have brought yoga to the general public and mainstream of society, truly making yoga a household word the world over.

The extraordinary quality of his being and spiritual attainments was recognized early in his life. While living in Rishikesh in the ashram of his guru, Swami Sivananda Saraswati, the young swami received glowing appreciation and admiration from guru-bhais, visitors and guests. To this day, tributes continue to express love and a sense of profound gratitude from all who have been touched by this modern day saint and his teachings. Sri Swami Satyananda, however, remained a disciple throughout his life and fulfilled his guru's mandate by making it his life's mission.

The Golden Collection is a true testimony to the wealth and depth of yoga and to its master exponent, Sri Swami Satyananda. In his early teachings he set the tone, purpose and aim of his mission. The reader is able to discover and connect with the roots of Satyananda Yoga, whilst appreciating its evolving contemporary nature, a trademark of this tradition.

Indeed, Sri Swamiji's prophecy, "yoga is the culture of tomorrow", has come true. His tomorrow is our today.

Words of Satyam

Extracts from letters of Satyam to a brother and sister

Swami Satyananda Saraswati

Yoga Publications Trust, Munger, Bihar, India

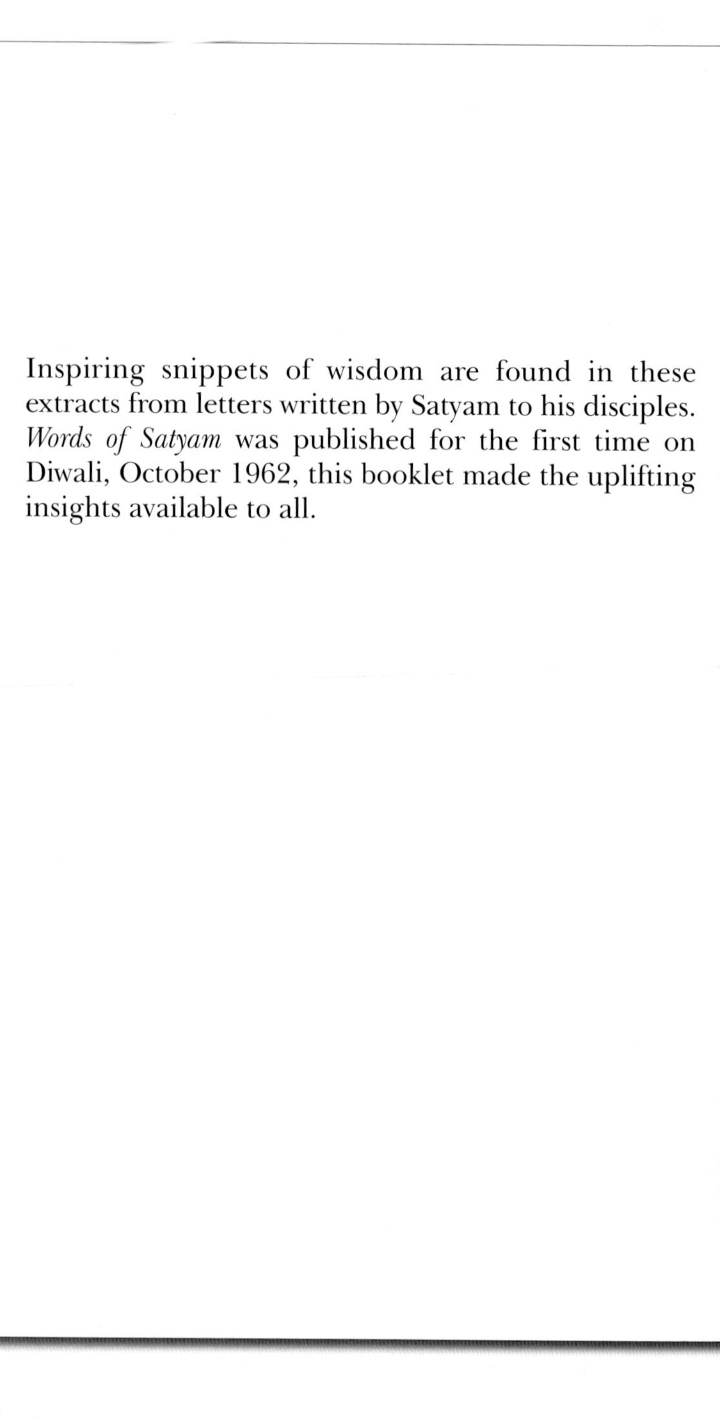

Inspiring snippets of wisdom are found in these extracts from letters written by Satyam to his disciples. *Words of Satyam* was published for the first time on Diwali, October 1962, this booklet made the uplifting insights available to all.

SATYAM – *who has humility of the great and greatness of the humble*

Preface

This little booklet comprises thoughts culled out at random from the letters of Gurudev to my sister and me. The words of Satyam are words in which eternal meanings and messages unfold themselves continuously. In these pages, one may say, greatness defines itself.

Satyam is a man with a mission. His mission is to construct a community of men whose culture is yogic, whose activities and modes of life are governed by the laws of yogic discipline, and informed by the essential knowledge of yoga. Satyam's personality acts like a philosopher's stone on those who go to him and transmutes the base metal of their beings to glorious gold of self-lucent awareness. In more ways than one, Satyam is the hope of mankind.

Man, it is said, has one foot in the finite and another in the infinite, and is torn asunder between these two worlds. Status quo in such position could only mean suffering to extinction. Satyam show we could emerge whole, unscathed, glorious, into each of these spheres. Yoga is a bridge through which man passes from finite to infinite.

—Bhai

Our Satyam

In the confusing labyrinth of unawareness, I heard a lingering cry. Bewildered and awed, I realized that the cry emanated from the deep, hidden recesses of my soul. It was the cry of my own inner self. But why this agony? Basking in the luxuries of life, revelling in the comforts of the world, what was it that I lacked? There commenced in me a ceaseless self-analysis which I tried hard to make impartial and objective. But self-analysis has misled many an old and many a wise man. How could I expect to acquire this confusing knowledge in a correct way? I was restless. I yearned for real knowledge and meaning of life. There were many learned teachers to solve the mathematical problems, but there was no one to understand my need and help me solve the puzzling problems of life.

I met a sannyasi – Satyam, they called him. Strong, serene, ever smiling and understanding. "I know you, but I want you to know what you are," he told me. He seemed to know my thoughts before I became aware of them, to divine my emotions before I felt them. He answered those questions which were just struggling to articulate in me. And all this happened after I had met him only twice! Then he went away, engrossed as usual in the work of his mission. I wondered whether in his over-busy mind I would ever have a place, but he did not forget. He immediately started sending me gifts of wonderful letters. He also wrote to my brother who became his ardent admirer much before he had even seen him. Every letter of Satyam brought knowledge and peace. Life took a new turn. The time which used to go by listlessly assumed a new urgency. The secrets of life opened up and we began feeling that life was a benediction.

It does not take Satyam half the life of a person to make him experience the power and glory of life. Satyam works miracles in minutes. He somehow brings up a deeper consciousness of life in you. He is dynamic and determined. Words like 'rest', 'lethargy', 'postponement' and 'delay', have no place in his dictionary. For him everything has to be immediate – ekdam! One has to run breathlessly to keep pace with him. I have spent some glorious days in his company and have never stopped wondering at his magical ways with which he transforms a person.

The works and wonders of Satyam cannot be described in a nutshell. One has to be with him to realize the glory that he brings to the lives of those who go to him. One goes to him for the solutions to selfish, personal problems, but the enormous work of Satyam's mission with which he overwhelms one's entire being, makes one forget the self, the epicentre of all conflicts. This, according to Satyam, is truly the only way to experience the fullness of life and to be able to 'live', not merely exist.

—Bahen

If you become what you wanted to, you will always remain restless. Real, eternal peace will descend upon you only if you become what He wants you to become. Always pray to the Almighty to make you aspire for your real aim.

* * *

You have to change – entirely, fully and wholly. The topsy-turvy centre of gravity will have to be shifted. Replace your aspirations. Think anew. Act anew. Talk in a new way.

* * *

A great time has already elapsed. Golden days of youth are flying away. Do you mean to offer unto Him an old, withered flower? Hurry up! Hurry up! Find out yourself. Rest in Him.

* * *

Prosperity, victory are your slaves,
Peace and happiness your birthright,
Infinitely powerful is your soul.
So, stand up my hero and walk forth!

* * *

You may not know what you are. I know it very well. At times, I think over this mysterious phenomenon, as to why one becomes unaware of one's own capacities.

* * *

A golden time of opportunities has been ignored because of the lack of true knowledge of your own self. Years and years have been wasted. So much has to be done! You cannot afford to sleep any longer. Wake up my child, and be up and doing. Help me to mould your life. Work hard. Inaugurate a better chapter of your life.

* * *

Let me tell you that human life is full of funny jokes. One complains of the lack of opportunities, but do you know how many times enlightenment comes and knocks at your door but returns disappointed, finding you in the sleep of unawareness? Understand this and rise above these funny jokes of life.

* * *

The world is a play of the mind. The mind creates various feelings. It gives shape to shapeless things. The mind alone attaches importance and also annihilates it. Annihilate the mind, and lo! The world is no more a real theme.

* * *

The mind plays havoc. It is the mind which is a veritable seat of pleasure and pain. Actually, events in life haven't got their own significance. It is the mind and the mind alone which attaches importance to those events in life.

* * *

The mind moves objects. The mind creates death. The mind moulds the life. The mind is a congregation of attitudes.

* * *

The mind cannot rest. Therefore, one should engage it in higher activities. The idle mind begets errors. The busy mind creates tensions. Only the sublimated mind gives rest.

* * *

The mind can be trained by *vairagya*, detachment, and *abhyasa*, studies. Realization of transitoriness is vairagya. Ceaseless meditation is abhyasa.

* * *

Yoga is not an ancient myth buried in oblivion; it is the most invaluable inheritance of the present. It is the essential need of today and the culture of tomorrow.

Yoga is not meant only for the bearded old rishis. It is the correct way of life, particularly for the modern youth, for yoga teaches the wandering mind discipline. It channels the aimless waves of thought.

I earnestly wish parents to realize the necessity of yogic discipline for our young generation, to ensure a clean atmosphere in minds and society.

* * *

Everything of this world with all its glories and beauties, prosperity and pomp is nothing in comparison to the eternal peace of *atma*, the soul. And no tragedy or anguish can disturb such divine peace.

* * *

Go in and search for real peace. Go in and find out the pearl of bliss. No, not outside! Not in the fulfilment of your whims, cravings, desires. Futile search, dear child! Go in every now and then, like a moneyed passenger who feels his pocket every now and then.

* * *

Peace, like the kingdom of heaven is within you. It is enveloped by cravings and hankerings of a dissipated nature. As one digs for diamonds, or fathoms the sea for pearls, one goes into the inner recesses of oneself to attain peace. Peace comes by attaining harmony between your external and inner selves.

* * *

Worry not about your temperamental weaknesses. Proceed with speed towards the goal of the noble ones.

* * *

Emotions which we imagine we feel are not enduring emotions. We are apt to imagine things in ourselves which have no existence within us. Maybe imagination is a natural function of the mind, but surely daydreaming and indulgence in fancies are not inherent functions of our mind.

A developed man dreams and has visions; an undeveloped man just daydreams and is purblind.

*　　*　　*

Preserve and protect your emotions in order to be given to Him, who is the only deserving recipient. Waste not the emotions upon this street! May your mind run up to your Lord!

*　　*　　*

So far, you served the world with your emotions. What, after all, did you get? You know it too well! Try these emotions for Him. Sing before Him! Weep only for Him! Eat in order to live for Him! Become sad because of the separation. Become unhappy just because you are away still. In short, use every emotion for Him, only for Him, and you will be blessed with divine grace.

*　　*　　*

Spiritual life is absolutely an inner process of 'no thinking' by following a method of 'blissful thinking'.

*　　*　　*

Thinking too much over anything is not a solution. The solution lies in not thinking about it. There are many things in life which are solved by stopping all activities of body and mind. There are many things in life which become knotty problems by trying to solve them. My experience is that most of the things would go smoothly if only we stopped wishing for them.

*　　*　　*

Think less. Work more. Talk less. Remember Him at all times. Constant *nama smaran*, repetition of His name, will give you health and peace. Make every day the beginning of a fruitful era of your life.

*　　*　　*

Repeat His name from deep within you. Remember Him as your dearest. Spend no moment in vain. Realize Him here and now. You are born to become a perfect human being. Assert your birthright. Be a humble offering at His feet. Take pledge that you will realize Him, see Him!

* * *

You will not forget that you, too, will be spiritually born. Your spirit is in the womb of sadhana. Light will shine. Knowledge will dawn.

* * *

Your inner soul was never born. It is plugged with eternity. Beyond birth and death, disease and old age, stands your atma, soul. Birthday indicates the manifestation of the physical body, whereas the soul, your inner ruler, is quite different from the body and its group.

* * *

Real birthday is the day when the spiritual self emerges from beyond and overpowers the entire being from every side. Real birthday is the day when divine virtues take birth within ourselves, and make us happy and peaceful. Real birthday is the day when old samskaras have died, giving birth to religious zeal.

* * *

Let your finite soul merge in the infinite ocean of lordly love. Let your mental separateness dispel in the light of meditation on one Lord. That alone will be your real birthday.

* * *

We are far, very far from our beloved God. That is why we are confused in the wilderness, and lost in the labyrinth of the world.

* * *

Long, long ago you were separated from Him. Since then you have been an aimless bird, weeping and laughing, suffering and singing, living and dying again and again. So, do as I say. Come back to reunite with Him!

* * *

Your Swan is wandering, separated from waters, which is its original abode. Discover your real home, which is situated in the Land of Dhyana, otherwise known as Kailash.

* * *

If this jungle were your home, you divine Swan, why did you feel unrest all along? If this condition of life were your home, why did you aspire for something unknown all along? For it is not your original nest at any cost!

So, may I ask you to look up towards a life which is undying; towards a nest, which is eternal? So, may I ask you to tune your soul to the song that is divine?

* * *

The search and the craving of the soul have continued for ages. The unrest continues also. The inability to realize the goal brings numerous pains and pangs, and ignorance brings sufferings. The strange thing is that true knowledge lies hidden within this erring self!

Your soul is in quest of something. It knows not what exactly it seeks. It will not rest, until it has realized itself.

* * *

There is something greater than this world. There is something more valuable than this life. There is something more exquisite than that what you have seen so far.

* * *

Never forget that you are born for a greater purpose. Your soul is powerful. Your samskaras are divine. Be up and doing.

I shall always be with you. You might wonder, but the fact is this, that I am, wherever you dear children feel me.

* * *

The thing that is essential is meditation. Let your time, some of it at least, be spent in japa, meditation and prayers. You will experience ineffable joy and peace. Only then all confusion will cease. Regular meditation will not only give you mental peace, but it will bestow upon you physical health also. Please note down this truth.

* * *

Let me explain the different words, like japa and dhyana, to you.

To repeat the mantra any number of times is japa. It is a form of worship.

To conceive His form mentally is dhyana.

To lay down inner emotions at His feet is prayer.

Pooja means worshipping Him by means of kirtan, bhajan and meditation.

Sadhana means setting the mind right, so that the light of God is seen directly.

Realization is a spiritual experience of God in meditation. It is a direct experience. Even as you meet your friend, likewise you realize your eternal friend.

Realization of God dawns upon man, when his mind has merged in ishta devata, during meditation.

* * *

Sincere and loving prayer will unify your mental tendencies and make you fit to receive the divine experience and light.

* * *

Yes, you are going to acquire His darshan. Life is given to you to achieve this aim. You are sure to manifest Him before you. Undoubtedly, you are going to perfect dhyana. Only keep the zeal alive and the practice regular.

Every moment is blissful! The entire life is an expression of the Divine! Radha, Mira, Gauranga, Surdas – may all of them inspire you. They are your ideals.

* * *

You have already stepped forward towards a divine pilgrimage for perfection, peace and purity. I am showing you the way. There are many more with you on this road. You are not alone. In your pilgrimage to perfection, you will never be alone.

* * *

The pilgrim is marching on and on upon the road of life, headed for the land of peace. There are many bypasses leading towards wilderness, confusion and many pitfalls of passion, anger and greed. You must know it well!

* * *

A guru does not merely help his child in spiritual matters only, but his help can be commanded – yes, not requested but commanded at every step of life. You can ask for my help and advice at any time for anything. This is my duty, my mission. I shall be thrice blessed, if I can help those who need and seek. I know that sometimes a little sincere guidance from the one who understands can destroy many self-invited frustrations and remove the imaginary layer of weakness in a man and bring out to the light the power that is there in every soul.

You might consider yourself the weakest one but I know you well. I am sure that by uncovering the superficial layer of *ajnana*, ignorance, you can also work wonders in the world. I know the fact and I am confident about those who sincerely wish to walk on the road to knowledge and enlightenment.

* * *

I understand your Bahen well. I know that one who cries knows too well its cure when she is honoured with the duty of curing them. I know that one who knows how to feel sad, broken and unhappy, also knows the way out. And I know she will do that, which I am doing now.

* * *

Make your spiritual aspirations sincere and keen. Resolve to keep the spiritual march uninterrupted. Dive deep and connect your soul with the Lord.

* * *

The path of sadhana is flooded with immense light of happiness and bliss. Pooja, prayer and meditation will lead you to a greater and richer part of life.

* * *

The inner soul is full of unsullied *ananda*, ecstasy. It is homogeneous ananda and *masti*, intoxication, irrespective of all events and moments. This inner ananda is your real nature. You can experience it in *dhyana*, meditation.

* * *

When you meditate, feel that He is in front of you, in you and everywhere. Remain merged in Him like Mirabai and Gauranga. Let every fibre of your heart cry aloud for Him, yearn for His darshan. Let every thought of yours run after His *sumiran*, repetition of His name. Live with Him! Be with Him.

* * *

There is nothing greater than sadhana. Nothing else can give you indestructible peace. Nothing can give you freedom from pain and agony except dhyana.

Human nature is dictated by the mind. The mind is controlled by thoughts. Thoughts are born of desires. Desires are born of ignorance. Cut every root of ajnana, ignorance, by sadhana, and you shall see your entire nature converted into saintliness and strength.

* * *

The superficial layer of ignorance will have to be removed by incessant practice. In the course of time, your real nature will express itself in all its glory.

* * *

If you keep your zeal alive and love for God unshaken, I am very much sure that you will gradually become inwardly receptive to the vibrations of spiritual inspiration. As and when your external person will be consumed by the inner pervasiveness of introversion, you will distinctly commune with your inner person.

* * *

Merge your mind and person in your *ishta*, god. Lo! You will see the real Self clearly. Every wonderful and thrilling secret of the Self will be unfolded for you if only you surrender yourself completely to your ishta.

Your inner self is the witness of your mind and its activities. Your inner self is the witness of your dreams and sleep. Don't you feel that someone is observing the dream affairs? Don't you feel that someone is aware of your process of thinking? Don't you feel that someone is aware of your physical existence? Behind all experiences of life, you will realize that someone is observing them from somewhere. Once you dive deep in meditation, you will come to see that witness of all affairs. That is self-awareness.

* * *

None can remain totally unaware. Realization is a part of our destiny. Spiritual evolution will terminate in supramental flights. Man will become superman. There is no other way than this.

* * *

I know that in all, including you, there is a store of infinite *ananda*, ecstasy, *shakti*, power, and *shanti*, peace. Let all tap the source. Let all go in through the passage of dhyana. And lo! They will come face to face with the eternal truth!

* * *

You have in you the capacities to dive deep within. Put off your superimposed mental cloaks of desires, prejudices, complexes, self-consciousness and brooding with the help of sincere and impartial self-analysis. Most important of all – let the constant remembrance of 'that' aim be the focal point of your consciousness.

* * *

Interrogation and rationalism are stepping stones to critical self-analysis. One who never asks questions, never gets answers, and the riddles of life remain unsolved. Doubt implies a desire to know, a will to understand, and a capacity to learn.

* * *

It is very easy to suffer from superiority complex and inferiority complex at the same time. But such an attitude is very confusing to the mind and harms mental balance a lot. You must become a stranger to superiority complex for it is very misleading. And at the same time refrain from inviting inferiority complex. No man is perfect here. Everybody is trying to become complete and perfect. So, I say, overcome these complexes and forget mental acrobatics. All that you have to do is to become a good seeker.

* * *

You have to go on building the material side of life, which is essential for bringing normality to life and also for bringing success in sadhana. But at the same time do not forget to take care of your spiritual side. Or, I may say, material advancement can very well accept spiritual enlightenment.

* * *

Religious life does not kill the emotional side of man. It is only a safety valve. Emotions are safe there, only to emerge when the proper atmosphere exists. Religion provides this safety through sublimation. If needed, sublimation can turn into vairagya. In normal cases, sublimated impulses can be re-channelled towards a happy emotional life.

* * *

Yes, what isprimitive should be dislodged. It is a simple matter of commonsense. Anything that is painful for our soul should be sensibly renounced. It is not difficult for the one who is determined.

* * *

True, you are saying that spiritual life presupposes a sense of aim, a devotion to higher discipline, a constant examination of oneself, purification of one's mind and development of serviceability, affection and competence in life, but you are talking about someone who has already become perfect, which none of us are and which each of us wants to be. You have in mind the thought of the goal, but what you have to bear in mind is the way to reach that goal. Do not forget that it is on the way that one finds many bypasses and many pitfalls! Many get lost on the way. Only a few reach the goal of perfection and realization.

* * *

You can very well say for anyone that he has not realized, but you cannot say that he is not spiritual. The consciousness of not being spiritual is just the consciousness of the urgent need of spiritual orientation.

* * *

Spiritual life or realization or perfection, as you call it (and I agree with your idea of a spiritual being), is not a joke, nor is it something like a university degree. Spirituality starts from that blessed hour when the lowest in us begins to strive, either positively or negatively, for the highest and noblest; and it culminates when one becomes unmindful or unaware of the highest or lowest. That is *jivanmukti*, salvation.

* * *

A spiritual personality should be above the trifles of life, master of low and high tides of emotion, a mountain of intelligent patience. But the fun is that nobody has the required strength to assimilate these virtues in practice.

There comes a day in everyone's life, when one truly becomes intelligent and great. Keen aspiration, sincere attitude and deep enthusiasm are the things which count for this.

* * *

Again a mistake. You write that nothing can change your destiny. You are wrong: *ekdam*, entirely, wrong. This is the same rigid faith which tightens the grips of destiny. Believe me that you can be free from it and you are an amendment in the rigid books of destiny.

Please correct yourself, child, in order to help me to help you, and then go on with your work.

* * *

Good that you are studying and working hard to make a good career for yourself. Go ahead with all the capacities at your command. I am sure those who work hard and never lose heart will rise very high in life. Greatness is never far from intelligent, honest and hardworking people. I am forever with those who have wedded industry to intelligence.

* * *

No drawbacks in you. And if there be any, I think you should not divert your intellectual mental and spiritual energies to that end. Instead, think of heading forward on material and spiritual planes. If you keep on reflecting and brooding over your drawbacks, be sure, you are going to lose the golden chances which pass by you from time to time.

* * *

He, who is ever conscious of his defects and drawbacks, so also in a wrong way, may turn into a hysteric or monomaniac. I do not ask you to err, I am just lifting unnecessary weight people put over the past and its tragedies and comedies, graces and disgraces. Yes, in order to take speed, one has just to run, run and run! That is all. Misfortune unsurpassed if one looks back and reflects. This is the point where we lose the most profitable game.

* * *

I believe in the laws of nature and the streams of thought motivated by that law. In this sense, I am said to constitute a total departure from the religious beliefs, which the majority of people hold so fervently. What I know is that actions are guided by motives, motives by instincts, instincts by the laws of evolution and evolution by the laws of a cosmic type of nature, which again derives its power of execution from the fountainhead, the Almighty God. Such is the trend of events in this vast universe, where you two, Bhai-Bahen, are perhaps not even a speck. How then can I dare to hold you responsible for faults, if any?

* * *

You two ask for my forgiveness for your shortcomings and faults. The question of forgiveness does not arise at all in my case, for I do not believe anyone to be at fault. Fault! It is beyond my conceptions and acceptances.

* * *

You can never dismiss my attention to you, consciously or unconsciously. Whether I receive regard or disregard, I do not care. I keep on hammering upon the truth of life and law.

* * *

Wherever I may be, I assure you, that you will be with me. It may not be physically. Nor do we need it. There is something more valuable and lasting than this physical sheath. I shall spare no effort to inspire you from any physical distance.

* * *

Please realize that your life is an expression of a great mission we have undertaken, and every act you do is for the mission. Dedicated and devoted souls never separate. They are bound and interlinked by a great purpose in life. It is our mission that spiritual ideals may hold the reins of the human race and conduct the world in a better and peaceful manner. For that we work together. You will not forget that you have an enlightened future.

* * *

Regarding Bahen – she has in her all those qualities, which help one to realize the gifts of higher life, in a very short time. I know her difficulties and agonies. She too knows them. I know her physical disabilities. A guru understands his disciple well.

Let her get down into the chamber of the inner being, in her purest, natural and noble form, and all her troubles, disabilities and agonies will dwindle into airy nothing.

May she meditate! May she live and move for her fulfilment! My blessings are always with her.

* * *

I am greatly impressed by your noble and divine inclinations. Believe in it that there is in you a divine potency. You are very much different from the normal type of children, who just walk upon this imperfect and perishable earth, and try to see no more the vistas of a more perfect and richer and fruitful and nobler life. This much of realization at present will suffice for you to keep your march to your goal – the Kailash – steady.

* * *

You say you are an ignorant child. Good! God loves those who are innocent and simple. Be constantly aware of Him as a child is of its mother, and never forget to reflect on His glories.

* * *

Try to give everything unto Him, when you sit for His worship. Constant japa of mantra will unfold the inner spiritual powers. It will intensify your affiliation with your preceptor. Remembrance must be in you always, without exception.

* * *

Let the worldly friends come. You remain consumed by the spiritual awareness of your beloved God. Talk to your friends physically. Let His name be constantly in your inner being. Gradually the name will become your spiritual comrade.

Even as a mother talks to so many persons about so many affairs, still retains in her inner mind the awareness of her sweet little child, likewise mix with all and still retain the remembrance of your God all throughout. Constant remembrance of His glory must become your very nature, even as constant thinking has been our nature so far.

* * *

Repeat the *nama*, name, mentally all throughout. Look within. Contact inner happiness. You will be able to be aware of the name and aim throughout day and night.

Revive your spiritual zeal every day.

Revise your resolves.

You must get spiritual light.

* * *

Life in constant prayer is a veritable blessing to such a one who is undergoing a nature-designed penance. For, it will not only make one free from the pains, it will show one more of the glories of God which are hidden inside one's inner chamber.

* * *

Man in his march to godhood comes across various phenomena which his own nature designs for him. Disease is one of those phenomena.

* * *

Usually, man curses his lot for having suffered miseries and pains, and thus drags on a hellish existence. His every attempt then is to get rid of the pains of life by any possible method next to hand, which only results, in repetition of the cycle of sufferings.

* * *

Once I thought deeply about the reason and the origin of pain of every nature and dimension. The conclusion that I reached was this. It is the *swabhava*, nature, of the body and mind to expel the useless but stored-up matter from it by any easy and possible means. I think that this theory is perfectly in tune with the view of our modern psychology.

Body and mind receive a lot of stuff from time to time and that gets piled up in the system, which, when in excess or very heavy to carry, is expelled by the system in the form of disease and agony.

* * *

We do everything to look after our physical comforts but we have neglected the inner requirements of our soul, which as human beings, we have developed in a natural course. That requirement was a spiritual mission in my case. That requirement can be anything in every individual, but the gist of it is, fulfilment of all that I want'. Yes, it is that alone.

* * *

We want fulfilment of our inner desires, desires which are unknown and unshaped, and in primitive and scattered dimensions. These peculiar and unknown forces of *vasanas*, inner desires, express themselves in all great achievements from national leadership to sainthood, if properly channelled; in disease, agony and frustration, if misunderstood and not attended to.

* * *

The negligence and misunderstanding of the longings of the soul are universal. There is hardly one man who is attending correctly and impartially to the requirements of his inner being. And the one who has done it has become something in life.

* * *

Life is an easy course of music, or life is a strenuous day of happy sports or a sleepless night at a dance party. There is only this much in life which has life, a first and eternal melody. The rest is only a process of self-gratification and self-satisfaction.

* * *

Life is a huge machine which can get jammed for want of a small spring. Even an insignificant deposit of carbon can cause choking. Wise ones are careful about minor events.

* * *

Man is helpless before the inevitable. The inevitable must happen. This realization comes with a harsh blow to everyone upon this earth at different times. There are moments when he stands, helpless and sad, doing nothing by the side of death, he cries and laments. Of what use is vanity or self-confidence of a man at such a time?

* * *

Karmas done in previous births bear fruits. The seed which is sown becomes a tree and bears fruits in the end. So, an individual has to suffer for the past deeds. This is the law. Biological, physical and psychological sufferings have a cause. Good results and bad ones have a previous cause.

The quick fruit-bearing tree will have to be hewn down. The seed will have to be destroyed. Previous *karmas*, actions, will have to be balanced, firstly, by spiritual merger of the mind in God; secondly, by the attainment of God in person.

* * *

To abide by the laws of karma yoga is an uphill task, but surely not an impossible one. The karma yogi goes his way through small day-to-day happenings. The test lies in trying the attitude of a man towards daily problems, severe and ordinary. The one who can detach himself from the exciting effects of joyful events and from the maddening effects of sorrowful events is a karma yogi in the true sense of the word, for he has offered all that he had at His feet. For such a man prayer does not mean His remembrance for a few routine minutes but it means the offering unto Him his whole, full life. For him then, life itself becomes a constant prayer.

Make your life a constant prayer by dedicating yourself to karma yoga.

* * *

Your principle should be this, to work splendidly for whatever you have before you at that particular time. There is only one thing you have to keep in mind. 'Not to mind, not to give a mind and not to be mind-minded', which every intellectual is. Remember always to give more and more of your time to the work at hand. Every immediate work is important. To abide by this principle is not as easy as many would think of.

* * *

You write that you are neck-deep in the sea of work. Let me understand it the other way. You are considerably free from the 'uchhal kood', the jumping jacks of the mind.

Blessed is he who is always neck-deep in work. Thrice blessed is he who has lost himself in the work. Unto such a man dynamism will be given. Rest? We do not need it at all!

Work? We need it very badly. Work of any virtue does purify the soul. Work saves the soul. It confers immunity from evil influences. Work awakens willpower. It paves a way towards the 'line of intuition'.

* * *

Work is rest. Rest is work. Change of work is rest. Be ever dynamic. Pray before you retire at night and when you inaugurate the day. Dedicate your life to a greater purpose.

* * *

Remember one thing – in future, when you become something in life, please do not forget to use everybody's energy without exception. This is the only thing you will have to keep before your mind in order to make yourself a tremendous success. One does not succeed merely by intellect or purse or dynamism or competence. A sure way to success is to put everyone to the yoke.

* * *

Your life will not be allowed to go in vain. Your powers will not be wasted. Your capacities will not remain condemned. Satyam will pull you on, drag you further, push you forward, even if you are lazy and passive. And imagine, how much can be done, if you strongly decide, surrender, feel and say, "Here I am, given to thee. Lead me anywhere!"

* * *

One request – you have to resign everything in toto. You have to stop desiring, wishing, brooding. 'Thy will be done; I have nothing to say', this should be your attitude. If you are able to shift everything here, I assure you, the best happiness will be waiting for you.

* * *

I do not mind your weaknesses and shortcomings. I do not care for any other thing. I want to know whether you will work hard or not. Your future is in the making. Your life is being carved. Obstructions are there. Remain unmindful. Offer your sincere attitude and hard work. It is not enough, if you call yourself as my child. You have to work ceaselessly and be indifferent to results.

* * *

In order to receive, assimilate and mobilize the divine blessings, what one has to do is to plunge in ceaseless activities, well-sustained and supported by confidence and faith.

* * *

Whether you are well in body or mind, I do not worry. I want to see you lost in regular, systematic work. No half measures are allowed! You must not forget the noble duty entrusted to you by me. You must dedicate yourself to this common cause of ours. I need you. You have to be aware of me and my mission. Can you tell me that you cannot?

* * *

Please shake yourself from slumber. Years have been wasted in unawareness. So much has to be done. I want work containing your sweat and sleep. I do not care what you feel about it. What I aim at is that you must do something I need from you. If you feel that you can keep on sleeping even now, you are entirely wrong. I know the way to put you on the anvil. I have this much of faith in myself that I can work through you. Your entire attention should be fixed towards this noble side. You must work for me and my mission for as long as I want it. Your abilities and talents should become manifest. I am all the while aware of you; see that you are too.

* * *

My children, who said that you do not deserve my love, affection and protection? If anyone says so, he is utterly and entirely wrong. I do not care whether one is dedicated to me or not. What I care for most is your wellbeing, material and spiritual both blended in each other. I am sure that I have a lot of place for you in my inner chamber. I have never felt like withdrawing the love and affection which I feel for both of you.

* * *

You have joined us in our humble task we have chosen for ourselves. It is a matter of delight to me to have a competent worker in you, about which you are not yet sure. We constitute one family, a large family indeed, to which you have now been introduced. You have become a dear member of the family. Welcome!

* * *

We are one family. We are trying to increase our dimensions and scope. On some bright day we shall be a huge family with improved visions and affectionate frictions. Noble and sacred ideals and actions will frame this family. Even as many men and women in the past lived together and performed sacrifices and offered oblations into the holy fire, likewise have we to meet and perform good acts and contribute our share of spiritual efforts to keep the fire of righteousness and happiness in ourselves ever lit. This is the fulfilment of the spiritual mission of which I am a visionary, not a leader.

* * *

The aspirations of those working for the same mission should be common; so be their slogans of life, so be their meetings all throughout, so be their endeavours in this field of life, and so be the diversity in life, for honest differences do not mar the rhythm and interrupt the melody, but add to the orchestration of life.

* * *

Look around yourself. You will find that everyone is wrapped up in their own self. Nobody goes out of this self to help others who are plunged in misery and suffering. To forget this narrow-minded outlook is a part of our mission. I am very much sure about our mission's great services to humanity. Those who sincerely intend to plunge in this sort of work will never bother about how. I have faith in those revelations, which inspired me for the establishment of this mission. I have faith in my inner voice.

You are there, Bahen is there, many others are there. Every inert stone will become a storehouse of dynamism. The pilot should be a yogi. The propeller should be a yogi. Every dead wire will become a good conductor of energy.

* * *

For a mission, a sort of definite outlook is required. I need all, young and old, for our mission. You will not believe me perhaps, but I assure you that the best way to bring instantaneous progress in ourselves is to live among the deficiencies of others! It is a fact that the mind is dormant at the time of watching its own defects but is quite alert at the time of watching others' defects. Here comes the sense of comparison and an urgency in us to be different from others, and thus gain praise.

* * *

I urgently want people with inadequate knowledge also. They will help others to gain knowledge quickly. I want critical observers in order to inspire my sleeping children. I want half-hearted devotees also to inspire others to long for full-hearted zeal and sincerity. Remember that Satyam will make use of every person who comes near his work and obtain mind, zeal, sincerity and everything else we should need for our mission. There will be many living examples of undying sincerity and enthusiasm. Yes, it must happen. Everybody's resources should be tackled.

You say that we lack good workers. Please do not worry about that. Every institution of this selfless kind, must suffer for want of sincere workers in the beginning. Moreover, every new work has to face triangular fights in order to become a straight-forward motion. Even if we have no workers, let us not worry. We are working, at least I am working, in the name of God and by His unseen inspiration.

*   *   *

I do not doubt my workers at all who, though not saints, are at least normal human beings. The greatest quality which success in a mission demands is what you have rightly pointed out – certitude about the mission and joyousness in working for it.

Of course, we should infuse the mission with a fitness to survive, but how? It is a burning question which every movement had to answer and which none could, so far as I know from history. Have the movements of Buddha and Christ survived? How has Hinduism survived?

*   *   *

The essential thing for us at present is to keep our movement aloof from the interferences and interests of politics, and also from the masses for some time, and watch with patience its unpopular or less popular progress solitarily carried out by its dedicated and devoted workers. I am quite clear about the values of survival needed for any movement.

*   *   *

I do not aspire to see humanity not differing, not quarrelling, not fighting. I only aspire to see that all of us believe in unity, peace, love and cooperation – in all that is good. I aspire to see the dream of man fulfilled.

*   *   *

I am not hopeless about anyone. I have a clear-cut vision of every condemnable stuff of today. Really speaking, there is nothing like de-spiritualization. Every act is an expression of atma, the soul, heading towards the pinnacle of evolution. The moment we are hopeless about a person or an object, we are frustrated and we are interrupted on the road to progress and peace. I believe in change, yes, change from the first to the next. And therefore, you should always have an optimistic and dynamic attitude.

* * *

Regarding meditation – you want things to come like leaves to the trees, while it is like water being pumped upstairs. This is the way, but in the beginning of course. Normally, the mind is running towards senses. One has to, by dint of sadhana, withdraw it inside, and ultimately go beyond its compass.

* * *

Meditation is more difficult than it is thought. It needs efforts, not exerting however. It is rendering the mind stuff subtler, keener and pointed, which it usually is not.

* * *

Life in meditation and prayer, coupled with total detachment, will lead one to a greater field of dynamism, wherein one will be able to manifest oneself in all beauty and grace, power and peace.

In as much as disease and frustration are the lower expressions, power and peace are the higher manifestations of the inner man. I have chosen the highest manifestations and ask others to choose the same, and I ask you too to choose it.

* * *

What is disease and what is suffering which we mortals suffer from? Is it atonement for our beginningless sins, which, however, I do not know or believe in, or is it a process of evolution of the soul, or is it just an invariable and essential physical concomitant?

My humble but incessant observances have brought me to this understanding, that diseases and the like are milestones to peace and perfection.

* * *

Diseases have their origin not in the body or mind, but in the inner cravings of the soul, which, in almost every case, are hidden from the outer observances of the individual. The cravings of the soul, when fulfilled, keep one fit and when neglected would expel through a form of disease, agony or frustration.

* * *

After all, disease is a transitory phase of the body. It is not permanent. What is permanent and of abiding value is *shanti*, the inner peace, the dynamic state of flawless happiness and bliss, which is immortal and eternal.

* * *

Untamed passion is a deadly poison. Untamed thoughts turn into obsessions in the vacant hours of rest. The mind is the stuff, seat and soul of evil thoughts. The ceaselessly occupied mind gradually loses the habit of delving in lower planes. One should, therefore, plan life with ceaseless engagements of engrossing nature. This is the beginning of sadhana.

* * *

After going through prolonged ceaseless engagements one becomes fit for devotion and capable of assimilating the truth of sadhana. Here he starts with sublimation by giving an upward push to his mental stuff. This is the second phase of sadhana.

* * *

Those who are sincere about sadhana and selfless about its results make great strides in the world of sadhana. For such a seeker, life becomes a field of endless work. He does not even find time to remember his own self. He becomes a constant source of joy to everyone. He works for others' happiness even at the cost of his own, regardless of his own hurts and troubles. So, I say, it is better to aspire for sincerity in word, thought and deed, which is a much more difficult task, before aspiring for success in sadhana.

* * *

To blend the melody of life with the melody of sadhana is a great achievement. The one who reaches this difficult goal is surely a hero. But this is possible only if one is able to transcend the normal abnormalities of day-to-day life and dealings. One needs immense power of resistance for this. Prayer is the resistance, for prayer fortifies the self.

* * *

People start to work for a mission with enthusiasm and sincerity alright. In the beginning, their aims and ideals are quite outspokenly high. But mostly they end in acquiring vanity and amassing self-deceit. Their precious time is then lost in empty boasts about their 'high-selves' and little-understood spirituality. Beware my child, of deception. It is very easy to suffer from self-deceit and become victims of vainglory while you are on the threshold of the world of sadhana.

* * *

I need your selfless hard work, though of course, no compliments will you ever receive from this end, nor even complaints. The work is yours – ours. We are laying the foundation of a spiritual mission; now every brick and every effort is welcome. Spiritual thoughts will certainly find a way into the minds of seekers.

* * *

God needs faith, implicit faith and unquestionable faith. Such faith is a sure answer to all queries. It is never blind. Rather it helps the blind to walk with eyes in the dark.

* * *

I am thine. I am in thee. We are one. There is a common essence, which underlies our existence. Bodies are many.

Minds are many. Soul is one, like a thread interpenetrating numerous beads.

* * *

My *ashish*, blessings, to you. Remember that you are going to be mobilized for a greater cause and greater happiness. Greater is your future, a future, which only a few can claim for. Every bit of your talent has to be recognized. Your usefulness will be unanimously accepted by many.

* * *

Regarding Bhai. I am always with him. Yes, he is brilliant, bright, honest and good. He deserves all blessings. Verily, God has appointed him to do good to humanity. Seek his help at all times. Be his help also. Bahen is a 'pavitra rakhi' (she herself is the pure bracelet of thread that sisters tie to the wrists of their brothers to give them strength and courage). Be a good sister to him. Help him to maintain mental balance. I know you can do that. He has a great duty to fulfil. He must maintain sincerity and determination. He must be calm and thoughtful.

* * *

I am here as a whip, a controller, a reminder. It is my sacred duty to see that you ply the boat of your lives well. I want to frame your destiny in such a way so that you reach your goal without any unnecessary mishap.

This will be as a token of my deep regards and total attention for your singular devotion.

* * *

I am ever conscious about you. You should remember that everybody in this world can betray and misunderstand, but guru can never. To me you are only a little child. I have never been able to consider you as a grown-up.

* * *

Please be clear in this respect that you are quite different from what you have seen of you in your physical covering. Body and mind are limited and are liable to perish at any time. Nothing physical or mental in anyone is permanent. Beyond all that the normal eyes can see, there is in everyone something else. It is possible to affiliate yourself to that something else during meditation.

Once you realize the value of sadness and momentary joy, you will never be swayed by the cyclones of experiences. Experiences which have a beginning rooted in a particular cause have an end as well. Experiences born of objects and men, impressions born of time and reason are bound to come to an end very soon. So the wise men do not mind these events. So the wise men care not for success or failure, weakness or strength, victory or defeat. So the wise men keep their mind unimpressed, untainted and unscathed at all the hours of life.

* * *

You write that your restless moments are always short-lived. Let me add that every mental phenomenon is short-lived, if one has the power of endurance and understanding. If one is just a little above that, then restless moments are not felt at all. I want you to climb up, a step higher at least. Then you will be immune to the charges of agreeable and disagreeable currents of life and love.

* * *

Sensations born of the normal experience of life trouble our mind only for the time being. They pass away like winter clouds, like the swift flowing waters of a river. Sad and vivifying experiences of life leave certain impressions upon the mind of those who are ignorant of this fact.

* * *

We have tender emotions. We get permanently influenced. At times of crisis one has to switch on to a nobler way of life to become normal and avoid havoc. One must never forget that for everyone, there will be a better time in life. The only thing to do is to plunge in engrossing activities which do not allow any free moments of vacillation to the shaky and unsteady mind.

* * *

Success and failure, life and death are minor accidents for one who has a greater future ahead. Criticism, failure, adversities, death and the like, when they come, come with a mission to mould the mind and personality. One knocks against a block only to become vigilant about the ditch ahead.

Never get depressed by passing phases of weakness. Weakness, sorrow and depression, all these are passing shows in the arena of life. Spiritual joy or ananda is the permanent factor of life.

* * *

Within ourselves beyond physical, mental and intellectual shores, there is a peaceful, diseaseless, deathless realm of ananda, ecstasy, which can be seen, felt and assimilated in the depth of dhyana.

* * *

In the realm of dhyana alone all pains end. There alone agonies are crushed. Let anyone go into that realm, and come out to tell me that what I claimed was wrong. I shall accept defeat. I shall accept the truth of his statement. I shall submit to his charges.

* * *

It is a true saying that if you cry, you cry alone. If you laugh, the world will laugh with you. So no tears, my child. The world will be the least impressed by them, and so shall I. I have dreamt the fulfilment of a great work through you. Do not waste mental energy for all and sundry. Conserve it. Who knows what is written in the books of fate! Please understand me, mission and yourself. There is nothing in the world that your well-developed willpower cannot give you.

*   *   *

If you feel you are an eyesore to others, then please understand that this is no punishment to you but to others. For whose eyesore are you? Theirs! Then they suffer. And if you suffer, then you are your own eyesore. When I say that I am an eyesore to them, actually I am an eyesore to myself.

*   *   *

Awareness of a heart-warming and sincere atmosphere is mental weakness. Candidates for unceasing joy must transcend this weakness.

*   *   *

Never be conscious of anyone's bitterness and coldness. For being thus conscious is a sure way of opening the way to others to intrude upon the peace of your inner chamber, which is your own sanctuary. You are not concerned with their ways of thinking and feeling. Do not let them be concerned with yours by being sensitively conscious of their ways of behaviour. Close the gates of your castle and dwell peacefully in it, keeping all intrusions away.

Let the tides come and go.
You remain tight and light.

*   *   *

Those who work ceaselessly and selflessly for a mission, and still are humble and sincere enough to be free of vanity can easily be called 'the wonders of this strange world'. Such well-trained and developed minds can surely work wonders in the dissemination of the spiritual gospel.

*   *   *

Love of God is a thrilling experience. It puts you in the state of unperishing ecstasy. To experience this, you have to be an embodiment of faith, endurance, patience and divinity. Be God-intoxicated!

* * *

God's helping hands in our day-to-day life work miracles. Let us behold His glory by day and meditate upon it by night!

* * *

You will have to tread the path which Mira undertook for herself. You will have to walk upon the path which Chaitanya walked upon. You will have to think in terms of God-realization. You will have to attain that stage anyhow. I understand you. You must dedicate sincerely.

* * *

Spiritual awareness is your heritage. That is your nature. Gold is gold, whether dormant in mines or ready with a goldsmith. That awareness will have to be experienced gradually. It is not a matter of days and months. The process is gradual, timed and regulated.

* * *

This world is a play of emotions and commotions. There is hardly anyone who is above these mental factors. When we review the past, we only find to our surprise that after all everything that we had cherished, carried no ultimate and abiding substance.

We are newcomers to this world. Many more things are waiting to enrich us from experiences of various natures. The mind wants something to linger over and after. It needs a prop. Giant men of psychology have also repeatedly hinted at this truth. There is no doubt in so far as the unseen truth is concerned that attraction and repulsion, *raga* and *dwesha*, are overwhelming every phase of existence. It is just a waste of time to expect something more from this world. This world is nothing but a whirlpool of raga and dwesha. I have it. You have it. They have it. Everyone without exception has it. There have been a few great men, who have been able to dominate these twin currents, but they are not many.

* * *

Great among men, Sri Ram, whom we directly identify with divinity, had to face the greatest calamities which can befall a man.

Greatest among men, Sri Krishna fought throughout his life right from the day he fell upon this mortal floor.

Yudhishthira, the great among the virtuous ones; Arjuna, the nearest of the Lord; Draupadi, the unforgettable heroine of the *Mahabharata*; what did they not face in their lives? Injustice, exploitation, oppression, scandal, exile and lastly the bloody war, where they lost all they fought for.

* * *

Life is a novel in which comedies are rare and tragedies very frequent and quite natural. It is a long story of various episodes. Neither free will of an egotist, nor predestination of a fatalist are true and loyal to the theme. What is true is the mind of the Author, who has written this life of yours, mine and others.

* * *

Desires, yes, desires cause actions and actions cause experiences. Experiences beget new and fresh cravings. This is how this world proceeds. The wise one takes the maximum of the sweet experiences and the unwise loses the thrills of all sweetness in the repentance of the bitter acquisitions.

* * *

All that we long for and everything we hold dear or nasty in our heart and eyes will one day or the other pass away from us, and we shall be left alone just to witness the departure with indescribable emotions and pathos.

* * *

The first and the last truth that can be said about the life of all on this plane is this much: either one should pick up life from the dead or else one should be dead while alive. Either one should be happy perpetually amidst the sorrows of life, or else one should be sorry even when happiness crosses one on the way.

Live life in any way, but live it fully. There is no use in grieving over the rest of the people of the world.

* * *

There comes a glorious day in the life of all those struggling and striving for truth, when wisdom dawns and all that we longed for, for here and hereafter, seems an illusion and mesmerism of an expert conjurer. It might be too early for you to realize this absolute truth of saints and science, but the time must come when you should also be well established in the knowledge that 'vanity of vanities and all is vanity'. The fragrance of flowers, the thorn that pricked, the snake that bit and the nightingale that sang the sweetest lore – all, yes, all were a series of dreams, only to be realized after the slumber breaks.

And there comes a glorious moment when the eternal light illumines the entire arena and every bit of fear vanishes.

Always pray for that moment alone!

The clouds will dispel!
Darkness will depart!
Peace and Bliss will prevail!
May the One descend upon thee!

* * *

Epilogue

It is extremely difficult to fathom the depth of the ocean for the sake of finding a few pearls, no matter how precious they are. Only a rare few would do that. But it is very easy to admire and possess those pearls once they are out of the ferocious ocean. Almost all do this.

We are among those common human beings who wish to acquire the pearls without toiling for them. Our Gurudev Satyam is one of those rare beings who fathom the ocean of existence and find out the pearls of true wisdom and eternal knowledge just to gift them to us, the fortunate, though undeserving us. It is thus that this priceless treasure of his words has been collected. But will it do to keep it to ourselves, selfishly, and niggardly? Certainly not! Such words should echo in every human heart. Hence they have been presented to you in this book.

Do not think that this is the end. This, believe me, is just the beginning.

—Raksha

The price of this book is:
"Your eager interest and your vigilant understanding."

Satyam Speaks

Extracts from *Lessons on Yoga*: Letters to Viswaprem and Satyabrat

Swami Satyananda Saraswati

Yoga Publications Trust, Munger, Bihar, India

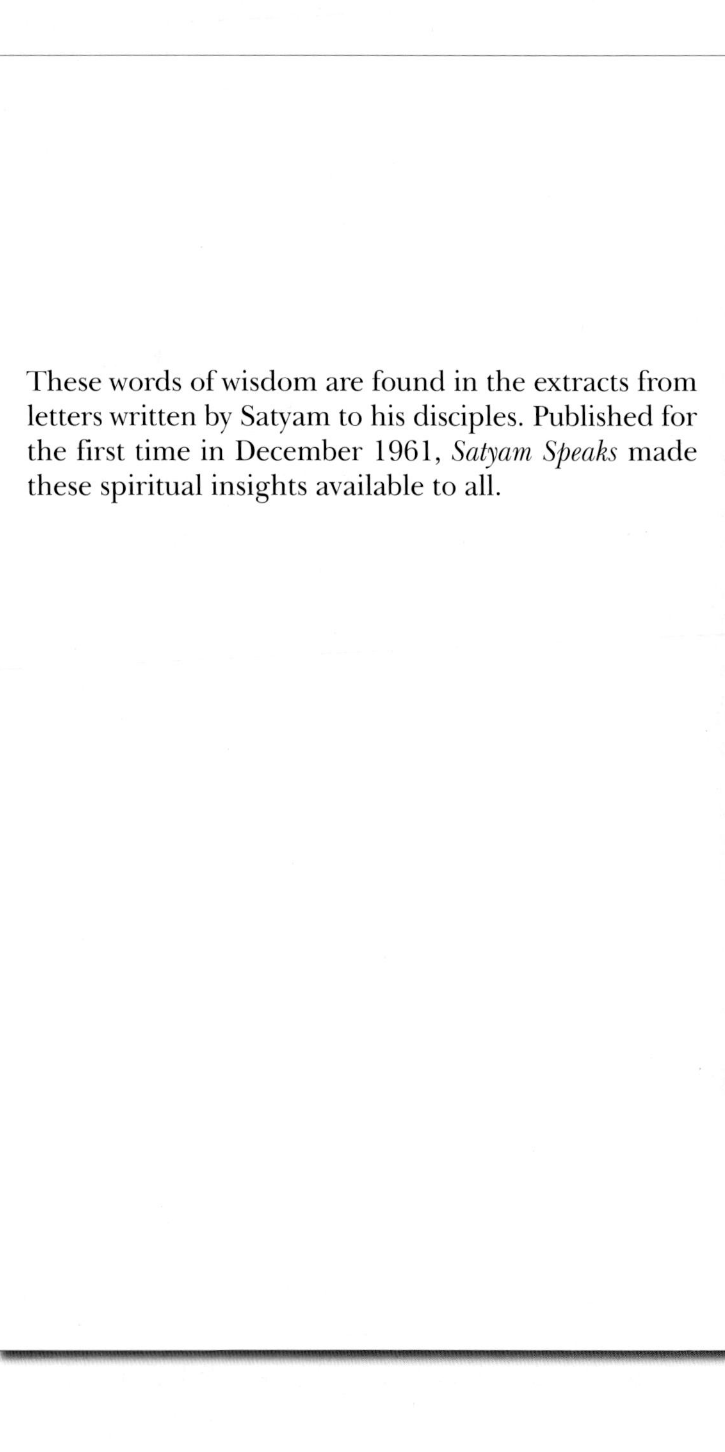

These words of wisdom are found in the extracts from letters written by Satyam to his disciples. Published for the first time in December 1961, *Satyam Speaks* made these spiritual insights available to all.

Swami Satyananda and Vishwaprem (Born: 16th July 1938, Diksha: 12th November 1958)

Swami Satyananda and Swami Satyabratananda
(Born: 26th June 1914, Sannyasa Diksha: 1967)

Yoga is a system of living with sense and science for the realization of ultimate values and altruistic missions of life. Yoga evolves a harmonious order in the mind, matter and man.

Yoga is an absolute departure from basic animal tendencies. Yoga is certainly renunciation of self-centrism and exploitation. Yoga is a state of aloofness from the artificialities of life and relationships.

Yoga is the culture of tomorrow.

—*Satyam*

A Few Words about Satyam

Satyam's ethereal life is one more assurance of the Divine to us that we, too, can make our lives sublime and lead ourselves to perfection through conscientious efforts. It shows clearly that no amount of distracting circumstances or no type of stifling environments can really arrest man's spiritual ascent.

This beautiful world of ours and this mystic life pulsating within us, incessantly remind us of the beauty and the mystery of the Divine, the realization of which could be the only justification for our living. So felt Dharmendra, Satyam's poorvashram name, born on 26th July 1923, in Almora, of rich, cultured parents, convent-educated, a literary prodigy and genius-in-making even in his Senior Cambridge days, when he left his fond home at the age of eighteen, impelled by this overpowering urge. For a full twelve years as an ashramite, Satyam did all sorts of work, from menial to mental and spiritual. By incandescent sadhana, he devoted himself to the task of continual demolition of the self and all the attributes that belonged to it.

Satyam's mission is to bring a spiritual awakening especially among the masses of Indian villages. So much has to be done there, from social service and reform to spiritual awakening. Satyam feels that in the lay village folk a spiritual renaissance could be touched off in which lies the only answer to the menacing, modern, Godless civilization. Satyam's mission is urgent and impatient of any procrastination. It is to disseminate, reinterpret and revive the order of true and eternal dharma and also to reawaken the dormant glories of spiritual sciences of ancient rishis.

And so, our Satyam is moving ceaselessly from place to place passing on the torch of knowledge, vanquishing atheism, doing social relief work on the material plane, and creating a new spiritual climate everywhere he goes.

—*Upen*

INVOCATION

Wake up, O Shiva, from within, from Kailash and dance on the bosom of thy Mansarovar. I know thee as my Shiva, as my inner-light. My Ram! Do thou descend upon thy children.

—*Satyam*

Days are flying away. You have wasted so many years in vain. Whether you are a father or a husband, you can walk upon this divine path. This path is not only accessible to a Brahmin or a sannyasin. Every sincere soul can start on his pilgrimage to peace and power. The path of God is the only path. The glory of God is the only glory. All else is transitory and evanescent.

*   *   *

Don't postpone the item of sadhana for old age. There is no guarantee that you will live for a hundred years. If there is a war in 1964, there is no surety of one's life. You cross the road; a motor truck overruns you. You talk to your friend; next moment you are down with a heart attack. Therefore, dear child, take to spiritual sadhana right now – this very moment.

*   *   *

Young age is the proper time to reap the divine harvest. While you are healthy, young, energetic and fresh, offer yourself unto Him. What is the use of offering an old, rotten flower, with no beauty and fragrance? Give Him your mind; give to the world the body. Give Him your soul; give to the world your hands and senses.

*   *   *

Life is wastage without God-realization. Youth is a waste without yoga. Intellectual achievements are futile without meditation. Prosperity is a curse without peace. Manhood is a mockery without brahmacharya. In short, you are dead without that eternal life.

*   *   *

What I want is to awaken thy soul. What I want of you is to realize thy prestige and glory. Thou are not a bundle of flesh and a bottle of blood. Thou art not a target of animal passion and a victim of romantic shows. Thou art not this physical body meant for exploitation. Thou art that spirit, which, when awakened, can move immovable mountains, bring the dead back to life, bestow sight to the blind and command nature. Never forget this great truth that thou art!

* * *

God is within you. The thing you want is already in you. It is outside also. But you will not get anything from outside. You will have to peep within in order to realize it.

* * *

Don't waste Sundays in socializing, 'chakkar-baji'. How many Sundays have been wasted so far! Use this day in mouna, japa and dhyana. Never give up japa. Let it continue along with concentration. Keep the mind calm, quiet and serene. There is no end to friendly invitations. Ye sadhaka, the destination is far, far, still far! Sail thy boat quickly. Don't waste even a single moment.

The aim of your life is self-realization. It is better to be born as a dog or a monkey than that man who leaves the world without realizing Him. What is the difference between such a man and an animal?

* * *

You will have to be sincere. You will have to give up hypocrisy. You go to temples and take His name twice a day. You feel as if you have discharged your duty towards God, while it takes you the whole day in discharging the duties towards your family and society. What a great pity!

* * *

It is not compulsory to sit at one place and take His name. On the other hand, your whole life must be dedicated to His awareness. Every act of yours must become His worship. Whenever you have time, merge yourself in His *sumiran*, remembrance, introvert your tendencies, peep within and experience joy.

* * *

Pain and pleasure may come your way. The clouds of calamities may eclipse your inner shrine. But with nothing should you barter the peace of your soul. He alone, who considers pain and pleasure as passing clouds and is always aware of his goal, will be really happy.

* * *

Neither in temples, nor by ringing the bells and blowing the conches, nor even by waving the arati and clapping the hands does one see Him; but verily it is love, a dynamic and creative type of love one holds and nourishes in his heart, by which he sees Him within as well as without.

* * *

Divine steps are mysterious. We, who are plunged in *avidya*, ignorance, cannot make out anything of His plans. To us, His plans seem to be whimsical and His orders beyond understanding. A bhakta has full faith in Him. He will accept His arrangements as a form of divine grace. A real devotee does not murmur, complain or grumble.

* * *

You are Gaya and Kashi. You have no other place for pilgrimage except your own atma. Awaken all *tirthas*, holy places, within yourself by realizing that atma.

* * *

Bhakti does not lie in renunciation. It is a limitless expression of one's all-round talents. Religion doesn't ask one to give up day-to-day duties. It only asks one to get rid of mental imbalance, moral evils and spiritual ignorance. Bhakti exhorts on ceaseless engagements from morning till night. Fie be upon that wretch, who underrates the value of work in the name of tyaga.

* * *

In order to realize God, one need not renounce home and join any ashram, nor need he wander hither and thither.

What exactly one needs is a guide, that is all. Further, one should strive under the guidance of his master.

* * *

If you can't realize and achieve the divine knowledge while you are at home, I can assure you that you can't do that anywhere else. The freedom, homeliness and security, which one enjoys at home, are absolutely absent in any ashram. Not only ladies, even males experience insecurity and an unhomely atmosphere there. A lot of artificiality comes in one's behaviour. None can realize God in an ashram, if he fails to do so at home.

* * *

Equilibrium is that quality when your Self has become a witness of all events. So long as you consider yourself a doer, you must enjoy as well as suffer the consequences.

* * *

Normal duties need neither be minimized, nor stopped. They do not come in the picture at all. When the atma is separated, then actions and mental workings do not bind the sadhaka. When the sadhaka brings in the bhava of instrumentality and considers himself working, thinking, and seeing at His will and for Him, then his mind is not at all affected. What one needs in cultivating vairagya, is to consider himself working at His orders, and remain ever balanced in thought, word and motions. This type of vairagya strengthens the powers of sadhana.

* * *

In fact, our sorrows and joys are nothing; our individual exaggerated fantasy makes them appear magnified a thousandfold.

* * *

Concentration is a faculty. This can be used in business, office, as well as elsewhere. Concentration helps in improving the personality of an individual. Concentration is a permanent aid to success in every sphere of life. It bestows keen insight and a ready reckoning intellectual capacity. It somehow acts as a potential medium to unearth occult treasures.

* * *

Karma yoga is a sublimated form of expression of suppressed passions.

* * *

You may go to temples and discharge all religious obligations as taught by your tradition, but that alone will not help you to unlock the secret chambers. At the best, they will maintain the brim of psychological conditioning. However much you may sit for pooja, please note that lack of concentration will render all your efforts futile. It is always best to aim first and then shoot. There is practically no use of shooting in the air.

* * *

Don't think of rest. To rest is to rust, nothing else but rust.

* * *

Do the best; leave the rest. Spare no effort. Care not for success and failure. Take care of your mental equilibrium. Remain as a *sakshi*, witness.

* * *

Pray unto Him in all love. Open your heart unto Him. Don't lock it with a big Godrej lock. Love is the key, which will help you to open the lock. It will open the door of the cage in which is enshrined the golden bird. The pathway towards it is sadhana. The strength to reach the cage is love. The key which opens the lock is concentration.

* * *

Let one remember Him as a lady would remember her precious golden necklace presented by her husband on the wedding night and which was stolen a few minutes back.

* * *

Bhakti is a divine gift; it is given by Him. Unfortunately, we have misappropriated the divine wealth in satisfying our worldly whims and fancies, passions and fashions. The gift of God, which is love, has been consumed by wife, children, property, kith and kin, name and fame. Thus man has lost the capital together with the interest. What remains with him now is a bundle of Reserve Bank notes; and that he, by the force of circumstances, offers to the Lord at Kedarnath as pooja. Now, let him withdraw the love from objects mundane, detach, and direct the same towards the Supreme Lord, attach. This is detach and attach.

* * *

Yes, do read the *Bhagavad Gita* whenever you get time. But, my child, this life itself is a never-ending-Gita. Study this wonderful life-Gita and put the same into practice.

* * *

Sakama bhakti is not inferior to nishkama bhakti. In the course of time, you will give up sakama bhakti of your own accord and start loving Him for the sake of love. Those who practise nishkama bhakti do not generally have so much of intense love. They are so dull and emotionless.

* * *

Work would become a source of happiness, if the spirit can recognize it as a stepping-stone towards the path of samadhi. Karma is an outlet to our mixed samskaras. Karma perfects our soul. It is a yoga or a method of self-control.

* * *

Surrender born of love is abiding and real.

* * *

Emotions make the senses behave unruly. Sensitiveness causes the mind to miss the judgment. Brooding destroys hard-earned self-confidence. Hatred pollutes the inner temple. Passions of all kinds persuade the jiva to undertake indiscriminate and feverish actions. Blessed be that man, who has turned his gaze, withdrawn his senses, dedicated his heart and started dhyana.

* * *

The sea tells a river, "Oh darling, if you want to become one with me, you will have to merge yourself in me and lose your individuality." In the same way, if you want to gain Him, you will have to take back all the attention you have given to the world and offer the same unto your Beloved.

* * *

We can change our lives by changing the mode of our thinking. As you think, so you become. Whatever you are today, is what you thought yesterday and what you will be tomorrow is what you think today. Surely a man becomes great not by anything, but by his *karma*, behaviour, and *swabhav*, temperament.

* * *

Give the gold to devil, but spare love and attention for Him. He is not in need of your gold, plantains or flowers. He is feeding infinite universes from that time. The only offering to be made unto Him is your attention and love. Unless you turn the gaze from the fleeting shadows and fading beauties, you can not expect redemption from sin and misery. Unless you turn the gaze from worldly pleasures and skin deep lust, how can you be happy and peaceful? How can you gain the best by slaying your own soul?

* * *

There is no 'kolahal', noise, in the world; there is no peace in the Himalayas! Both are within you.

* * *

Speak out everything unto Him. Ye, go to Him all naked and all empty. Though our Beloved Lord knows everything, still we have to tell Him in order to empty our minds of the filth. Place before Him all your defects and actions.

* * *

Prayer is a most effective medicine which won't cost you anything. Feel as if He is standing before you, you at His feet, kneeling down and saying unto Him all your troubles, karmas, accomplishments, emotions and worries.

* * *

Great difficulties confuse us. Clouds surround us all over. Criticism creates restlessness. But with all that if we sincerely take his name, adversities will pass away like winter clouds. We will be able to maintain high-rated stamina and a balanced mind. We will not be puffed up by prosperity, nor shall we be disappointed in forced austerities. Take this divine anaesthesia.

* * *

A home, where there is mutual peace, where husband and wife do not quarrel, where bitter taunts and harsh words are totally prohibited, where husband and wife respect each other at every step of life, where every family member knows to 'forgive and forget', where every affair is treated in a spiritual light, verily, that home is really a heaven on earth, a lovely divine garden laden with beautiful flowers of eternal fragrance.

* * *

Bring peace into your home. Keep the garden of family forever green and fragrant. Reorganize the scattered patterns of your home. Rebuild your house on the strong foundation of love, peace, unity and strength. Let every one of you have a different flute, let the tunes of all be the same. If everyone starts playing different tunes, there will be a mess. No bullet can really kill a man, as the tongue does it.

* * *

Let it happen, if it happens and as it happens. Never worry over anything. Events take their destined course automatically. You are not to break the head. You are just to cooperate with the plan.

* * *

Speak only when necessary. God has given you a soft tongue encased in two sets of strong teeth, for speaking always sweet. If you speak sweet, you will see that the person, who is incorrigible and who dislikes you, will be drawn to you as if by a magnet. You do not realize this great secret. When a person is calm and quiet, he becomes powerful and attractive. He can bring the others under control very easily. Let not the family members have 'quinine or castor oil' faces. Learn from the *Gita* the art of living and the act of loving.

* * *

In order to develop love for God in your heart, express love through the service of and sympathy for mankind. See God in them. They are conscious forms of God, 'chalta-phirta Ram'.

* * *

Love all. Did I ask you to love physically? I only asked you to stop reflecting over others' misbehaviour, jealousy and evil nature. Harbour no thought against anyone in your mind. I didn't mean that you should submit and yield, shampoo and flatter, beg pardon and sell away your soul. No and never! Love is a spiritual experience of the inner being. Its other name is strong and tolerant dedication. It can be best expressed in the service of mankind. Love can be better practised by keeping the soul under religious control.

* * *

Love is a divine force for annihilating worries. It is one of those heavenly drinks, which freed man from the thraldoms of dissatisfaction and spiritual unrest. Love – we have misspelt it. We say 'lao' which means 'bring it'. I say 'lov' or 'take it'. Love knows nothing but sacrifice. Yes, at the altar of love, I sacrificed my body, my soul, my all! All that I claimed to possess. 'Take it' is the real meaning of love! 'Give me' is the watchword of an exploiter. Love does not exploit, love only enriches. Love is the only fertilizer of the soil of life.

* * *

Passion is not love. Greed is not love. Romance is not love. Attachment or attraction is not love. Love is an innermost feeling of the soul. Love is a state when strains and burdens have been set aside and when our soul relaxes its tensions and rests in the blissful lap of someone divine.

* * *

What is love? Constant remembrance and awareness of the Beloved Lord and a keen longing to unite with Him. If there is no love in you, rest assured that you won't have His darshan. There is no fun in your going to Badrinath, if you fail to love God. Renunciation is fun, sannyasa a mockery, if the aspirant lacks in bhakti. No man who has no love for God will ever realize the divine glory.

* * *

If sadhana cannot enrich your present existence with beauty and health, success and gold, kick it off. We do not want these things at all, if they are only for *paraloka*, the world of hereafter. I love this life. I care to make this existence better. I wish to make this body hale and hearty, this mind quiet and peaceful. I love men more than they love stone gods. The more I mix with people, the more I have begun to love them. Love is a greater force than the law of religion. If water cannot cool your body, food cannot appease your hunger, love can do that.

* * *

Whether you are a devotee of God or an atheist, you can realize the divine glory through meditation. A person having faith in God can meditate on any choicest form of God, through which he will realize Him. An atheist also can be given a way to reach the destination. He can either meditate on a flower or on a star, or on the tip of the nose, or between the eyebrows, or on the heart and so on. He can concentrate on *nada*, sound and vibration, according to the advice of an experienced master of nada yoga.

* * *

So long as you don't realize your real swaroopa, you will continue to suffer from positive and negative charges of nature; you will not experience that supreme bliss which is your personal property. This is your first and foremost duty.

* * *

Love! It is an inexplicable attitude towards one's ishta devata. It is not passion, not lust, not romance. It is an unceasing thirst, unforgettable remembrance and eternal application for uniting with one's ishta. Love is not madness. Love is constant awareness. It is the totality of dedication.

* * *

Repetition of the name is divine bangles and rings. Sadhana is the best of all beautifying agents. Japa is a never-fading lipstick. Yoga is the only pancake, which can produce everlasting lustre. Annihilation of ego is the real process of taking a wash. Can the soap clean the dirt of our souls? So, it has been said that simplicity opens the gates which lead to heaven and God.

*   *   *

Keep a cool head and a balanced mind. Excitement brings about depression, consequently a terrible fatigue. Balance of the mind and efficiency in one's duties is yoga.

*   *   *

Pain is a cross unto which Nature hangs a man whenever She wishes to make him a sublime superman!

*   *   *

The mind plays havoc. It advances lame excuses. It creates many obstacles. One has to tackle the mind tactfully. Control of habits plays a very prominent role during the initial stages of sadhana. The sadhaka should have a fuller understanding of the mind and its habits.

*   *   *

Now, about mental silence. This is really very important. Mental silence is not what they call 'not thinking'. Mental silence is really a positive state, when the sadhaka is either remembering the name or the form of his ishta devata, instead of all and sundry things.

*   *   *

Thoughts of various kinds kill the spiritual stamina. "Stop thinking" is the open-sesame of Ali Baba. The less you think, the greater you become.

*   *   *

Spiritual life is long, strenuous, barren and fruitless at its very outset. It is a plunge into the unknown. Its rewards are beyond intelligence, therefore, uncertain. One has to strive, strive and strive, sometimes for lives together. It needs constant vigilance and care. It is a mission fit for heroes. The cowards and timid will find it terribly hard and hot. Bold and brave soldiers alone can undertake this mission. Emotional and passionate individuals will find it troublesome. After all, who can bear the rigours of vairagya?

* * *

The path of sadhana is hard to walk upon. The path of the world is easier. The fruit of sadhana is eternal power. The fruit of the world is perpetual frustration. One is hard in the beginning, another is easier. The wise one chooses one of them, considering the fruits thereof. Sugar is sweet but it acts as acid. Neem is bitter but it kills poison.

* * *

Success knows no rest. Faith knows no defeat, no frustration and no 'stop' order. Suspense and uncertainty do not trouble one who has faith. Life needs no procrastination. The death of your near and dear ones should not put your spirit low. Death is a challenge, a warning, a call to get ready to face the realities of life, which are so thrilling, so romantic and so new.

* * *

There is no meaning in having faith in the master only after he has performed certain miracles. Real faith and love are independent experiences which one develops even before knowing a person. Faith is the first and foremost condition. God-realization is an outcome of intense, unflinching and non-dual faith. Faith does not demand any proof or epistemological conclusions. Faith is that intuitive attitude which one cultivates inwardly even before he comes across an object or a person. Of course, faith presupposes love. Thus, we love the object of our faith, then awareness, then merging, finally realization. This is how the whole matter progresses.

* * *

Bliss is thy birth-right. Not sorrow.
Freedom is thy heritage. Not bondage.

* * *

Is it of any use to perform miracles just to convince the dull heads of your type, especially when eternal-infinite miracles of the Almighty in the cosmos have not opened your eyes? None can see Him so long as he is seeing the rest. None can hear the divine music so long as he is concerned with worldly tumults. It is only after the external perceptions have been withdrawn and the last trace of lower love and passions has also diminished that He comes, sings, loves and makes one blessed.

* * *

Guru, God and devotee are essentially One. Perfected faith can work miracles. Let not any amount of failures depress one's heart; and let not success snatch from him his mental equilibrium.

* * *

When love becomes overpowering, faith reaches the final point of culmination, then He is in front of you in flesh and blood. Now, you can talk to Him. You can sit by Him. He will reveal unto you the power of consciousness. He will give you all you asked for. Let the wise one understand this.

* * *

Worldly objects won't give you lasting happiness. You shouldn't be enamoured by their quixotic fancies and magnifications. As a witness, let ye transcend the realms of maya. Live in the world as a lotus leaf lives in the water, as the tongue lives in between the two sets of sharp teeth, as Shiva lives in the wilderness of life.

* * *

God is not separate from the creation. He has expressed Himself in these creations. Even as from gold, many ornaments are made, the ornaments being nothing but gold in fact; even as from mud, various pots are fashioned, those being nothing but mud in fact; likewise the creation is but His manifestation. It is not different from Him. Ornaments without gold are nowhere. Pots without mud are nowhere. Similarly, the creation is nowhere without Him. Everything here is an expression of Consciousness-Absolute.

* * *

You should always bear in mind that not only this body, but your wife and relatives and property also are His gifts. Not for a moment should you forget this fact that He alone looks after all your needs. This attitude will not only remove worries and fears but it will also bestow immense spiritual stamina.

* * *

So long as the wife does not submit herself to her husband in her entirety, she cannot be close to him to the extent she expects to be. When she submits herself entirely, she undoubtedly gets complete right over him and all that belongs to him. The secret of this 'gain' is hidden in 'totally giving' – the things of fleeting values against the 'thing' of absolute value. Yes, you give yourself, and you not only gain Him, you regain yourself also. This is surrender of ego unto the Lord!

* * *

How do you cure physical constipation? By taking Purgolax or fruit salt. Thereby, the constipated matter is thrown out of your body and you feel light and healthy. But, how will you cure mental constipation? Give a purgative to your mind! Prayer is the purgative which removes the fermented filth out of the system.

* * *

No use of fasting, if your mind is fast running after evil-mindedness. What is the harm, if you eat and drink well and lead an inner life of purity and peace? A non-vegetarian friend, with altruism in his head and hands, and sacrifice in his every nerve, is by all means better than that vegetarian and self-styled pundit, who is engrossed in black-marketing, adulteration, exploitation and antisocial activities. Therefore, it is better to be a simple man with noble virtues than to be a nobleman with ignoble vices. Then what? Be a man of God, a friend of all, brother of all believers and a master of your own self.

* * *

Don't get disturbed by noise. This is a test of your progress. It is only after the external sounds have stopped irritating you that you should realize you have really made initial progress. Never until then!

* * *

It is always better to work than to renounce it. If it were not so, saints would have never worked after achieving jnana. Not by the total renunciation of karmas that one attains jnana; the fact is just the opposite. That is this; one has to work in perfect awareness with fullest ability at one's command. The three gunas of prakriti will compel him to act elsewhere, even if he renounces this work.

* * *

Jagate rah, be eternally aware of thy *atma*, the all pervading consciousness.

* * *

A king's son enacted the part of a 'dhobi', washerman.
He did not play it well; he could not adjust.
A king's son enacted the part of a dhobi.
He did play marvellously, yet he was a prince.
Similarly, we play the part of jiva.
Let us play it marvellously,
Yet we are Consciousness-Absolute.

* * *

One work at one time. Total absorption in any work will gradually train the mind to forget its usual fickleness and unsteady character. If you plunge in any work at hand with non-dual keenness and attention, you will only derive immense help in meditation.

* * *

The pathway to His palace is sadhana. The zeal to reach the palace is divine love, *bhakti*. The key to open the lock of the gate is concentration. The attempt to enter is *pratyahara*, withdrawal of senses. The transcendence of three chambers is meditation. And, the fourth chamber is where He IS.

* * *

Empty the vessel of its various contents! How? When the consciousness would be saturated in His awareness, when the ideal, ambition, reflection, anticipation, love, hatred, action, rest and all movements would be diverted for His cause; when rains and thunders, winter and chill, night and wilderness, birth and death, praise and insult would lose their effects in the wake of overwhelming awareness of One; when Bilwamangal would become unmindful of torrents, jungles, thorns, an over flooded river, a dead body and the hanging snake for his Chintamani and for her love and in her constant awareness – it is then, verily then, that the vessel would really become empty of its confusing contents.

* * *

Him alone, who has united in Godly love, no sense-pleasure can affect, no spring tide can upset and no flesh can attract.

* * *

Domestic responsibilities give one a chance to cultivate patience, forbearance, and to develop a hippopotamic constitution. Unfavourable conditions pave a way to everlasting spiritual strength. It is only under adverse circumstances that the mind of a sadhaka really becomes steady and strong.

*　　*　　*

Never give up remembering, admiring and recognizing other's importance. This will purify your *vyavaharic*, materialistic mind.

*　　*　　*

Whenever the mind loses the divine touch and identifies itself with happiness and sorrow it becomes a victim of the three gunas.

*　　*　　*

How does a child feel for his mother in her absence as well as in her presence? Likewise you must awaken the dormant *prem* and *bhakti*, love and devotion. Lukewarm prem will not do. Overwhelming, overpowering and intoxicating love is the secret.

*　　*　　*

Constant work and mental engagements keep the inner instruments in order. Arguments and reflections weaken the mind. Feelings and opinions are detrimental to normal progress in life.

*　　*　　*

We want events to move according to our personal choice, so we suffer, repent and live a dead existence with frustrations all throughout our life. Why not obey the commands of the Divine for there alone lies happiness. Let us, therefore, leave everything to be worked out by His mercy.

*　　*　　*

Trials and tribulations are but the forms of His grace. They serve as a thermometer to indicate the seriousness and grossness of an imperfect personality. But for the trying conditions, one couldn't have gauged his personality.

* * *

God creates every event with a great purpose behind it. Wise men don't oppose it for they know His mission.

* * *

Every moment of leisure is to be used for a flight in spiritual land. Every minute is precious for a yogi. Every second is precious for a real sadhu. Time is fleeting away, therefore, let us stop unyogic thinking. Maintain yogic introversion all throughout. No holiday from sadhana. No reserved hours for sadhana. Let it be regular, constant, unceasing and in various ways and activities. No reflection of the past, no anticipation of the future. Always be in the present, immediate present.

* * *

Electricity comes from the powerhouse. But His grace is everywhere. All India Radio is broadcasting music even now. You must tune your radio. So His grace is also ever upon you. You must only tune your mental radio. Switch on. Have faith in Him.

* * *

Just as you can not see thoughts, can't see the air or fragrance or pain, can't see the butter in the milk, a tree in the seed, a hen in an egg, or a child in the womb, likewise there is something which you cannot see, and which is beyond the reach of the five senses and the mind.

* * *

In order to see a distant object you must take the help of binoculars. Even so, in order to see Him, you must possess inner vision or *sukshmadarshi*.

* * *

In order to solve an algebraic sum, you have to say, "Supposing 3 X plus Y is equal to 3." If while solving a sum, we have to have faith in the supposed formulas, what to talk of solving this greatest problem involving God and His creations!

* * *

Just as a king, in dream, sees himself as a beggar, while in reality he is a king; in the same way, this soul imagines the feelings of sorrow and joy.

* * *

If someone insults you, you will definitely feel bad, because your indriyas are receptive to this. Once you sleep, even if he insults you, you will not be affected by it. So this soul, when connected with maya, experiences sorrow and joy, and becomes as if it were a victim of the positive and negative charges of nature.

* * *

The electric bulb shines, while the fan stands still, although both are connected with the powerhouse through wires. Why? Because the bulb is plugged and the fan stands disconnected. In the same way, when we plug ourselves with the world and its objects, we are affected by them, and consequently, we experience sorrow and joy.

* * *

Take a fresh coconut; break the shell. The inner thing, kernel, also will be broken. Now take another dry coconut and break it. The shell will break, but the inner portion will remain unaffected. Why? Because, the kernel has now detached itself from the shell. So, if we disidentify our soul from the body, we will not be affected by what happens to the body.

* * *

The Satyananda Yoga Tradition
YOGA KEERTI STAMBHA
YOGA WILL EMERGE AS A MIGHTY WORLD CULTURE AND CHANGE THE COURSE OF WORLD EVENTS
SWAMI SATYANANDA
Yoga Publications Trust, Munger, India

Munger

Housing the institutions of Bihar School of Yoga, Bihar Yoga Bharati, Yoga Research Foundation and Yoga Publications Trust, Munger aims to integrate yogic education with a traditional gurukul lifestyle, providing the ideal environment for spiritual growth.

At present, the centre offers courses in yogic studies, health management, gurukul lifestyle, sannyasa training and yoga teacher training.

Munger also conducts a number of cultural and spiritual events during the year.

Swami Sivananda Saraswati

Swami Sivananda was born at Pattamadai (Tamil Nadu) in 1887. After serving as a medical doctor in Malaya, he returned to India to pursue his spiritual aspirations, and in 1924 he was initiated into Dashnami sannyasa in Rishikesh by Swami Vishwananda Saraswati. In subsequent years he toured India extensively and wrote hundreds of books and articles on yoga and spirituality, inspiring people to practise yoga and lead a divine life. Swami Sivananda founded the Divine Life Society at Rishikesh in 1936, the Sivananda Publication League in 1939, the Sivananda Ayurvedic Pharmacy in 1945, the Yoga Vedanta Forest Academy in 1948 and the Sivananda Eye Hospital in 1957. As a spiritual luminary of his time, he guided thousands of spiritual seekers, disciples and aspirants all over the world. His eightfold path of yoga: serve, love, give, purify, do good, be good, meditate, realize, continues to guide the work of the Bihar Yoga branch of his lineage. Swami Sivananda attained mahasamadhi in 1963. His last message to the world was, "Happiness comes when the individual merges in God."

Swami Satyananda Saraswati

Swami Satyananda was born in Almora (Uttaranchal) in 1923. Drawn to spiritual life from an early age, he left home at the age of eighteen, and in 1943 surrendered himself to Swami Sivananda in Rishikesh who initiated him into Dashnami sannyasa in 1947. He served his guru for twelve years, perfecting every aspect of spiritual life. Thereafter, he travelled throughout the Indian subcontinent as a wandering ascetic. Realizing the need of the times as scientific rendition of the ancient system of yoga, he founded the International Yoga Fellowship in 1956 and the Bihar School of Yoga in 1963. During the next twenty years Swami Satyananda hoisted the flag of yoga in every corner of the world, consolidated BSY into a foremost institution of yoga, and authored over eighty major texts on yoga, tantra and spiritual life.

Satyananda Yoga became a tradition which combines classical knowledge with experiential understanding and a modern outlook. In 1984 he founded the Yoga Research Foundation to synchronize scientific research and yoga, and Sivananda Math to assist the underprivileged. In 1988, at the peak of his achievements, he renounced everything and adopted kshetra sannyasa, living as a paramahamsa ascetic. In 1989 Rikhia was revealed to him, where he came to live and performed higher vedic sadhanas in seclusion. Receiving the command to provide for his neighbours in 1991, he allowed the ashram to help the underprivileged villages in the region. From 1995 onwards, he performed a twelve-year Rajasooya Yajna with the sankalpa of peace, plenty and prosperity for all, and in 2007 he announced the establishment of Rikhiapeeth with its mandate to 'serve, love, give'.

Swami Satyananda attained mahasamadhi, a yogic accomplishment of discarding the body at will to become one with the universal consciousness, in 2009, in the presence of his disciples.

Swami Niranjanananda Saraswati

Swami Niranjanananda was born in Rajnandgaon (Chhattisgarh) in 1960. Guided by his guru, Swami Satyananda Saraswati, from birth, at the age of four he came to live with him at the Bihar School of Yoga (BSY) in Munger where he received training in yogic and spiritual sciences through yoga nidra. In 1971, he was initiated into Dashnami sannyasa, and thereafter for twelve years he lived overseas, mastering skills in varied areas, acquiring an understanding of different cultures and helping establish Satyananda Yoga ashrams and centres in Europe, Australia, North and South America.

At the behest of his guru, he returned to India in 1983 to guide the activities of Bihar School of Yoga, Sivananda Math and the Yoga Research Foundation at Ganga Darshan, and assumed the presidentship of BSY. In 1990 he was initiated as a paramahamsa sannyasin by his guru and in 1993 anointed spiritual preceptor in succession to Swami Satyananda Saraswati by the luminaties of the sannyasa tradition. His guru transmitted his spiritual shakti to Swami Niranjan during the Sat Chandi Mahayajna 1995 and declared him as the guru and paramacharya of the tradition. Swami Niranjan established Bihar Yoga Bharati, the first university of yoga, in 1994 and the Yoga Publications Trust in 2000 in Munger. He also initiated a children's yoga movement, Bal Yoga Mitra Mandal, in 1995. In addition to steering the activities at Munger, he travelled extensively to guide seekers around the world till 2009, when he received the command to embark on a new phase of sannyasa life. In 2010, he established Sannyasa Peeth, to reintegrate India's spiritual heritage and culture into the fabric of modern society.

Author of many classic books on yoga, tantra and the upanishads, Swami Niranjan is a magnetic source of wisdom on all aspects of yogic philosophy, practice and lifestyle.

Swami Satyasangananda Saraswati

Swami Satyasangananda Saraswati, popularly known as Swami Satsangi, was born in 1953, in the small town of Chandernagore, West Bengal, India. In her youth she had a series of inner awakenings, which led her to Swami Satyananda Saraswati, who initiated her into the tradition of Dashnami sannyasa on 6th July 1982 at Ganga Darshan, Munger. Thereafter she travelled extensively with Swami Satyananda on his tours in India and abroad. This experience contributed to her development into a scholar with deep insight into the yogic and tantric traditions as well as modern sciences and philosophies, leading to the writing of authoritative commentaries on classical texts.

In 1989, Swami Satyananda, ordained by an inner mandate, went to live in seclusion in Rikhia, and Swami Satyasangananda accompanied her guru to serve him there. Since that time, Swami Satsangi is fulfilling her guru's vision of uplifting the neglected, impoverished and downtrodden villagers in the surrounding areas of the ashram, by implementing the cardinal teachings of paramguru Swami Sivananda: serve, love, give. Her tireless efforts, which are carried out under the banner of Sivananda Math, have transformed the entire area into a vibrant centre of spirituality where people throng in large numbers for spiritual solace. On 1st January 2007, she was initiated into the paramahamsa tradition and appointed Peethadhishwari of Rikhiapeeth by Swami Satyananda. In 2009, when Swami Satyananda attained mahasamadhi, she entered a new phase of inspiring and guiding the multifarious activities at Rikhiapeeth and travelling extensively around the world, spreading the light of her guru's teachings. She embodies compassion with clear reason and is the foundation of her guru's vision.

Swami Suryaprakash Saraswati

Swami Suryaprakash was born in 1982, in San Francisco (USA), to Indian parents. His birth took place with the blessings of Swami Satyananda when Swami Niranjan was touring in the USA and was a frequent visitor to his home. He was raised in an environment that encouraged a deep sense of spiritual commitment, his grandfather and family members being dedicated disciples and associates of Swami Satyananda.

In 1999, after completing his education in the USA and Spain, he came to India to join the ashram and serve in the guru's mission. On 14th January 2000, he was initiated into Dashnami sannyasa by Swami Niranjanananda. After undergoing intense training in ashram and spiritual life, he was appointed president of Bihar School of Yoga on Basant Panchami, 11th February 2008.

Swami Suryaprakash oversees the management of ashram activities and is a shining example of unswerving commitment to the guru's mission. He represents the new generation where the classical spiritual tradition easily blends with the latest technical knowhow. Fluent in English, Hindi and Spanish, he has a flair for many languages including Catalan, French, Italian, Greek as well as Sanskrit. He is also a gifted musician and orator.

International Yoga Fellowship Movement (IYFM)

The International Yoga Fellowship Movement is a yoga movement founded by Swami Satyananda at Rajnandgaon (Chhattisgarh) in 1956 to disseminate the yogic tradition throughout the world. As the movement spread, taking the message of yoga from door to door and from shore to shore, Bihar School of Yoga became its head office. IYFM provides guidance, systematized yoga training programs and sets teaching standards for all affiliated yoga teachers, centres and ashrams around the world. A yoga charter to consolidate and unify the humanitarian efforts of sannyasin disciples, yoga teachers, spiritual seekers and well-wishers was introduced in 1993. Affiliation enables one to become a messenger of goodwill and peace in the world through active involvement in various yoga projects. Today, with Swami Niranjanananda as paramacharya, the IYFM has become a global community which unites, inspires and coordinates the family of practitioners who propagate Bihar Yoga all over the world.

Bihar School of Yoga (BSY)

Bihar School of Yoga is a charitable and educational institution founded by Swami Satyananda at Munger in 1963 to impart yogic training to all nationalities, householders and sannyasins alike, and to provide a focal point for the global revival of the ancient science of yoga. The yogic techniques that evolved are a synthesis of many yogic approaches to personal development, based on vedantic and tantric teachings in conjunction with contemporary physical and mental health sciences. Today, BSY continues to further develop the Bihar Yoga system and guides yoga research projects in association with hospitals and other organizations. BSY yoga training programs are applied in education, prisons, hospitals, the defence services, private and public sector industries and other areas. Yoga health management, teacher training, sadhana, kriya yoga and other specialized courses are held regularly. BSY is renowned for its sannyasa training and the initiation of female and foreign sannyasins. Trained sannyasins and teachers travel around the world to conduct yoga conventions, seminars and lecture tours.

Bihar Yoga Bharati (BYB)

Bihar Yoga Bharati, an Institute for Advanced Studies in Yogic Sciences, was established by Swami Niranjanananda at Munger in 1994 to preserve and regenerate the yogic sciences by combining academic and scientific methodology with a spiritual vision. The culmination of the vision of Swami Sivananda and Swami Satyananda, this gurukul based institute is the first of its kind in the world wholly devoted to the subject of yoga. BYB offers a comprehensive scientific and yogic education according to today's needs, with provision to grant certificates and diplomas in yogic studies in the areas of yoga philosophy, yoga psychology, applied yogic science and yogic ecology. Four month and one year residential courses are conducted in a gurukul environment, so that along with yogic education, students also imbibe the spirit of *seva* (selfless service), *samarpan* (dedication) and *karuna* (compassion) for humankind. Satellite academies in Australia, Europe, North and South America continue to bring the teachings of BYB to a wide range of aspirants.

Yoga Research Foundation (YRF)

The Yoga Research Foundation is a scientific research institute founded by Swami Satyananda at Munger in 1984. It aims to provide an accurate assessment of yogic practices within a scientific framework, and to establish yoga as an essential science for human development. YRF is actively engaged in research into the benefits and applications of the yogic science. The result is an alignment of spirituality and science with unlimited possibilities for the creative enhancement of society and the environment. At present YRF is working on projects involving fundamental research, clinical research and applied research. Future plans include literary, scriptural, medical and scientific investigations into other little-known aspects of yoga for physical health, mental wellbeing and spiritual upliftment.

Yoga Publications Trust (YPT)

Yoga Publications Trust (YPT) was established by Swami Niranjanananda in 2000 to disseminate and promote yogic and spiritual knowledge, lifestyle and practice, nationally and internationally. YPT publishes and distributes text books, magazines, research materials, practice texts, audio and video cassettes and multimedia presentations in the fields of yoga psychology, applied yogic science, yoga ecology, vedic, upanishadic and tantric darshanas, yogic and spiritual philosophy, mysticism, as well as the inspiring talks of eminent spiritual personalities and authors. For a complete list of YPT's comprehensive range of publications, contact Bihar School of Yoga. Globally acclaimed as a leading publishing house in the field of yoga and spirituality, YPT has published hundreds of books, which are available nationally and internationally. Universally recognized as essential reading for spiritual aspirants, yoga students and teachers alike, YPT books are heralded as salient treatises on yoga and spiritual knowledge, practice and life.

Sannyasa Peeth (SP)

Sannyasa Peeth, the vision of Sri Swami Satyananda, was entrusted to his successor, Swami Niranjanananda Saraswati, with the mandate to establish the spiritual teachings of sannyasa as a lifestyle to cultivate and nourish creative expression. Founded on 6th December 2010, the *punya tithi*, first anniversary of Sri Swamiji's mahasamadhi, Sannyasa Peeth was established by Swami Niranjanananda at Paduka Darshan, beside the banks of the sacred river Ganga in Munger.

The training of sannyasa is the means of imbuing perfection into life, and the sannyasa lifestyle aims towards awakening and expanding the mind and human potential to its fullest extent in order to enhance and achieve positive, complete and creative participation in life. Sannyasa Peeth has set out to make the teachings, ideals and values of sannyasa accessible to all, under Swami Niranjanananda's inspiration and guidance.

Sivananda Math (SM)

Sivananda Math is a philanthropic organization founded by Swami Satyananda at Munger in 1984, in memory of his guru, Swami Sivananda Saraswati of Rishikesh. The head office is situated at Rikhia, Deoghar (Jharkhand). Sivananda Math aims to uplift the neglected, underprivileged sections of society, especially in rural areas, by following the precepts of *seva* (service), *karuna* (compassion), *prem* (love) and *sneha* (affection). Activities include: educational assistance for children, distribution of clothing, blankets, grains, household necessities and livestock according to need, installing tube-wells and constructing low-cost housing, assisting farmers with ploughing and irrigation, providing self-employment opportunities and promoting self-sufficiency. A medical clinic, Sivananda Charitable Dispensary, established in 1991, provides medical treatment, advice and education. All services are provided free and universally to everyone, regardless of caste and creed.

Sivananda Ashram (SA)

Sivananda Ashram is a philanthropic institution founded by Swami Satyasangananda in 2004 under the inspiration of Swami Satyananda. The ashram's centre of activities is at Rikhia, Deoghar (Jharkhand). The aim of Sivananda Ashram is to provide spiritual education and knowledge through the medium of yogic science and culture, as originally inspired by Swami Sivananda of Rishikesh. At present, the children (kanyas and batuks) of the Rikhia area receive education in yoga, kirtan, Ramayana, Bhagavad Gita, English, Sanskrit and computer skills. In this way, the children are imbibing the spiritual culture of India as well as receiving modern education, thus creating the blueprint for an evolved society.

Sri Panchdashnam Paramahamsa Alakh Bara (PPAB)

Sri Panchdashnam Paramahamsa Alakh Bara was established in 1990 at Rikhia, Deoghar (Jharkhand), the *tapobhoomi* (sadhana place) of Swami Satyananda. A philanthropic and spiritual institution, it aims to uphold and propagate the highest tradition of sannyasa: *vairagya* (dispassion), *tyaga* (renunciation) and *tapasya* (austerity). Intended for sannyasins, renunciates, ascetics, tapasvis and paramahamsas, it propounds the tapovan style of living adopted by the rishis and munis of the vedic era. Swami Satyananda, whilst residing at the Alakh Bara, performed the Panchagni Vidya and other higher vedic sadhanas, thus paving the way for future paramahamsas to uphold their tradition.

Rikhiapeeth (RP)

Rikhiapeeth was born on 25 November 2006 during the Sat Chandi Mahayajna, when Swami Satyananda proclaimed that in future Rikhia ashram would be known as Rikhiapeeth. A philanthropic institution and modern day gurukul, Rikhiapeeth aims to disseminate the ancient spiritual knowledge as propagated by the vedic lineage of rishis in the Vedas, Upanishads and Puranas to all, regardless of caste, creed, nationality, religion and gender. The first peethadhishwari of Rikhiapeeth is Swami Satyasangananda, who has the mandate to implement Swami Sivananda's three cardinal teachings of serve, love and give.

The Satyananda Yoga – Bihar Yoga Tradition

At the beginning of the twenty-first century, humankind stands at a crossroads. Technological progress and economic development have created immense wealth for some, but not all. Globalization has linked the world out of economic necessity. Rapid urbanization has harmed the environment and disconnected the individual from nature. Voices are raised about pollution, environmental damage, both inner and outer, and the need to uplift the poor. On an inner level, people are unhappy, unhealthy, stressed and unsure about the direction of life. There is increasing awareness that human beings have a choice about whether to blindly pursue a non-existent utopia or to live in harmony and find inner fulfilment.

Bihar Yoga provides a system that restores order to our lives, creating harmony so that imbalances in the form of disease and neurosis drop away. The mind regains its peace, the emotions begin to harmonize and the body recovers its vital capacity, so that the individual can face life and its distractions with a greater sense of inner serenity and balance.

The Bihar Yoga system is a complete science of harmonious living, suitable for everyone, regardless of age, gender, nationality, religion, mental condition or level of fitness. It is a holistic system which addresses all aspects of human life in the spheres of physical health, mental well-being, emotional behaviour and work environment. Awareness is emphasized and practitioners are encouraged to learn about all aspects of their personality through yoga. Adjustment in stages is emphasized, not a total change in one's lifestyle and environment.

The beauty of Bihar Yoga is that it slowly grows on one, and it is totally up to the practitioner to decide how much to implement. If the need is relief from chronic diseases, such as asthma, diabetes or hypertension, then a simple package of practices can be implemented. If the need is to improve one's physical fitness, or one's mental abilities, or take up yoga teaching, or find a direction in life, or live a spiritual life, then Bihar Yoga also provides that opportunity.

Bihar Yoga is a living tradition based on the realizations of two masters, Swami Sivananda and Swami Satyananda. Swami Sivananda was the first spiritual personality in the twentieth century to emphasize that divine life was everyone's birthright and could be practised in simple ways even while living in the normal social environment. He introduced the concept of integral yoga for harmonious development of the personality, incorporating a practical philosophy and a holistic lifestyle.

Swami Satyananda was given the mandate of taking yoga to humanity 'from door to door and from shore to shore'. During nine years as a wandering ascetic, he discerned the needs of the general public, and then travelled around the world teaching the practices of yoga in a systematic and easily comprehensible way. He simplified and systematized the yogic practices, and at the same time added depth to every dimension of yoga. *Shankhaprakshalana* (intestinal cleansing) was made a practical and effective technique in the hatha yoga shatkarma series for physical purification. Asanas were classified and grouped according to position and sequence, and prefaced with the pawanmuktasana series, so that everyone could benefit. Pranayama as a complete system was revealed for the first time. The deep relaxation practice of yoga nidra provided major relief from stress as well as a means of personality transformation. Swami Satyananda taught yoga in practically every country around the world. He found total acceptance everywhere due to his simple approach and universality. His successor, Swami Niranjanananda, has built up and consolidated this solid foundation of yoga.

Thus Bihar Yoga evolved into a complete and integrated system of yoga with its practices and philosophy culled from the vedic and tantric traditions. Swami Satyananda gave tantra its rightful place as a science for the expansion of consciousness, removing misconceptions and adapting the techniques and philosophy into the Bihar Yoga system. All the systems of yoga: hatha yoga, raja yoga, mantra yoga, bhakti yoga, jnana yoga, kriya yoga, kundalini yoga, nada yoga, swara yoga and other yogas, have been applied and adapted according to current need. For example, three specific mantras have been adopted for daily practice from amongst a vast collection of mantras. Meditation practices have been systematized as pratyahara and dharana practices. For the serious spiritual aspirant the practices of kundalini yoga and kriya yoga have been brought into the open.

Karma yoga as a distinct path for evolution and self-purification has been given a practical shape as part of ashram life. People have been given the opportunity to experience ashram life and offload the stresses of daily life. Within the ashram environment aspirants have the chance to experience *seva* or selfless service, and to come into contact with sannyasa, a tradition which has been given a new lease of life worldwide by Swami Satyananda. His sannyasa is not withdrawal from society, but a dynamic and service-oriented life with inner renunciation.

Bihar Yoga supports its yoga teaching with a comprehensive range of publications on all aspects of yoga: hatha yoga, raja yoga, kriya yoga, kundalini yoga, bhakti yoga, karma yoga, swara yoga, yoga philosophy, both traditional and practical, yoga psychology, yoga therapy, applied yoga, yoga for women and children, etc., as well as the teachings of Swami Satyananda and Swami Niranjanananda.

Experimentation and research has been one of the hallmarks of the Bihar Yoga tradition. Thus Bihar Yoga is a continuously evolving yoga, while at the same time retaining its classical base. Swami Satyananda experimented with scriptural knowledge, extracted whatever was relevant and reintroduced it in a practical form. Various meditation and concentration techniques, including antar mouna, ajapa japa, trataka, chidakasha dharana and prana vidya, were developed from the tantras. He experimented with yoga nidra, and instigated research in hospitals and medical colleges into the effects of yoga on the management of common diseases such as asthma, diabetes, digestive ailments, obesity, arthritis, hypertension and cardiovascular disorders. The aim of this research was to investigate scientifically and to document the therapeutic and mind-expanding benefits of the yoga techniques.

Bihar Yoga has been effectively integrated into society for the development of human resources. It is applied in stress management and business management programs, yoga health management training and research, training programs for the defence forces, prisons, the police force, railways, private and public organizations, sporting associations, educational institutes, medical colleges and hospitals, in private and public sector industries, and for rural upliftment. Internationally, the application of Bihar Yoga addresses current issues within society such as addiction, drug and alcohol rehabilitation, troubled or homeless teenagers, prisoners, abused women, HIV-positive patients, as well as the needs of the physically and mentally challenged, autistic adults, children and the elderly, and encouraging creative development through yoga nidra.

A unique children's yogic movement managed and conducted by children has been successfully established. Internationally, research into yoga for children's education has been pioneered in France and Canada. Satyananda Yoga Academies in Australia, Europe, North and South America, in cooperation with the IYFM, ensure a high, uniform standard of yoga propagation. Thus Bihar Yoga, or the Satyananda Yoga system, is an interconnected and vibrant holistic system spread all over the world, meeting the physical, psychological and spiritual needs of the current generation.

Synopsis of the Life of Swami Satyananda Saraswati

Swami Satyananda Saraswati was born in 1923 at Almora (Uttaranchal) into a family of farmers. His ancestors were warriors and many of his kith and kin down the line, including his father, served in the army and police force.

However, it became evident that Sri Swamiji had a different bent of mind, as he began to have spiritual experiences at the age of six, when his awareness spontaneously left the body and he saw himself lying motionless on the floor. Many saints and sadhus blessed him and reassured his parents that he had a very developed awareness. This experience of disembodied awareness continued, which led him to many saints of that time such as Anandamayi Ma. Sri Swamiji also met a tantric bhairavi, Sukhman Giri, who gave him *shaktipat*, transmission of energy, and directed him to find a guru in order to stabilize his spiritual experiences.

In 1943, at the age of 20, he renounced his home and went in search of a guru. This search ultimately led him to Swami Sivananda Saraswati at Rishikesh, who initiated him into the Dashnami order of sannyasa on 12th September 1947 on the banks of the Ganges and gave him the name of Swami Satyananda Saraswati.

In those early years at Rishikesh, Sri Swamiji immersed himself in guru seva. At that time the ashram was still in its infancy and even the basic amenities such as buildings and toilets were absent. The forests surrounding the small ashram were infested with snakes, scorpions, mosquitoes, monkeys and even tigers. The ashram work too was heavy and hard, requiring Sri Swamiji to toil like a labourer carrying bucket loads of water from the Ganga up to the ashram and digging canals from the high mountain streams down to the ashram many kilometres away, in order to store water for constructing the ashram.

Rishikesh was then a small town and all the ashram requirements had to be brought by foot from far away. In addition there were varied duties, including the daily pooja at Vishwanath Mandir, for which Sri Swamiji would go into the dense forests to collect bael leaves. If anyone fell sick there was no medical care and no one to attend to them. All the sannyasins had to go out for bhiksha or alms as the ashram did not have a mess or kitchen.

Of that glorious time when he lived and served his guru, Sri Swamiji says that it was a period of total communion and surrender to the guru tattwa, whereby he felt that just to hear, speak of or see Swami Sivananda was yoga. But most of all through his nishkama seva he gained an enlightened understanding of the secrets of spiritual life and became an authority on yoga, tantra, Vedanta, Samkhya and kundalini yoga. Swami Sivananda said of Swami Satyananda, "Few would exhibit such intense vairagya at such an early age. Swami Satyananda is full of the Nachiketa element." Although he had a photographic memory, a keen intellect, and his guru described him as a versatile genius, Swami Satyananda's learning did not come from books and study in the ashram. His knowledge unfolded from within through his untiring seva as well as his abiding faith and love for Swami Sivananda, who told him, "Work hard and you will be purified. You do not have to search for the light; the light will unfold from within you."

In 1956, after spending twelve years in guru seva, Swami Satyananda set out as a wanderer (*parivrajaka*). Before his departure Swami Sivananda taught him kriya yoga and gave him the mission to "spread yoga from door to door and shore to shore".

As a wandering sannyasin, Swami Satyananda travelled extensively by foot, train, horse, boat, bullock-cart and elephant throughout India, Afghanistan, Burma, Nepal and Ceylon. During his sojourns, he met people from all strata of society and began formulating his ideas on how to spread the yogic techniques. Although his formal education and spiritual tradition was that of Vedanta, the task of disseminating yoga became his movement.

His mission unfolded before him in 1962 when he founded the International Yoga Fellowship Movement with the aim of creating a global fraternity of yoga. As his mission was revealed to him at Munger, Bihar, he established the Bihar School of Yoga in Munger. Before long his teachings were rapidly spreading throughout the world. From 1963 to 1982, Swami Satyananda took yoga to each and every corner of the world, to people of every caste, creed, religion and nationality. He guided millions of seekers in all continents and established centres and ashrams in different countries.

His frequent travel took him to Australia, New Zealand, Japan, China, the Philippines, Hong Kong, Malaysia, Thailand, Singapore, USA, England, Ireland, France, Italy, Germany, Switzerland, Denmark, Sweden, Yugoslavia, Poland, Hungary, Bulgaria, Slovenia, Russia, Czechoslovakia, Greece, Saudi Arabia, Kuwait, Bahrain, Dubai, Iraq, Iran, Pakistan, Afghanistan, Colombia, Brazil, Uruguay, Chile, Argentina, Santo Domingo, Puerto Rico, Sudan, Egypt, Nairobi, Ghana, Mauritius, Alaska and Iceland. One can easily say that Sri Swamiji hoisted the flag of yoga in every nook and cranny of the world.

Nowhere did he face opposition, resistance or criticism. His way was unique. Well-versed in all religions and scriptures, he incorporated their wisdom with such a natural flair that people of all faiths were drawn to him. His teaching was not just confined to yoga but covered the wisdom of many millenniums.

Sri Swamiji brought to light the knowledge of tantra, the mother of all philosophies, the sublime truths of Vedanta, the Upanishads and Puranas, Buddhism, Jainism, Sikhism, Zoroastrianism, Islam and Christianity, including a modern scientific analysis of matter and creation. He interpreted, explained and gave precise, accurate and systematic explanations of the ancient systems of tantra and yoga, revealing practices hitherto unknown.

It can be said that Sri Swamiji was a pioneer in the field of yoga because his presentation had a novelty and freshness. Ajapa japa, antar mouna, pawanmuktasana, kriya yoga and prana vidya are just some of the practices which he introduced in such a methodical and simple manner that it became possible for everyone to delve into this valuable and hitherto inaccessible science for their physical, mental, emotional and spiritual development.

Yoga nidra was Sri Swamiji's interpretation of the tantric system of nyasa. With his deep insight into this knowledge, he was able to realize the potential of this practice of nyasa in a manner which gave it a practical utility for each and every individual, rather than just remaining a prerequisite for worship. Yoga nidra is but one example of his acumen and penetrating insight into the ancient systems.

Sri Swamiji's outlook was inspiring, uplifting as well as in-depth and penetrating. Yet his language and explanations were always simple and easy to comprehend. During this period he authored over eighty books on yoga and tantra which, due to their authenticity, are accepted as textbooks in schools and universities throughout the world. These books have been translated into Italian, German, Spanish, Russian, Yugoslavian, Chinese, French, Greek, Iranian and most other prominent languages of the world.

People took to his ideas and spiritual seekers of all faiths and nationalities flocked to him. He initiated thousands into mantra and sannyasa, sowing in them the seed to live the divine life. He exhibited tremendous zeal and energy in spreading the light of yoga, and in the short span of twenty years Sri Swamiji fulfilled the mandate of his guru.

Thus, by 1983, Swami Satyananda's tireless efforts to spread the message of yoga had touched the whole world. He had also trained a core of sannyasins to transmit the yogic techniques for different needs and cultures, and they had established many Satyananda Yoga ashrams, schools and centres around India and the world. Bihar School of Yoga was well established and recognized throughout the world as a reputed and authentic centre for learning yoga and the spiritual sciences. More than that, yoga had moved out of the caves of hermits and ascetics into the mainstream of society. Whether in hospitals, jails, schools, colleges, business houses, the sporting and fashion arenas, the army or navy, yoga was in demand. Scientific research into yogic techniques was being conducted all over the world. Professionals such as lawyers, engineers, doctors, business magnates and professors were incorporating yoga into their lives. So too were the masses. Yoga had become a household word.

Then, at the peak of his accomplishment, Sri Swamiji renounced all that he created. He appointed Swami Niranjanananda as his successor and gave him the mandate to continue the work, and then began to gradually withdraw from the teaching and administering of the yoga movement. In 1988, Sri Swamiji renounced disciples, establishments and institutions, and departed from Munger, never to return again. He went on a pilgrimage through the *siddha teerthas* (spiritual centres) of India as a mendicant, without any personal belonging or assistance from the ashram or institutions he had founded.

At Tryambakeshwar, before the jyotirlingam of Lord Mrityunjaya, his ishta devata, he renounced his garb and lived as an avadhoota. And here, at the source of the Godavari River near Neel Parbat, while performing chaturmas anushthana, his future place of abode and sadhana were revealed to him. He received the mandate for a new mission, to progress toward the cosmic dimension through unbroken remembrance and repetition of the Lord's name with every breath. On 8th September, 1989, birthday of his guru Swami Sivananda, he heard the voice loud and clear, "Chitabhoomi", and saw a vision of the place where he was intended to go.

Swami Satyananda did not choose Rikhia, it was chosen for him. After leaving Munger, while roaming the length and breadth of India, he came across many beautiful places where he was invited to take up residence. However, in keeping with his style of surrender he awaited the mandate of his ishta and guru, which guided him to the small nondescript, unknown village of Rikhia, on the outskirts of Baba Baidyanath Dham in Deoghar (Jharkhand), the *chitabhoomi* or cremation ground of Sati, consort of Shiva.

Sri Swamiji arrived at Rikhia on 23rd September 1989, at midday, the day of vernal equinox, when nature is in perfect balance as the day and night are equal. Soon after, he lit a *dhuni* or fire and called it Mahakal Chita Dhuni. Lighting a dhuni is a very ancient tradition among sadhus. It is believed that the ash from a sadhu's dhuni is very potent, for his entire day is spent in front of the dhuni and all his acts are performed with the fire as witness.

The Rikhia that Swami Satyananda arrived in was still living in the sixteenth century. There were no roads, electricity, telephones, newspapers, television or shops. However, its vibrations were pure and spiritual, providing an ideal climate for the seclusion which he imposed on himself. He began a life of intensive spiritual practice, entering the lifestyle of paramahamsas who do not work for their flock and mission alone, but have a universal vision. His first anushthana commenced in 1989 during Ashwin Navaratri: the performance of ashtottar-shat-laksh (108 lakh) mantra purascharana which took him three hundred days to complete. He gave up the geru cloth and donned the kaupeen, loin cloth, an important hallmark in the life of a sadhu denoting that vairagya and dispassion are an inherent part of his being. He no longer associated with any institutions, nor gave diksha, upadesh or received dakshina, but remained in seclusion and sadhana.

In a conclusive message, he told all, "I have nothing more to say to anyone and no further guidance to give. For over twenty years I have lived with the people answering their questions and helping them on their spiritual path. Now I withdraw my responsibility. Those who are receptive, they will surely benefit from what I have told them, but those who are not, they will now have to find their own way."

In 1990, he designated the sadhana sthal as Sri Panch Dashnam Paramahamsa Alakh Bara, denoting it as a place where a sannyasin who has perfected himself consolidates his learning and gives it momentum to attain greater spiritual heights. The *ishta devi*, presiding goddess, of the akhara was established as Tulsi Ma, the benevolent force presiding over all spheres. Now Sri Swamiji undertook the vow of *panchagni*, the five-fire austerity, in which he performed higher sadhanas sitting before five blazing fires outdoors during the hottest months of the year. The vow culminated in 1998. The fire lit by Sri Swamiji is still burning at Rikhiapeeth and is worshipped daily at sunrise and sunset with aromatic herbs amidst the chanting of vedic mantras.

In 1991, Swami Satyananda received another divine mandate: "Take care of your neighbours as I have taken care of you." Seeking to strike a balance between the personal aspect of spiritual liberation and the social aspect of helping others, he gave Swami Niranjanananda a new task for Sivananda Math: service to and improvement of the living conditions of the tribal people in the thousands of villages surrounding Rikhiadham. Thus, from 1991 onwards, Sivananda Math undertook

to finance and construct homes for the homeless, provide for clean drinking water, essential medical facilities, free clothing and household items. In the second phase of assistance, means of sustainable livelihood were provided.

In 1994, in a month-long darshan, Sri Swamiji gave a new message, of bhakti yoga. He said that the purpose of human life is to realize God through love and to serve God by helping humanity. He prophesied that while hatha yoga and raja yoga were the panacea of the twentieth century, devotion to God and bhakti yoga would be the panacea of the twenty-first.

In 1995, Sri Swamiji held the first Sat Chandi Maha Yajna, invoking the Cosmic Mother through a tantric ceremony hitherto not witnessed by common people. During this event, Sri Swamiji also passed on his spiritual and sannyasa sankalpa to Swami Niranjanananda.

In 1996, the annual event included Rama Naam Aradhana and Sita-Rama Vivaha, and in 1997, Sri Swamiji declared it as Sita Kalyanam. In 2001, for the first time he revealed that the yajna was part of the 12-year Rajasooya Yajna, a ceremony that is traditionally performed by a conqueror.

"I am performing the Rajasooya Yajna not as a conqueror of land, wealth or people, but because I was able to establish an empire of yoga, which is the need of today in our civilization," said Sri Swamiji. "Yoga works at the spiritual, mental and physical levels to improve the quality of life, and that is also the concept of prosperity in today's society. We have wealth, but we lack quality of life and peace of mind. I am performing the Rajasooya Yajna to re-establish peace of mind, to re-equip people with the riches of contentment, happiness, joy and wellbeing."

In 1998, Sri Swamiji also inspired Sivananda Math to undertake an education project. Thus scholarships were given to deserving students of Rikhia panchayat with special emphasis on the education of girls. English classes were also started at the ashram. By 2001, nearly all eligible children aged between 6–12 years of Rikhia panchayat had been adopted into the ever-expanding family of Swami Satyananda. In 2003, computer training was started. The girls, called *kanyas*, were also taught chanting of Sanskrit stotras. The boys, *batuks*, were simultaneously introduced to Gayatri mantra, Bhagavad Gita, surya namaskara, and rituals of havan and worship. Today these little children confidently conduct all the ceremonies and rituals at Rikhiapeeth before thousands of devotees who come to participate in these events.

In 2004, Sivananda Ashram was formed with the main thrust of looking after the elderly and infirm, including widows. It has also undertaken a project to provide one wholesome meal a day to the children and elderly of Rikhia panchayat.

Thus, in a short span of time, a silent revolution has taken place in Rikhia. It was all made possible by a sannyasin who came to this place to live in solitude. Sri Swamiji says, "After coming to Rikhia my cataracted vision was corrected. I have lived a spiritual life for more than sixty years. I have practised every form of yoga, but ultimately I found that when I began to think about others, God began to think about me. On my guru's instructions, I lit the flame of yoga in Munger and the light of seva in Rikhia. This is the requirement of humanity today."

In 2007, Sri Swamiji announced the formation of Rikhiapeeth. He said, "The Rikhia ashram will now be known as Rikhiapeeth. Peeth means 'seat', an apt term for Rikhia as the instructions given to me by Swami Sivananda have culminated and fructified here. Rikhia is an ashram in the original sense of the word because here a lifestyle is lived. Swami Satyasangananda is the Peethadhishwari of Rikhiapeeth and has been given the sankalpa that the three cardinal teachings of Swami Sivananda, serve, love and give, will be practised and lived here. This is the future vision of Rikhiapeeth."

In 2009, after participating in and giving darshan during Sat Chandi Mahayajna and Yoga Poornima where Sri Swamiji inspired everyone to lead the righteous life and bid final farewell to the thousands who had gathered to participate in these events, he entered into mahasamadhi on the midnight of 5th December and merged into Swami Sivananda, our sadguru.

Synopsis of the Life of Swami Niranjanananda Saraswati

Swami Niranjanananda Saraswati was born on 14th February 1960 in Rajnandgaon (Chattisgarh). A month after his birth, Sri Swami Satyananda Saraswati took Swami Niranjan in his lap, blessed him and said:

> *The light of God has descended in the form of this child to illuminate the darkest corners of this earth. He has been born through a pure, divine sankalpa. He has come to fulfil a grand purpose and mission. All of us owe him a debt of duty and responsibility. We have to prepare him for the great task he has come to undertake, a task that will involve countless other souls. He is an embodiment of divine light and he has come with the requisite ingredients. Water this young seedling . . . and in the course of time, this precious flower will spread its divine fragrance throughout the world.*

Swami Niranjan's parents, Swami Dharmashakti and Swami Satyabratananda, were Sri Swamiji's first and closest disciples. They were childless and were inspired to ask Sri Swamiji for a child. On a trip to Gangotri, Sri Swamiji agreed and blessed them, but told them that the child would belong to him. Even before conception, Sri Swamiji had appointed Swami Niranjan as his successor. Thus, Swami Niranjan is the *manas putra*, mind-born son, of Sri Swamiji.

By the age of three, Swami Niranjan had made up his mind that he wanted to be a sannyasin, in service of guru. He first visited the Munger ashram when he was four years old with a resolve to enter the path of sannyasa.

In 1967, Swami Niranjan formally withdrew from school to live with Sri Swamiji, much to the disappointment of his teachers, as he was a star student. Thus, at the age of seven, Swami Niranjan was brought to the ashram, and he lived there until 1971. Under the tutelage of Sri Swamiji, he received intense gurukul education and training. Swami Niranjan was educated in languages, scriptures, philosophy, art, ethics, sciences and contemporary subjects through yoga nidra. While he slept, Sri Swamiji taught him to awaken the seed of knowledge within him

At the age of ten, on 11th January 1971, Swami Niranjan was initiated into Dashnami sannyasa by Sri Swamiji. On 1st March, 1971, Sri Swamiji left for Ireland with the eleven-year-old Swami Niranjan. He was left at the Belfast ashram where he remained with Swami Atmananda to assist in the development of the Satyananda Yoga Centre in Belfast and also to live and learn without the physical presence of Sri Swamiji. He also lived at Satyananda Yoga Ashram in Newcastle-on-Tyne with Rishis Arundhati and Vasishtha, furthering his cultural education. During this time, he travelled through Scotland, France, Belgium, Switzerland, Germany and Austria, conducting yoga classes and yoga training courses.

After that, although they met several times at different destinations, including Munger, Swami Niranjan and Sri Swamiji never really lived together. Their contact, however, has been total. Swami Niranjan lived and moved thousands of miles away, yet his spirit of dedication remained with his guru at all times. Swami Niranjan faced difficulties of every kind. Nevertheless, he did not compromise himself in the face of them and remained undaunted in his discipleship. In Ireland, he built bridges of tolerance between the Catholics as well as the Protestants, becoming an icon of neutrality between the two warring sides.

After spending time in Ireland, Swami Niranjan spent his childhood in London at the home of Swami Pragyamurti. There were many children around at that time who observed that Swami Niranjan exuded joy all the time, and anyone in his company always felt uplifted and experienced inner joy.

In the articulate, intellectual, progressive and scientific environment of the western world, Swami Niranjan impressed all who he came in touch with through the maturity of his knowledge and insight into their needs and problems. At the age of eleven, Swami Niranjan was giving discourses and teaching yoga techniques such as hatha yoga, raja yoga and sadhanas such as prana vidya, often to people more than thrice his age.

In 1972, at the age of twelve, Swami Niranjan had his first encounter with the medical fraternity in London. The day before the lecture he found himself wondering what he would say. That night he dreamt of giving the lecture. On waking, he noted down all the points. After the lecture, the doctors were surprised to hear that he had never completed formal school education. Yet he spoke to the doctors of biofeedback, a recently emerging subject, which most did not know of. He attributed that knowledge to the information given to his subconscious mind in yoga nidra by his guru.

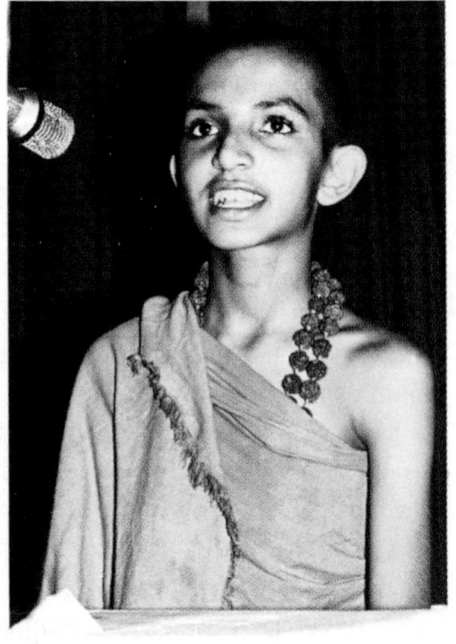

On 11th January 1973, Swami Niranjan travelled from England to Bogota in Colombia, South

America, and extensively toured Colombia and Ecuador. Then he returned to India with a delegation of South American yoga aspirants to participate in the Golden Jubilee Celebrations and the World Yoga Convention being held in Munger.

He now travelled with Sri Swamiji to participate in yoga conventions throughout India. In July 1974 he returned to Colombia and travelled extensively through El Salvador, Guatemala, Mexico, Venezuela, Ecuador and Chile, conducting yoga training programs and establishing yoga teaching centres. During this period he also researched the existence of yoga systems, practices and theories in the pre-Columbian culture of South America, gathering pictorial, sculpted and documented evidence.

In 1976, en route to Australia, Swami Niranjan conducted yoga programs in Chile and French Polynesia. He then participated in the World Yoga Convention in Sydney with Sri Swamiji in 1976. He remained in Australia and carried out research on pranayama in Sydney, and music and mantra in Queensland. He assisted in the formation of ashrams throughout Australia including Sydney, Brisbane and Canberra. He also travelled to New Zealand to guide yoga programs.

Returning to India in July 1977, he became the editor of the monthly magazine *Yoga Vidya* and worked as Sri Swamiji's secretary. He also lived and worked to develop the Satyananda Yoga Ashram in Kolkata and conducted extensive yoga programs within India.

In 1979, Swami Niranjan travelled to Europe where he conducted yoga programs in Greece, Switzerland, England, Ireland and Italy, and assisted in establishing yoga centres in Spain.

Travelling to the US on 1st March 1980, Swami Niranjan conducted two whirlwind tours, visiting, teaching, training, guiding and lecturing yoga aspirants in all the major cities: New York, New Jersey, Virginia, Washington DC, Michigan, Illinois, Georgia, Louisiana, Missouri, Montana, Arizona, Colorado, New Mexico, Utah, Nevada and California. Subsequently, Satyananda Yoga Ashram USA was formed in October 1980. Residential ashram and teaching centres were established in key locations including New York City, Salt Lake City, Berkeley and San Jose among others.

During this period, Swami Niranjan interacted, worked and lived with eminent scientists, spiritual masters, Buddhist, Jewish, Christian groups and heads of different organizations. He conducted research on drug addiction and relaxation response at Gladman Memorial Centre, and on meditation with Dr Joe Kamiya, Nobel Laureate in alpha research. At this time he also acquired skills in audiovisual technologies and flying a Cessna plane.

Thus, for twelve years Swami Niranjan lived and travelled overseas, mastering skills in varied areas, acquiring an understanding of different cultures and helping establish Satyananda Yoga ashrams and centres in

Europe, Australia, North and South America, and New Zealand. During this time, he taught and spread the message of yoga to people from all walks of life. It was during this period that he decided to further strengthen his resolve to live the life of dedication, commitment, upliftment, and responsibility as a sannyasin.

By 1982, the yoga movement started by Sri Swamiji was flourishing and spiritual seekers were flocking to the remote town of Munger. In accordance with the wishes of Sri Swamiji, Swami Niranjan returned to Munger on 16th January 1983. A few days later, on 19th January, the day of Basant Panchami and the foundation day of Bihar School of Yoga (BSY), Sri Swamiji inducted him into the presidency of BSY and handed over full charge and responsibility to him, to also steer the activities of Sivananda Math and the Yoga Research Foundation.

Swami Niranjan served as president of BSY for twenty-five years, from 1983 till 2008. In that time he took the yoga movement and the establishment at Ganga Darshan, Munger, to new heights. During his term, Swami Niranjan was actively involved in lecturing, teaching, travelling and administering the establishment at Munger and the ever-increasing centres throughout the world. He took yoga to different sectors of society, uncovered more scriptural sciences and started new movements.

Under Swami Niranjan's guidance, BSY made significant advances in the application of yoga to address the needs of various groups of people in society including professionals, medics, sportsmen, prison inmates, army, school children, people with cancer, special needs, and people with addictions.

Since the 1990s, BSY has undertaken various projects for professional groups in the state of Bihar, delivering stress management and self-development courses to groups such as income tax officers, central excise, customs and service tax officers, Government of India staff, the Office of Ministerial Staff Training unit and employees of the Indian Railways.

At the request of the Sports Authority of India (SAI), BSY began conducting both short- and long-term training programs for athletes, coaches, physical training teachers, SAI unit heads, coaches and administrative officers. These programs included preparation for the Commonwealth Games in archery and gymnastics; judo, boxing and volleyball teams; and the world cadet wrestling championship medal winner.

A major project of teaching yoga in all medical colleges in the state of Bihar was undertaken at the request of the Bihar Ministry of Health. The Bihar Government sanctioned teaching of yoga therapy to 16,000 registered medical students and doctors.

Since 1994, yoga training has been imparted in twenty-four prisons in Bihar to thousands of prisoners in Bihar jails, hundreds of which have also been trained as yoga teachers.

The Indian Army has introduced yoga into their training programs, for both physical fitness and mental health, especially in high altitude and desert areas. Courses have been conducted for the soldiers and officers and troops at a number of locations. Training programs are also provided for trainees, instructors, inspectors and officers from a number of police academies throughout India.

In 1995, under the guidance of Swami Niranjan, sannyasins on *pad yatra*, walking pilgrimage, took yoga to 108 remote villages of Bihar. The sannyasins engaged in various activities, from clearing roads and drains to teaching yoga, conducting satsang and kirtans. Due to the positive influence of yoga in several villages in the most crime-infested areas of Bihar, hundreds of people resolved to leave the life of crime.

Combining philosophical, scriptural and empirical experience, Swami Niranjan's insight into the benefits of yoga for children has been accepted worldwide. In 1994 and again in March 2000, Swami Niranjan was the Guest Speaker at international conferences organized by UNESCO in France. His exposition on the role and benefits of yoga for children and possibilities for the integration of yoga into classical education was highly acclaimed and generated a new approach to education in Europe.

For people suffering with drug addictions, under the direction of Swami Niranjan, research and investigations undertaken in Greece, Italy and Czechoslovakia have conclusively shown that yoga can dynamically improve the ability of people to make positive qualitative changes in their lifestyle and move beyond the grip of obsessive desire.

On 31st December 1989, Swami Niranjan was initiated as a paramahamsa sannyasin by his guru, Swami Satyananda. The symbol of the paramahamsa is the graceful swan. Long before this initiation, people the world over started to call him 'Swan', due to the qualities of grace and balance which he embodied. In 1993, Swami Niranjan was anointed spiritual successor to Sri Swamiji by the luminaries of the sannyasa tradition. In 1995, at the first Sat Chandi Mahayajna, Sri Swamiji passed on his spiritual shakti and sannyasa sankalpa to Swami Niranjan and declared him as the guru and paramacharya of the tradition.

A rare combination of inherent wisdom, insight and incisive genius, the depth of Swami Niranjan's contributions to the understanding of yoga is remarkable. His exposition of *dharana*, the sixth stage in the raja yoga of Sage Patanjali, is unparalleled. Combining scriptural and personal experiential research, Swami Niranjan expounded upon a collection of dharana practices from ancient yogic, tantric and upanishadic texts. Published in 1993, his book *Dharana Darshan* systematized these practices and made them accessible.

His interest in scriptural research inspired Swami Niranjan to reveal the unknown practice of yoga derived from vedic thought and tradition, laya yoga. A highly advanced practice, laya deals with the dissolution of the manifest nature and experience into the unmanifest, and is seldom taught.

Bihar Yoga Bharati, an institute for advanced studies in Yogic Sciences, was established in Munger 1994 by Swami Niranjan to preserve and regenerate the yogic sciences by integrating science and spirituality. The gurukul-based institute is the first of its kind in the world wholly devoted to the subject of yoga, offering a comprehensive scientific and yogic education and provision to grant certificates and diplomas in yogic studies. Satellite academies in Australia, Europe, the US and South America continue to bring the teachings of BYB to aspirants worldwide.

In 1995, Swami Niranjan initiated a children's yoga movement, Bal Yoga Mitra Mandal (BYMM), under which the children of Munger and surrounding areas imbibe the yogic culture. Started with just seven children, today it has grown to include over 1,20,000 children devoted to yoga.

In 2000, Swami Niranjan established the Yoga Publications Trust (YPT) to disseminate and promote yogic and spiritual knowledge, lifestyle and practice, nationally and internationally, through the publication and distribution of text books, magazines, research materials, practice texts, audio and video cassettes and multimedia presentations.

For the period of Swami Niranjan's leadership, BSY ensured the continuity of both the ancient yogic culture and the tradition of sannyasa. In addition to steering the activities at Munger, Swami Niranjan travelled extensively to guide seekers around the globe. His fresh approach and innate humanity inspired countless aspirants around the globe to take up not only yoga practice, but a yogic lifestyle and yogic culture.

In 2008, he handed over the presidentship of BSY to the third generation, led by Swami Suryaprakash. In 2009, before attaining mahasamadhi, Sri Swamiji gave Swami Niranjan the command to embark on a new phase of sannyasa life, discontinue travel, focus on sadhana, base himself in Munger, and develop a new chapter. This new vision manifested in the form of Sannyasa Peeth.

On 6th December 2010, the auspicious one-year anniversary date of the mahasamadhi of Sri Swamiji, Sannyasa Peeth was formally established by Swami Niranjan at Paduka Darshan, beside the banks of the sacred river Ganga in Munger, with the aim to reintegrate the ancient vedic spiritual heritage and culture into the fabric of modern society.

As the first major project towards implementing the vision of Sannyasa Peeth, Swami Niranjan inaugurated a three-year sannyasa training on Basant Panchami, 28th January 2012, in Munger. To fulfil the mandates given by Sri Swamiji to Swami Niranjan, in 2010 he initiated the Yogadrishti (Yogavision) Satsang Series in which virtually every month a new topic of yoga and spiritual life is expounded upon. Under Swami Niranjan's keen sight, Sannyasa Peeth hosted the first Lakshmi-Narayana Mahayajna from 8th to 12th September, 2011, and since then, the event is being held annually at Sannyasa Peeth. As part of the new phase of his sannyasa life, Swami Niranjan has also undertaken a number of pilgrimages, in particular to those places which Sri Swamiji had visited. In conjunction with the Bihar School of Yoga, Swami Niranjan launches a World Yoga Convention in October 2013. The event marks the next yogic and spiritual revolution, awakening a deeper insight and understanding of the ancient yogic science.

Having handed over the reins of BSY to Swami Suryaprakash and successfully spreading 'yoga from shore to shore' as part of his guru's mandate, Swami Niranjan now spends more time in solitude and sadhana, perfecting the ancient yogic techniques, at the command of his guru.

Tradition

The essence of all tradition is continuity. It is this factor alone that gives birth to tradition. In order to understand this, all we need to do is observe nature. Some of the best examples of tradition can be drawn from it. The planets, the seasons, the plant, animal, mineral and human kingdoms are all governed by their own set of rules. Nature has bestowed these in the form of tradition. These rules never change.

The purpose of tradition is to pass on useful knowledge. All that we know today about ourselves and the world we live in is through the traditions formulated throughout the ages by different civilizations. Thus we see a variety of traditions existing in the world today.

Traditions lend stability to life. Through stability, growth ensues, society evolves and cultures flourish. New discoveries are made and difficult tasks accomplished. This stability is exemplified in the traditions of nature. How impossible it would have been for man to reach his present level of achievement if nature was erratic and whimsical in its traditions.

The Sanskrit word for tradition is parampara. This word also lays emphasis on continuity. Literally it means that which was present yesterday, is there today and will exist tomorrow.

—Swami Satyasangananda Saraswati

Rikhia

Rikhia houses the institutions of Sivananda Math, Sivananda Ashram, Sri Panchdashnam Paramahamsa Alakh Bara and Rikhiapeeth. Primarily a centre for seva (selfless service), Rikhia aims at cultivating social growth and upliftment in the surrounding rural areas, including education and medical care. Another important function of Rikhia is to disseminate ancient spiritual knowledge passed down from the rishis of the vedic era.

Rikhia also hosts many spiritual and cultural events throughout the year.

Contact details

Munger

Bihar School of Yoga, Ganga Darshan, Munger, Bihar 811201, India

Tel: 06344-222430, 06344-228603, 09304799615
Fax: 06344-220169

Website: www.biharyoga.net

✉A self-addressed, stamped envelope must be sent along with enquiries to ensure a response to your request

Rikhia

Rikhiapeeth, P.O. Rikhia, Dist. Deoghar, Jharkhand 814113, India

Tel: 06432-290870, 09304-488889, 09204-080006

Website: www.rikhiapeeth.net

✉A self-addressed, stamped envelope must be sent along with enquiries to ensure a response to your request

How to disidentify the soul from prakriti? Just as we separate butter from milk or rice from its chaff, in the same way, we have to separate the purusha and prakriti tattwas through sadhana.

* * *

What I want to tell you is that this body is not only as much as you see. Beyond the phases of perception and experience we have seen in it an infinite power. Within the folds of the body, there lies the power of homogeneous consciousness.

* * *

How to control the mind? Here is the easiest method: when a box of precious ornaments is lost, we become introvert. When there is some great problem confronting us, we do not even notice our surroundings. Many people pass by, but we see none. When a lady does some stitching work, she sings a lullaby to her baby, her hands automatically move, side by side she talks to her friend. This shows that work can go on even if our mind is introvert. A poet writes the best poem when he rises above the feeling that he is writing something. So is the case with doctors, scientists and others.

* * *

The indriyas are gopis and worldly objects are their husbands. So long as the gopis, indriyas, are busy with their husbands, objects, they will not hear the flute of Krishna. Let the indriyas withdraw from the objects. Lo, now they can listen to the divine music of the soul!

* * *

How to achieve success in every field? You just have to be sure and definite about your success in the work you have undertaken. You should relax your mind while feeling sure about the success. Indifference and relaxation coupled with definiteness and surety lead one to success.

* * *

Surrender to guru or God is the easiest way to ensure mental equilibrium as well as worldly success. Therefore, I say, "Simply resign to His will." This is the secret.

* * *

Fortunate was Christ who was crucified.

Fortunate were Socrates and Mansoor; what about Mira and Dayananda?

How unfortunate are we, when we find ourselves allured by praises and favours, flowers and merits?

Misfortune unsurpassed! When trials come to our door, we cry out aloud to help us kick them away. Yet we only kick divine chances. So do you understand!

Satyam feels His grace and mercy, when tempests try to move him. Oh yes, Satyam thanks all of them, because they come to judge and confirm his strength. You call them shoes; I call them flowers.

Flowers! Verily, they are the destroyers of my soul.

Abuses, insults, injuries, taunts, harassments, discomforts, have all strengthened my personality. Let me repeat my mantra, which my guru whispered into my soul . . .

"Adapt, adjust, accommodate;
Bear insult, bear injury; highest sadhana."

* * *

Those who are suffering may come to me. Those who wish to know Him may come to me. Those who love me may come to me. Those who deny God may come to me. Let them surround me in any manner they like. I will give them a way of life which will be practical, divine and trouble free. And, thus we end the logical discussions about God's existence and absence, for both are His attributes and attributes are inseparably integrated with the object proper.

* * *

This booklet is our small offering of love to Satyam, our beloved Guruji, as a token of our deep regard and gratitude for his consenting to conduct the Spiritual Training-Camp in Bombay from 24th December 1961 to 1st January 1962.

Dissemination of Satyam's message of peace, love and happiness is the sacred and foremost duty of us all. At our first camp at Rajgirh, we decided to set up the first of the four printing presses in Chapra, Bihar. It was also decided to form a cooperative society with an authorized capital simultaneously with the establishment of a Publication Fund for crediting those donations and subscriptions which do not form a share.

Hearty cooperation of all in order to motivate this spirit into action is cordially invited. I thank all my friends who have helped me in making this camp a great success. My special thanks go to Upen who has given me enormous help in editing and printing this booklet. But for him, the publication of this booklet would have remained a dream.

—Viswaprem, Bombay

Satyam Speaks

Part II

Swami Satyananda Saraswati

Yoga Publications Trust, Munger, Bihar, India

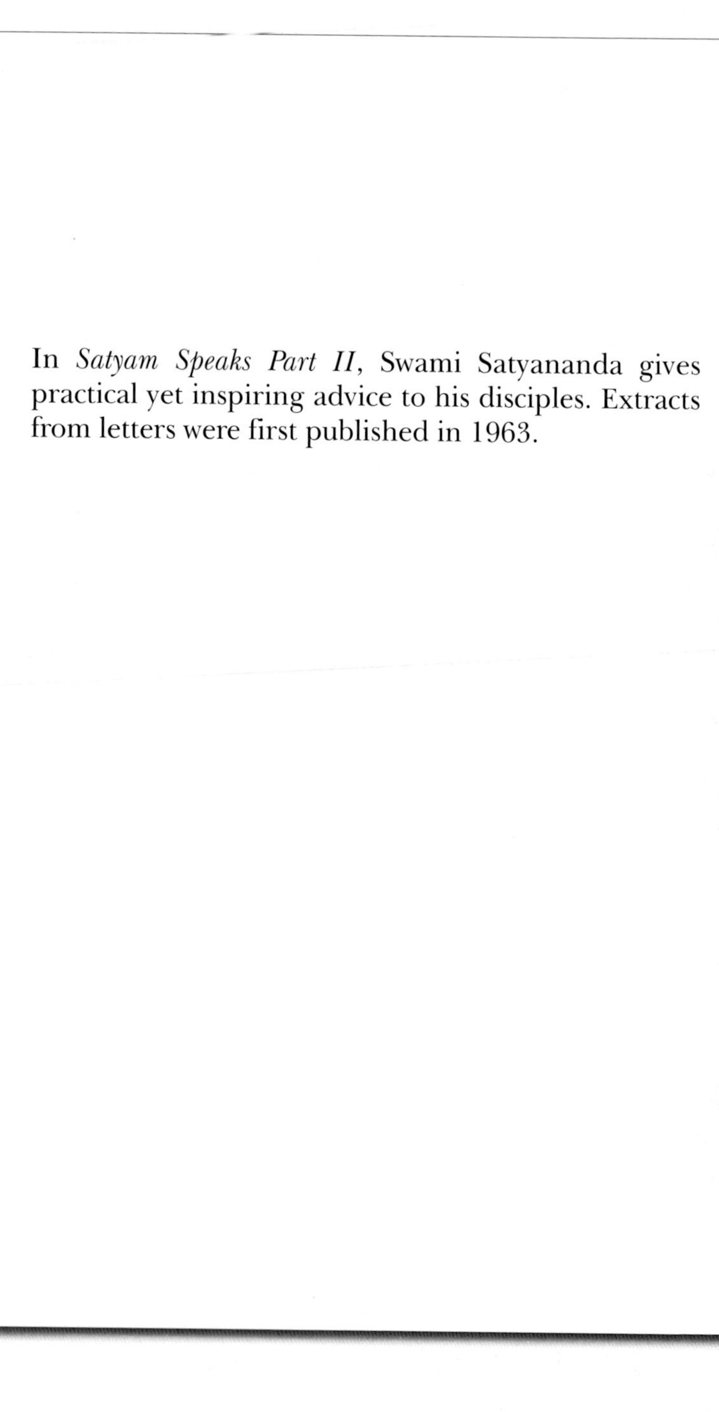

In *Satyam Speaks Part II*, Swami Satyananda gives practical yet inspiring advice to his disciples. Extracts from letters were first published in 1963.

Side Light

This is a collection of gems taken out of a chaplet of epistolary jewels prepared by Satyam as a gift to his disciples. The selection, if it could be called one, has been difficult, for, almost each expression is rich in thought, pregnant with meaning and replete with seeds of divine thoughts, and yet a choice had to be made.

Truth is self-luminous. Self-effulgence is its essence. Devoid of it, it would not be truth. Satyam, as his very name implies, is the apostle of truth and in the samplings of his writings which are given here, one finds a forthrightness of expression, a clarity of thought, a penetrating insight into the ways of life, its problems, its complications and their almost very simple and easy solution, if one has the tenacity to persevere on the path indicated by him. Blessed are those who have achieved that state, twice blessed are those to whom truth is brought as if on a platter and served as a delicious spicy morsel.

There could be no introduction to Satyam, for, as is said above, truth is self-effulgent and one who reads this scintillating starlet of thoughts will know not only the man but his mission.

—V. V. Baxi

Preface

We have great pleasure in placing in your hands the second part of the booklet *Satyam Speaks*. The first part was published in December 1961 and is now out of stock. The popular acclaim that the booklet received has encouraged us to bring out the second volume in the series.

This booklet consists of extracts from *Yoga Sadhana, Part 2*. As this book is also out of stock, we hope that this small booklet will meet the needs of many aspirants who have been requesting us for the same since long. The original book was in Hindi and the extracts have been rendered into English.

It will be seen that this booklet aims at giving in a nutshell a glimpse of elements which fashion the yogic disposition. The main theme of Swamiji's writings has always centred round the vision that commitment to yogic disciplines is possible for all. Although variously misunderstood, yoga comes to the rescue of the harassed householder as well as to the bewildered aspirant. It is one of the cardinal aims of our movement to establish yoga as a culture of tomorrow.

—Editor, June 1963

PART I

The mind alone becomes the helper or the bar on the path of knowledge. Therefore, the mind is first to be controlled. On this path of discipline, faith must be dominant and all-pervasive.

* * *

Prayer should be pure, straight and spontaneous. On prayer alone depends the success of other things. One should have full faith that the object of prayer listens to everything. Prayer has the power to destroy the rough elements in one's culture. Thus prayer is also a destroyer of sin. None should doubt this. Prayer is also a form of self-realization.

* * *

What is the power of sound? Sound waves quickly affect the subconscious mind. Sweet song relaxes muscular tensions; then alone proper aid is received in reaching the goal. With mental tensions continuing, no concentration can be achieved. Holy songs remove the unholy tendencies of the mind. The senses of hearing are drawn inward. The external sound turns inward and purifies the veins, and the mind full of pleasure becomes qualified to visualize easily the form of God.

* * *

The accident of life and death or happiness and misery which stand in front of you are like so many eye-openers. They open the divine vision. The sense of discrimination between the substance and the shadow becomes intensified. The heart is softened by the increase of grace and the path of final emancipation becomes free of obstructions.

* * *

A life without struggles is no life at all. In other words, the conflicts inherent in life, its ups and downs, are true life. Do not think that life will run smoothly in the same channel. The conflicts of happiness and misery, life and death, constitute the essence of life.

* * *

Before every act of grace of the Mahamaya, one must bow low and each such act has to be accepted with humility and reverence. We ignorant men never know where imperishable and enjoyable bliss lies. The Mahamaya alone knows by which act of grace an individual could be blessed. Therefore, the ignorant jiva for all time should surrender himself to God, because God alone is omniscient, all the rest are ignorant.

* * *

Worldly pleasures are transitory and are the harbingers of discontentment and sorrow. No man who loved the world has succeeded in making himself happy. He whose mind hankers after the fruits of actions, is full of longing, desires and discontentment. He whose ideals are shallow and yet aims high will remain discontented even if he gets the plenitude of the three worlds. Turn all the desires towards God. Thus only life can be made happy and successful.

* * *

Remain absorbed in the pursuit of God and your daily duties like the bee. Do not for a moment give the mind an opportunity to wander. The control of the mind is the first essential for the development of a life of yoga. In other words, do not let the mind wander here and there. He whose mind wanders, never attains to yoga.

* * *

To my mind, the first and foremost remedy to control the mind is to keep it occupied. This will deprive it of any opportunity to create desires. If you can keep your mind constantly busy, it will come under your control and then you will be able to mould it according to your desire. Remember that an active person crosses the confines of happiness and misery.

* * *

While attending to household duties, perform japa or prayers loudly or in silence, so that you may not have time to worry uselessly. Do not move about with a long face. Always remain cheerful, buoyant and calm. Learn to laugh and make others laugh. Do not fret. Just as a vehicle does not move on one wheel, so also without any effort, fortune never smiles. Only cowards believe in fate.

* * *

Nothing is achieved by worrying over difficulties. The fact is that worries deplete our energies to make efforts, whereas by doing efforts the cares are reduced. Between the funeral pyre and worries the latter are more consuming. While the funeral pyre burns the dead, worries burn the living. What a flame worry is! Worry is like a terrible serpent.

* * *

Have full faith in God. Accept His commands or directions as the only way and go on performing your duties as mere instruments. Such people alone have glorified the pages of history as highly successful individuals and immortalized themselves.

* * *

The fact is that man has less work and more time; less yoga and more enjoyment; less detachment and more attachment; less contentment and more desires; less hope and more despair; less confidence and more diffidence. This is the reason why he remains constantly afflicted by thoughts of worries and cares, attachment and unhappiness, failure and evils. Therefore, one should practise karma yoga, undertake the study of yoga, develop detachment, contentment and faith to make life successful and happy.

* * *

What should you ask in prayer? Remember that the only thing to be asked is devotion at the feet of God. Prayer should be offered only to secure the love of God.

* * *

Association with the low soils the intellect; association with one's equals, keeps the intellect even and association with the great makes the intellect great. That is why satsang is more valuable, for it is said that an insect by association with a flower is able to sit on the head of the great ones, and even a stone when installed by the great is worshipped as a divine image.

As soon as faith in the grace of God wavers, life also wavers. Even though one is conscious of the grace of God, the balance of life sometimes wavers. Why does it happen? Because the devotee has no patience. He desires that each movement must take place in tune with his own wishes. Here it is where the ego enters. The sadhaka comes to grief and becomes miserable. Ego is the greatest obstacle in the development of faith in God.

* * *

I do concede that the problems of domestic life are always difficult, especially when there is an absence of mutual cooperation between its members and when each one is trying to trouble the other. It is curious how while the family was founded in search for happiness and peace by man, in the end he gets these problems.

* * *

Develop self-confidence. All power is within you. Always think that you are capable of doing everything. This is the key to success. Do not despair till the last moment of defeat.

Therein lies courage. Self-confidence is the celestial treasure of man. It was on the strength of this that heroic deeds which altered the course of history, society and religion were performed. Those who lead nations and society should possess an abundance of self-confidence.

* * *

There is a great difference between ego and self-confidence, even as there is a difference between modesty and humility. As the bondage of worldly desires loosens, self-confidence grows. As physical, mental weaknesses and defects of character are removed, self-confidence appears. Ego is not necessary for the development of self-confidence. On the other hand, what is necessary is the removal of our ordinary defects. Correct your life and think that you possess the ability to do everything.

* * *

We are such stuff as are afraid of pain and desire happiness and ease. Such an attitude is the result of desires. We call the fulfilment of desires happiness and their non-fulfilment misery. If things turn out according to our desires there is pleasure, otherwise sorrow. We want to cling to happiness which kicks us and then we cry.

* * *

Therefore, do not treat the entire life as full of roses or a uniform flow. Wise men have treated life as a play. Those who are detached treat it as a dream. Devotees treat it as a play of the Lord. Remember further that he who changes himself with the changing pattern of life will laugh as well as cry but he who remains as a witness will remain steady. Better it is that we appraise each situation and assess each change. Here lies the beginning of yoga.

* * *

Sadhana is the gateway of liberation. To remain in a state of continuous bliss in life by means of sadhana is the realization of divine experience.

* * *

A sadhaka need not be troubled by attachment or consumed by jealousy. A sadhaka who has possessed himself completely by separating the senses, playing with the sense objects from attachment and jealousy, attains bliss. Attachment and jealousy imply that the sadhaka is still attached to the duality of the pleasant and the painful. Renunciation of family life does not bring an end to attachment and jealousy. The turmoil of attachment and jealousy only end through *viveka*, discrimination, a result of renunciation. Only then detachment and love come. You are not the leader of the world. Continue to remain its spectator.

* * *

Whenever worries invade the mind, take it that the mind is ill and that it needs rest and fast cure. Physical ailments are prescribed rest, even so when mental worries pervade the mind, one should cultivate satsang and also say prayers. Just as in physical ailments fasting is prescribed even so in mental ailments the ingress and egress of various thoughts should be prevented and only one thought which is light and peaceful should be created. Truly the mind should first be purged; prayer and repentance are purgatives. In addition satsang, initiation into mantra and sadhana should take the place of medicines, wholesome nutrition and nourishment. Then the disease of worry will be cured.

* * *

Do you know what the remedy for cares is? It lies in the giving up of one's desires and surrendering oneself to that Great Power.

* * *

Why not try to experiment for a few days to lead a desireless life? Your nature will automatically be transformed. Wailings of sorrow will cease.

* * *

You are sinful! Even to say that, is sin. To act in sin is not as sinful as to nourish a belief that it is so. Sin in itself is not as harmful as the fear of the sin. Sin! This is the great hurdle in the path of those devoted to actions. It is the great obstacle in the path of those heroes who wish to perform great deeds. It is the great python lying stretched across the path of life. Who created sin? Who created repentance? Those mentors who felt floored by the ignorance and indiscipline of the human race? Sin! Who does not commit sin? Sin! Who is sinless? If you are able to show me a single instance of sinlessness right from the prophets of the old to the most ignorant man, I shall accept the theory of sin. Remove such feelings; cut down those weaknesses of the mind. I say, rise. Free yourself from worries and continue to do your daily duties. Your home is your Vrindavan, Mathura and Kashi; your children are Radha, Sita, Rama and Shyam; your food is prasad of a temple; the water of your house is the sacred *charanamrita*, the water of holy abhisheka, of the temple; your room is your Saketpuri and Kailash. Divine power is another name for the holy powers of gods which are reflected in you.

* * *

It is sheer madness to attach any importance to the ups and downs in one's worldly life. He who gives importance to this sinks and forever goes down. It is the way of this world that it accepts those who suit its purpose. Where it finds that its ends are not served, it kicks. If you have art in you, people will sit at your feet, and if you have nothing in you, none will look at you. Therefore, believe me, social beliefs have no permanent or dependable values. The best course will be for you to tread the path of religion and to make you more and more enlightened. If you continue to think as to what the world will say about you, your mind will remain constantly troubled. Look upon the world as a strange country where the vision of the people is perverse, where each individual tries to look at the other one from his own standpoint and assesses him according to his own standards. It should be learnt from wise men what our attitude should be in such a world. Day and night you are occupied in trying to impress others. All your activities are concentrated towards impressing others but are they really impressed? If not then go to that plane where purity, knowledge, charity, pity and sympathy forever abide. That region is within you. That region is the region of *sahaja samadhi*, spontaneous samadhi, where the jiva attains the highest bliss and great power. Tread this path. It is the last resort of humanity.

* * *

Try to realize the blessed Divine Self in your daily meditation and deposit these experiences as if in a bank in your heart. But beware, lest these six robbers either by force or fraud break open the windows and steal this treasure of experiences. Therefore, repeat the secret mantra *Om Namah Shivaya* because that alone is such a key known to you as well as to the bank of your heart. Whenever you want to use these experiences for the benefit of people repeat this *panchakshara*, five-syllable, mantra and bring it out. Distribute this wealth between the poor and afflicted. Give it in guru dakshina to your preceptor and sustain yourself on the treasure of the Self; and I say that the plenitude of the entire universe is incomplete and I declare that the treasure of the Self is inexhaustible. Have you not seen that the rich are miserable and the wise are blissful?

* * *

Blessed are those who meditate. Our wise ancestors have, therefore, said, "Shut the nine gates so that external light may not enter inside; let the tenant remain confined and place four guards on the main gates. Now go into the harem. You will meet the Supreme Being."

*　　*　　*

If in one's daily domestic duties situations arise which cause anxiety and affliction, regard these as tests. If worries overpower you, then you fail. If worries come and pass away, then you are promoted, and if you do not treat worries as worries but regard them as signs of the grace of God, believe me, you are successful; and if worries lead you to higher knowledge, then you take it that you pass first class. Brave!

*　　*　　*

If you treat yourself as the doer then you will be the sufferer and worries also will be there. But if you know the doer, you will also know the enjoyer. To tell you the truth, it is here that the whole train gets derailed. The doer remains indeterminate. In ignorance, we regard ourselves as the doers. If we have not been fools in any other manner, it is here that we have made fools of ourselves. What vanity! Somebody else does the work and you call yourself the doer? Do you believe that in this world all work will be done through you? There are also four other companions. This life is a limited company of five shareholders. If one of them tries to exercise his right, he will be thrown out. His body belongs to *panchas*, the five tattwas. Is it you alone who have made this house?

*　　*　　*

The fulfilment of all actions is achieved through these five means. Take for instance, food, agriculturist or even yourself. See whether there is not the rule of panchayat? Then who is the doer and who is responsible? It has been said that if these five combine and act there would be no experiences of joy or sorrow, victory or defeat. In this mental attitude the question of good or bad results does not arise. The body, the jiva, twelve elements, ten pranas and the Unseen One, through these five instruments, all actions are accomplished.

You have wrongly believed yourself to be the doer and the enjoyer. I once again repeat that these five and not you, are the doers of actions.

* * *

Just as the stationary sun appears to be moving, the immovable road appears to be in motion; just as the stationary streets appear to be in motion with the movements of the wind, even so because of the play of prakriti, activities appear to be reflected in you even though you are the immovable atma. Only because of your identification with the functioning of nature you have believed yourself to be the doer of deeds and the enjoyer of fruits.

* * *

Just as the soldier who goes to battle by Royal Command acquires no sin of killing, even so treat yourself as the soldier of God. For even in domestic matters these five elements prevail. A physician who gives medicine to a patient is not tainted with sin if the patient dies. So also you should carry on your daily life with the objective of being serviceable to mankind while renouncing the feeling of happiness and misery; for, by being devoid of ego, the liberated souls have neither any selfish motive in good deeds nor are they harmed by bad deeds. The sadhaka, who treads the path of karma yoga with detachment while surrendering unto God the fruits of his actions, is like the lotus in water, not bound by the fruits of good or bad actions.

* * *

Just as the priest who performs ceremonies, penances and observes vows for the benefit of and on behalf of his host, is not responsible for the fruits of these actions, even so you should perform all your actions without a sense of ego for the benefit of all persons of the family.

* * *

Perform your duties for you are made to do them. You are merely an instrument. Therefore, you must carry on your daily duties without hesitation. Only if you realize that in this world of yours, there are crores of miserable people, you will at once cease to feel miserable at your own conditions. You have to learn the lesson of contentment. You have to change your outlook. Do not remain unnecessarily worried. Oh, if these wailings were for the sake of God-realization, the face of your situations would have been changed.

* * *

Oh, you are pure and stainless. Your soul is above all taints. It transcends the dualities. You are the symbol of truth, knowledge, existence and bliss. The pure and omnipresent power of *Aum* pervades every core of your being. You are not what is called of the earth and, therefore, earthly. You are that which is truth. Know this for certain.

* * *

The poor are unhappy because of want of wealth, but until such time only as they do not acquire wealth. The day they acquire the highest treasure, they exclaim, "We have got the jewelled treasure, our Rama." Thereafter, they do not remain unhappy for want of wealth.

* * *

A sonless man is unhappy so long as he has no son, but the day he finds the greatest of all sons, that moment he declares, "Rama is everything to me; my, son, my friend, my relation." Thereafter, he is not aggrieved at the absence of a son, a friend, or relation. He alone is the richest of the poor, the vision of the blind, the support of the afflicted, the curer of all faults. The day you realize Him, from that day, the sense of loss disappears.

* * *

Sometimes I used to feel so miserable at the thought, why there should be so much misery and trouble in this world. Will I not be ever able to find a solution for it? One day I became aware that there was no misery, no trouble in the world. Everything was within the mind. Therefore, once the misery in the mind is removed, the affliction of the world disappears.

* * *

If you are able to persuade your mind that the real brother, friend, mother, father, husband is Rama, will your mind go about wandering in search of another friend, mother, father or husband? Accept Rama as your only shelter, the higher treasure and the great beloved. Weep for Him, laugh for Him, sleep for Him, work for Him. We are all Radhas of Krishna, ever afflicted by His separation. We have not found Him that is why the miseries of this world affect us. Do you think that the experiences of pain will continue even after God-realization? The child is stretched happily in the mother's lap, the wife in the husband's and this world in the lap of Sri Krishna. Come, cease to worry. Weep for Rama. To wail for the fulfilment of desires is to be more miserable; service at the feet of Rama gives pleasure and removes the pains of life. The service for the sake of desires creates mental afflictions, makes life one long cry of wail. Rama is immortal. He is deathless. Desires are false. They do not endure.

* * *

Learn to be happy in all acts. Laugh with contentment at the time of work. Mental conflicts break in a variety of ways. Today, let us surrender everything at the feet of our great friend Rama.

* * *

We do not want anything from Him. Neither are we losing our prestige, nor do we need clothes to cover us. Neither is anyone coming to beat us nor do we want the help. Neither is anyone going to rob us of our belongings nor do we need Narayana. Give us the pure and sweet prema bhakti so that in every atom we can realize our great friend and get His glimpse. If we get the Shyam of Radha then it is foolish to ask for the insignificant things of the world.

* * *

You have struck the bonanza of gold and found forests of sandalwood. Then why are you worried about stone and fuel? *Moha*, attachment, is the root cause of all misery. Its result is sin, which again is the result of ignorance. Try to understand the nature of this world. Try to understand the greatness of Rama. Understand what happiness is and what misery is, and then judge for yourself how misery is experienced.

* * *

The whole world is unhappy. He alone is happy whose mind is attuned to the service of God. He who wants to keep both, the world and God, always stands on the danger zone. If you want to be happy, transform your thoughts and your attitudes. Try to understand the significance of each event. Behind each event there is a mysterious object of God.

* * *

Have you ever been unhappy for the sake of Shyam? Have you ever experienced unhappiness or shed tears like Mira? Have you ever experienced the anguish of separation from Krishna, the Lord of the universe like Chaitanya? Then what wrong is there if by crying for the world you have not been able to acquire the world.

* * *

When you were a baby you were trying to catch the shadow of the moon. When you were a deer, you were running after the mirage to satisfy your thirst. Today also having acquired human birth you are trying to run after shadows. That is why I say that worldly desires do not contain pleasure, only infinite unhappiness. Therefore change and transform yourself.

* * *

Transform your love, alter your vision, change your speech, search for Him from whom you have been separated for ages, for He is also searching for you.

* * *

Sound thoughts come in a sound mind. An unhealthy person is not able to overcome emotions of lust or anger.

* * *

There are too many temptations to spoil life, and many more complications. Beware, do not give up your path. That path is the path of truth. Of course, there are many more paths. But in all of them there is an end and death. All other paths ultimately lead to misery, despair, fear and death. It is best, therefore, to depend upon truth. The one who chooses to tread the higher path will go along fearlessly. One who chooses to go along the lower path of material pursuits will experience happiness and misery, but ordinary people prefer this path because they can get material prosperity in this manner. Only those who are free from bondage choose the higher path of spiritual pursuits.

The path of material pursuits is the path which follows the behests of the senses and therefore, the harbinger of evil results. The path of meditation is the path of spiritual pursuit and results in the attainment of samadhi. Therefore, proceed along this path of spirituality by taking resort to japa, meditation, asana, pranayama and kirtan. In brief, man is confronted with two paths: the spiritual and material. The wise men assess the relative merit of both of these separately. The man of higher understanding accepts the path of final bliss in preference to the other one, but the unenlightened one who desires the fulfilment of his longings chooses the path of material pursuits.

* * *

The world is full of selfishness. There is no question of doubt about it. Those who are ours deceive us. Some are selfishly inclined towards the body; some have a selfish nature while some are interested in wealth. Nobody cares for anybody in a disinterested manner. The love of the husband also falls in the same category.

* * *

The conjugal relationship is nature's arrangement to make it an instrument to lead to the path of yoga and samadhi. Ignorant men do not know that behind the physical, mental and allied relationship between man and woman lies concealed a scheme for spiritual unity. Such a man treats the body as everything, poetic language as all and thus sabotages the broad aims of Nature.

* * *

Without God-realization, life is worse than death. One, who even after attaining this rare human birth does not achieve self-realization, is born to no purpose. Man fulfils his mission of life only when he attains to God-realization.

* * *

Girls must have that vitality, that life and strength that they could even twist steel by their grasp. Do not teach them to weep. Do not teach them to blush red with shame. Do not tell them to look askance with lowered eyes and cover their heads and bodies every now and then. Let them not be taught to be suspicious. On the other hand let every atom of their being be made aflame with ideas of service and renunciation. Let every limb of theirs be made of finely tempered steel. Let their ideas bubble like hot water.

* * *

Man is foolish. He does not renounce the enjoyments of sense objects but dreams to be immortal. Renounce worldly pleasures – this is immortality. Repeat His name, do asana and pranayama – this is nectar. This is the way to be immortal. Oh, but who worries for all these? Everybody here has become lazy. We all seem to be concerned with pleasure and ease. People say, "We will continue to sin in life; for the panditji is in charge of the dry-cleaning department." They treat the pandit as a mechanical washerman. This is all self-deception.

* * *

Men of the world will prevent you from treading this path, for the world knows that it will not be able to deceive you or obstruct you once you take to this path. People always take advantage of our mistakes. If we are weak, they exploit our weakness and serve their own ends. If we want to be strong, we are prevented from gaining strength. The world wants us to fail. Society wants us to remain immersed in worldliness and in the end fall, get a bad name and weep. If we try to go on a nobler and purer path, we will be happy, will rise and will finally be honoured by society. This squint-eyed society is never able to see this. That is precisely why our friends prevent us from taking to japa, prayers and meditation. But ask them, "Have you ever prevented us from seeing pictures, from being disintegrated; from drinking and gambling? Did you object to our leading a humdrum life? Then why do these people prevent us from treading the path of truth? You may become a member of the club and take active part in politics, there is no objection, but why do you create obstructions in the path leading to strength and peace?"

* * *

Life never becomes happy by the acquisition of material comforts. Can anybody continue to live on bread alone? Is devotion to God never necessary for him? If so, his belly will always be full but his mind hungry and the soul thirsty.

He who is chary and wary of nourishing his mind and soul, suffers indefinable anguish but he who nourishes his mind and soul, gets his belly filled automatically.

* * *

What is the aim of life? What should it be? Ask those old fogies? What will you gain by asking those who have consumed cups after cups and bottles after bottles? Would those who have bargained their lives for bottles of blood, bundles of flesh, bank balances and plenitude of maya, ever be able to lead you to the goal of life? Will a blind man lead the blind or a lame man cross the river? For finding the right objective, surrender yourself at the feet of those who have divine and pure vision, whose mind is fixed on a single ideal. It is not easy to understand the goal of life. Men certified by colleges and universities as geniuses have also failed. But a man with common sense will certainly find out the real aim of life. Have we come here only to live? Is this all an accidental show? Is all confusion here or is life a vast experiment and a pilgrimage towards the infinite, where step by step we are marching forward towards peace and highest bliss?

* * *

If the mind of a sadhaka is afflicted, he has to sleep more because the reactions of rajoguna project into tamoguna. If there is peace in the heart, sattwa guna rises of its own accord. Then no exhaustion is felt in doing one's duty. Exhaustion is the result of worries, mental conflict or joy, sorrow and desires. In brief, indulging in senses brings the exhaustion and gives rise to tamoguna.

* * *

If the body is light and the mind is light, meditation is deep and, therefore, I am drawing you nearer to that. But first know what is the state of sleep and the state of wakefulness. When fear, delusion, infatuation and pride disappear then take it that you are awake. When life becomes easy; when one does not stumble or commit mistakes; when the self is controlled and one remains in a state of blessed tranquillity, then take it that one is awake. When petrol does not burn in spite of the nearness of fire; when a piece of paper does not get wet in spite of being dropped in water; when trees do not get uprooted in spite of a storm, then know that you are awake.

* * *

Know that the jiva is now asleep and is indulging in dreams of happiness and misery, and is drinking deep both of nectar and poison; it is alive as well as dead. Is there no remedy to save it? Yes, it is there. It is knowledge. When the walls of ignorance are broken, only Brahman remains and not the jiva; when sleep is broken I remain; not the tendencies of dreams. How can it ever happen that in a state of samadhi this jiva-consciousness, this bondage, would not go? Does it ever happen that a person who is dead in dreams remains dead when he wakes? Therefore, give up sleep. Cross the darkness of tamoguna. Raise sattwa guna and proceed.

* * *

In how many ways does God test us? Such tests continue only till such time as the devotee's surrender is complete. When the mind transcends happiness and misery and is permeated by unbroken peace then only He stops His play.

* * *

Spiritual, celestial or physical troubles and happiness through sense enjoyment are given only to lead the life to its proper fulfilment. Even though happiness and misery are experiences of the mind, its aim is to throw out quickly the imperfections of the jiva which is engrossed in darkness and confusion.

* * *

When by the wings of sadhana, Hanuman in the shape of sovereign power is realized, then only the quest of Sita becomes successful and the ten-headed monster is destroyed. If therefore, you desire to cultivate self-confidence and high thoughts, make sadhana a part of your life's activities, and as far as possible stop giving it publicity.

* * *

So long as individuals are immersed in self-interest, they feel unhappy. When there is a conflict of interests, trouble begins. Then they call each other selfish or false. In this neither the husband nor the wife believes each other. The wise know this. Therefore, they do not stumble. In this world we must know the origin of the world.

* * *

Behind love or hatred, praise or censure, gratitude or ingratitude, cooperation or apathy of this world, lies selfishness. The wise knowing this, behave in a disinterested manner with everybody. Do not seek for the cause of mental unrest outside you. You are the cause; the attachment, *moha*, concealed within you is the cause. Believe it or not but you are full of infatuations. That is misery and you too want to welcome this moha by calling it duty. What could be done? Even if a dog is beaten he comes back again. This is the state of everybody. How often has it been told that physical love is painful and transitory? Love is the bondage of the mind. Real love is only devoted towards God.

* * *

So long as you run after the shadow, the shadow will also continue to run. If you turn your back, the shadow will also turn to your back. This is the state of affairs with all worldly objects. So long as you have in your mind the desire for any object of the world, that object will continue to go away from you. Leave all desires and the same thing will automatically be drawn unto you. This is the secret of success.

* * *

Man shapes his activities in tune with his longing and thus falls into a vicious circle which does not leave him till his death. If one desire is fulfilled, the other is created and thus they swell.

*   *   *

There are two obstructions in the path of God-realization. The All-Knowing Soul is hidden by these. Lust and anger are permanent enemies of knowledge. So long as these exist, no real knowledge comes. Aided by the senses, mind and intellect, they exist. So long as you do not remove these two from within you, you will never reach the state of samadhi even in dreams, for, they degenerate the mind. You have been told, "Make the Meghnath quiet and then run after the Ravana for unseen enemies attack you from above." Even careful and self-possessed sadhakas sometimes get into their toils. Therefore, keep awake.

*   *   *

Happiness? That is that wine which is the share of the demons. Having drunk deep of that wine, we forget our higher object and fall from the path of immortality. Happiness? It is the most insignificant thing which has come out of the ocean of the mind. It is delicious, fragrant and intoxicating, but in the end it is harmful. If the wine of Holi defeats even the brave, this happiness which is the wine of life makes the living almost lifeless and dead. Remember, that the seeker after happiness has so far never been immortal.

*   *   *

He who like Lord Shiva drinks the poison of the conflicts of life relying on the name of Rama and keeps on his head the crescent moon in the shape of quiet thoughts, will get his share of nectar in a large measure. Yes, it is true that the man who drinks the poison of this world becomes good and also a harbinger of peace and happiness, and free from fear. Therefore, transform your attitude towards happiness and misery.

* * *

Nothing comes out of renouncing the world. It is the nature of the mind to play pranks even in the ashrams and tapovans. Then what is the good of renunciation? The man, who is ever awake wherever he goes, should transform his internal atmosphere and stay there; by correcting his spiritual, domestic and financial considerations, much of the difficulties in the way of the man are cleared.

* * *

In brief, in order to bring out the holy powers that reside in you, it is necessary that your thoughts should be pure, your speech should be pure, your conduct should be pure, your food should be pure; your character should be pure, your vision should be pure.

* * *

The world believes that because a person studies the Vedas and the scriptures, he will realize God; that because he performs sacrifices, he will realize God, that because he performs penances, he will realize God, and that because he has given alms, he will realize God! But, so long as there is no love for God, all rituals and ceremonies performed with a view to realize God bear no fruit. So long as the mind does not think of God in the same manner as a worldly-minded man thinks of his sense objects, the lustful about his lust, the deer about music, the poor about wealth, the butterfly about the flame, the fish about water, till then it will ever remain restless. Look upon God as the final aim and end of life and remain occupied in devotion. Keep away from sense objects, but love all.

* * *

Worries are attitudes of the mind which arise out of ignorance. They are in fact the habits of the mind which could be moulded or broken. When our minds are not engrossed in ourselves or in God and the universe that he has created, then worries arise. Worries are negative attitudes which should be removed. Their positive aspect is continuous contemplation on God.

* * *

Is there anyone amongst you who does not sleep by day and night, so absorbed is he in the thought of his beloved God? Is there anyone who has abjured food, clothes or love for the self and others for this end, but continues to pass day after day in the remembrance of that One? If such a person exists, there is no need of sadhana for him. I stand guarantee that he will realize Him because he has lost himself. Or, if it is not so, then continue to turn the wheel of sadhana and grind to dust the mind; destroy the ego remove the conflicts of the mind, awaken the soul. Let the treasures of your heart be lost and then you will be a fit and proper person to receive the grace.

* * *

Who does not want to be a siddha? Who does not want to be a yogi? But my Lords, what have you done? You want to do something and be something but you fail in the very fundamentals. You want to sleep for eight hours, you want to rest also, you want name and fame and also gossip. You want all and along with these, you want samadhi and siddhi!

* * *

Listen, you cannot make God or the devil both your servants. You should take to one path, one objective, one madness and one absorption. My guarantee is to such sadhakas that they will attain the highest because they have left everything.

* * *

What is all this folly that for a month you are fasting? To realize God you have left eating salt and also abandoned sleep. If you do that, your body will be a resthouse of diseases and the mind will become weak; then how will you realize God?

* * *

Steadiness, peace, absence of turmoil, purity and love of God – when the mind acquires these five qualities, then the Luminous One is seen; but if there is a slight disturbance in these five qualities, the vision will be lost. Therefore, your conduct of life should be sweet; free from anger, full of love. You should give up slander but continue to think well. Be fearless and practise continence. Remember that so long as external events continue to influence the mind, that vision will not be revealed to you.

* * *

Have you got that instrument with you by which the influence of external events could be prevented from affecting the astral body? There is only one instrument but its names are two. Some know it by the name of renunciation, *vairagya*, some call it devotion, *bhakti*. But it is one and the same. If the mind liberates itself from attachment to senses, then know it to be renunciation. When it attaches itself to God know it to be devotion. Vibhishana left Ravana and accepted Rama. When love comes, the superimposition of the world disappears. If bhakti is strong the state of renunciation comes effortlessly. This is the only instrument by which the daily impact of existence does not influence the inner being. This is the major condition for the fulfilment of meditation.

* * *

Thus it was that Jesus said, "Become you like little children," for, simplicity and straightforwardness of childhood are dear to God. Therefore, I have told others and tell everyone not to come to me as sophisticated individuals. If you want to come to me, keep your heart open in the palm of your hand, to surrender it to me. Come to me like little children. Come to me untrammelled by your external accretions. Empty yourself and come to me then you will be pure. Then you will get new clothes to wear and a novel light will be reflected upon you.

* * *

This indeed is the state of affairs in this world. Everyone is becoming clever. Even children are trained in fraud and deception. Everyone understands religion but none practises. Everyone wants peace but collects only those elements which cause restlessness.

* * *

Once again I repeat to you the essentials of meditation. They are: solitude, remembrance of God, guru, absence of desires, detachment, visiting holy places, conquest over postures, withdrawal, trance, a disciplined mind, a straight spine, fearlessness, all pervasive continence, surrender, a sense of bliss. If you have these fifteen with you, no power on earth can disturb your meditation.

* * *

The yogi is able to see his thoughts. He is able to give form to the object of his thoughts. He is able to transform the thoughts of others and also to have knowledge of the past and the future. He becomes the master of all the siddhis but he is able also to cast aside these things as useless, for these siddhis are obstacles in the path of God-realization. By being caught in the vicious circle of siddhis, the sadhaka falls prey to the six robbers. Be he a yogi or a householder, he who gives importance to siddhis falls.

* * *

Who is this Rama? Who pervades the expanse of the heart in 72,000 different ways? Just as the spider brings forth threads and sparks flow out of a burning timber, even so the universal life, all gods and all sentient and insentient beings, have come out of that Mighty Being and spread themselves. He sits in you, me and in everybody in the seventh region, seventh centre, seventh sky and on the seventh storey and plays about.

* * *

He who does not surrender himself to this Mighty Being but follows the natural propensities of the senses, can he ever get joy in place of miseries and anxieties? By following the propensities of even one sense, the butterfly, the deer, the elephant, the fish and the bee destroy themselves; then God alone helps him who is subservient to the five senses!

* * *

It should also be realized that anxieties are endless. They go on growing. They are the greatest sorrow. Even if you know very well that every event happens according to the grace of God and that He has been looking after your welfare in His great bounty, still diffidence of long-standing often or at times makes your faith waver. It is true that those who are given to worries do not become happy even by securing all their desires. Therefore, if you want to lead a happy life, leave everything to that beneficent God. Remain satisfied and pleased in whatever conditions He wants you to remain.

* * *

If you think of the good of the world, then you will be able to cross the ocean of life. If you think of God, you will transcend life, but if you reflect on this limited world you will die. When cares attack you, sin comes. Away, therefore, with these cares. A lot of work remains to be done. Though your vessel is purified yet a little more purity is necessary. Japa makes the heart pure, meditation makes it purer and samadhi makes it shine.

* * *

Constant worries give rise to depression, fear, heart disease, blood pressure and a variety of diseases, even cancer. A worried man in order to release his mental tension gives himself up to drinking, going to clubs, smoking, sleeping and indulging in loose living. Worry is the root cause of all troubles and the reason of worry is the absence of faith in the greatness of God, His omniscience, His all – pervasiveness and His grace.

* * *

Therefore, in the very root of anxieties lie embedded the ego and the desires of the jiva. As soon as the ego disappears, desires disappear and so do anxieties. Therefore, know this truth that ego comes because of ignorance and with it come desires and worries, and the jiva becomes unhappy. Hear also this final truth, that by knowledge alone, the ego will disappear and so also desires will disappear, anxieties vanish and the jiva attains to liberation.

* * *

Develop, therefore, internal and external faith and remain always rich in faith; smile within and smile without. Make your actions, religion and their practice blissful. God knows your needs. You have only to make efforts and these too with a sense of detachment; free yourself from the sense of being the doer; like the maidservant who completes the household work and remains detached, you should do all your work in a detached manner.

* * *

This body is the only instrument through which God could be realized. Preserve it. To call it sinful is itself a sin. In a healthy body, control of senses can be achieved and yoga realized. How can a diseased body achieve yoga? It would be enough if it could have enjoyment. The soul can never be realized by anyone but by the strong.

* * *

Look upon the jiva as your husband and consider yourself to be Parvati. This is called *madhurya bhakti*. The entire universe is a projection of Parvati. God alone is the master of this world. A devotee should not have any feeling of separateness between Him and himself for, He is the God and he is the devotee. He should treat the relationship as between a husband and a wife. To the exclusion of this everyone else should be looked upon as a brother or a relation.

* * *

In times of misery and stress, try to listen to His consoling words and secure His blessings. The gradual adoption of such an attitude will give you thrills, tears will flow from your eyes; the voice will be soft and the entire life will be one movement of joy. Slowly you will realize that He wakes you up in the morning, He performs japa with you, eats with you, bathes with you.

* * *

This body is ultimately going to end. There is no point in being attached to it. A saintly soul should lose body consciousness as quickly as possible. Those, who are enamoured of this world and engrossed in body consciousness, sinking in the eddies of pleasure, will never realize final beatitude.

* * *

He who listens to the opinions of the world will go mad. He who listens to the immortal music of the soul will reach the correct path. He who forgets the One, the controller of his very life breath, is mad. He who glories in his egoism when sorrows pervade the life is mad. But he who has surrendered himself at the feet of God is surely the best man.

* * *

A person whose mind is full of desires, whose speech is coated with untruth and who is false at heart is looked upon by people as a leader of men but such a person is mad. His speech may be sweet but his thoughts are bitter. People call such a person a gentleman. I call him mad for a person of an abnormal mind is mad.

* * *

In the present day some educated people try to live on an absolutely superficial plane and adopt a way of life according to their imagination, and also nourish such ideas. But subsequently they are troubled by neurosis. These are mad men of the rocket age. They go to the picture house in dignity and try to attract the attention of almost everybody towards them, but they feel shy of going to a temple and bow down. Should these be called normal or something else? This is an every day illustration. They sit in style in a hotel, but in a pooja they sit as if in agony.

* * *

This is the way of the world. It misguides the travellers, confuses and slanders them. So long as I was a fool, the world was pulling my leg; now that I have known the inside and outside of this world, it calls me mad.

* * *

Remember, therefore that as long as these insignificant interests of the world attract you, you will wander, you will be exploited. Some have interest in the body, some in wealth. As long as you have wealth, strength, youth and art, everybody will bow down to you, but when the bonds of self-interest between you and the world are broken, the world will drive you out like a dog.

* * *

Blessed is he who, in spite of youth and wealth, learning and intellect, becomes a real devotee. So long as the body is not disintegrated, the senses are strong, the intellect is steady and death is afar, build your temple by continued efforts. How else would you be able to surrender at the feet of God? This body and mind have become polluted by the inroads of the world. With what face will you offer them to God? Oh man, give to your God fresh and blooming flowers, but not dried and rotten ones. If you surrender your healthy life to God, you will become blessed. He who surrenders to Him realizes Him.

* * *

Understand correctly that sannyasa, or renunciation, is not the name of a stage of life signified by a change of dress or that it belongs to a particular sect. It is the symbol, signifying one of the highest impulses of man. Thus, if it is useless to leave the house and go to a forest, why not cultivate the attitude of renunciation staying with one's own family? My own view is that following one's dharma, one should try to make oneself useful to society and offer all actions to Brahman. This is intensive sannyasa. Renunciation does not mean renunciation of actions, but of attachment.

* * *

God is one. He is what He is. He is regarded as one with form when He is experienced through the instrumentality of the senses. But this consciousness of sakara should not be treated as a mistaken attitude because it is an attitude or feeling. How does it happen that knowing God as infinite we accept His finite form? Is He also without a form? Those who have experienced the formless will treat the personal God as an intermediary form of the Paramatma. Just as innumerable drops of water are in the ocean, even so innumerable forms, some of which are finite, are included in the Paramatma.

* * *

The truth is that there are two ways of realizing God, the way of worshipping the formless and the way of worshipping the One with a form. These are two specialized features of the same God, *sakara*, with form, or *nirakara*, without form. The difference lies only in this that the worship of the formless is difficult and that of the personal God easy. The formless is complicated, the personal is straight. In the worship of the personal God, even the most ordinary mind gets fixed, while the worship of the formless is for rare souls. Those souls alone who have become steady can worship the formless.

* * *

Both the devotees are equally entitled to the final emancipation, yet from the point of view of realization, the divine worship of the personal God is considered easy and praiseworthy because in this worship the mind experiences impulses of love, happiness, affability and concentration. If the sadhaka is not able to concentrate on the personal God, how would he be able to worship the formless, the immanent, who is beyond the senses? Without deep detachment the formless cannot be worshipped. By giving up attachment for the body, caste, wealth and other attitudes born out of ignorance, worship of the formless can be realized. But in this world the person who is not even able to give up tobacco, is he ready to worship the formless?

* * *

Just as a tired traveller does not have to make efforts to sleep but falls into deep slumber as soon as he lies down, so a sadhaka who has acquired control over his senses dwells within immediately as soon as he takes his seat. Just as a driver performs an easy operation in driving a car, even so a sadhaka only performs sadhana which comes naturally to him.

* * *

A strong sense of detachment and overall indifference towards desires, a turning away from the five senses, and a state of complete and sustained mental peace – these are the conditions precedent for the worship of the formless.

* * *

Therefore, we have made God an object of images, the object of prayer, the subject matter for pilgrimages. We accept both the impersonal and personal. We treat both as the instruments for final emancipation. Both these are considered beyond speech yet are made the subject matter of speech.

* * *

The worshipper of a personal God must cultivate such an attitude of the mind that he comes to believe that he is not the doer and that the senses are acting according to their natural propensities. Those who tread the path of worship of a personal God should not try to store up anything. They should consider this body as the treasure of God and their actions as the inspirations of the Divine. They must learn to accept happiness as a gift of God. They should accept miseries on their head as commands from God. Life and death, gain or loss, success or failure, religion or irreligion, faith or disbelief, all these phases must be treated as the reflection of the Divine and accepted. There should be a continual awareness that He is getting all done.

* * *

In single-minded yoga, your mind remains attuned only to one. As soon as the mind is entangled in two, that single-mindedness is broken. Therefore, the implication of single-mindedness is that the doer, the supporter and the destroyer is nobody else but He alone. The propeller of all actions, all religions, all inactions and non-religions is also He alone and none else. In this world He alone is my true companion, none else. This is called the worship of the personal God. This is called single-minded devotion.

* * *

In the ocean of this world, there is a boat. The mind is one oar and the intellect the other. The jiva is tired of rowing. He is defeated. What will he do in this condition? Either sit in despair or make attempts to draw his boat near a passing ship. This is called complete surrender. Its meaning is this:

Let all your thoughts and beliefs be absorbed in God and let your life be lived on His mercy.

*   *   *

Everybody says that he belongs to God, everything belongs to God, His will is supreme, but at each step they act contrary to this faith.

*   *   *

Let us be His machines and He, the machine man. Let us be ready every moment to act according to His commands. Slowly, slowly our mind will be emptied of egoism. Then He will shine through one medium.

*   *   *

Through the instruments of sadhanas let His consciousness be awakened. Try to spiritualize His form. To develop love for Him, let the mind dwell on His *lilas*, his play and sport. Hear His stories and continue to recite His name. By degrees you will be convinced that He has become a part of your being and that He is running the whole show. Do not treat your mind as your own, but let it be a servant at the feet of God. Is He not the real master? When the mind is engrossed in the love of God, the intellect steadies itself in Him. When the temptations of the senses are ended and anxieties die, the world of dualities disappears, and His grace is made visible. Surrender becomes more perfect and that long-dormant power of yoga, which is His mighty power, awakens.

*   *   *

This mind is full of impressions, is always engrossed in its tendencies and continues to think about something or the other. To make it steady is no joke, because that is its nature, but as the ideas of love slowly sink in, its old habits will start breaking. If the love is deep, intense and true, the old impressions of the mind are easily broken. Even if the mind of the sadhaka does not get steady in this, let the practice be continued. Slowly it will be steady.

These practices are of two types, concentration and remembrance. To sit at one place and continue to think of God is concentration, *nishtha*. But remembrance means to remember Him always. In other words, remember His name, remember His play, remember His grace, call to mind His experiences, His presence, His absence, His association, His separation, His form, His continued blessings and nothing else. This is called remembrance or concentration. The success of the concentration depends on remembrance.

* * *

Who should be remembered? Who should not be remembered? Understand this also. The impermanence of all enjoyments, the futility of all confused thinking, the complications of actions and the selfishness of the world – a constant awareness of these is known as *vairagya*, renunciation. The remembrance of God's name, His form, His play, His grace, His experiences, go by the name of bhakti. A sadhaka should carry on His remembrance in these two ways, but remembrance by way of bhakti is very pleasant, enjoyable and agreeable to our nature. Remembrance with a full heart achieves renunciation. No special effort is necessary.

* * *

When pure and noble thoughts pervade the mind, take it to be due to the prevalence of sattwa guna. When greed, activity, restlessness and desires increase attribute them to the prevalence of rajoguna. When the intellect becomes perverse, when common sense fails, the mind ceases to take interest in activity, and lassitude and moha are experienced, take it to be the effects of tamoguna.

* * *

Believe this much, that all troubles finally disappear. Just as happiness is transient, so also is misery. Unnecessary worries add to the discomforts. If you are in a state of trouble, remember that it will also pass away. He who is able to keep equipoise in happiness is able to live through periods of misery.

* * *

Every person considers his troubles great, but in fact, he is not as unhappy as he believes himself to be. How difficult it is for ordinary people to understand this? Just as every person exaggerates his own position and experiences a sense of pride; even so he exaggerates his state of misery and experiences the same feeling. Believe it or not, but I tell you the truth, that each one of us tends to put a premium to our happiness or misery, high state or low state, wealth, intellect and society. The nature of the mind is such that barely anyone knows its original nature. Mostly everyone is suffering from the disease of his beliefs. Know yourself well and all the agitation will cease.

* * *

Sinlessness and good conduct are ordained by scriptures. These can obstruct the path of sadhana. The yogi should transcend these beliefs and think of other things. The devotee should depend upon God and proceed. For him, to surrender to the will of God is the highest religion. The conflict between religion and irreligion is never solved by intellect. Even the scriptures are unable to explain. It is for us to be guided by the will of God and work as His instrument. We have to go through life accepting the greatness of God as all powerful.

* * *

If we surrender ourselves to God and work our way in life, the ego will become lifeless. Thereafter, we will act only in that way which our sinless, pure and changeless soul impels us to do. I do not mean to tell anyone that he should continue to misbehave in society. What I mean is that one who lives surrounded by soot will gain nothing except restlessness by worrying over the dark spots he will get because this worldly maze is the treasure house of vice and virtue.

* * *

Even if the circumstances force you to accept the desires, you should continue to keep yourself above these. The body, the mind, the intellect and the senses may continue to perform actions with certain desires. But if the sadhaka so wishes, he can give up attachment and do the work. One who fully realizes that a particular activity is natural to a particular sense organ, or that a particular phase is the natural state of the antahkarana, or that a particular state is a natural function of the body and in that awareness he acts, does not reap the fruits of his actions.

* * *

One who is absorbed in his desires and continues to work in this way, first experiences happiness and thereafter misery. Those activities which are performed just as a matter of duty, if they are performed with detachment, do not disturb the sadhaka's mind.

* * *

Remember, that activities induced by desires create obstacles in the path of sadhana. Lift the soul above these and if you carry on your worldly activities in this manner, you will not commit any sin.

* * *

So long as there are desires in the mind, the activities will continue and the cycle of happiness and misery will go on revolving. Therefore, you should take your mind away from thoughts about your family and happenings, and surrender your mind and soul entirely to God.

* * *

See for yourself how much blood, sweat and tears and pleasure your mother has given to this world? How thin has she become by swelling after this world, given sons and everything, even the golden days of happiness in life, but what did she give to Rama? Useless flowers, cheap sweets for a few hours. Therefore, the world gave her what she wanted. Now nothing remains to be given to the world but something still remains to be given to Rama.

* * *

In spite of obstacles and troubles, let your sadhana continue to proceed steadily. Worries are the worst obstacles. If you are within you and very keen on sadhana, who can stop you?

* * *

All of us have to find a proper way so that the natural aptitudes of every individual get a smooth outlet. We have to open up the volcano concealed within this earth and properly harness it. Each person is a sort of earth which conceals beneath it a volcano in the shape of desires, ambitions and so on.

* * *

The yogi achieves great peace by giving up desires for the fruits of actions, but as long as he is impelled by longings of the world and has a desire to reap the fruits of his actions, he remains bound. The sadhaka who has conquered his sleep, surrenders all his actions at the feet of God and remains happy in this very body neither without being anything nor without being asked to do anything.

* * *

It is no sin to remain in this world. Sin lies in keeping the world stored up in the mind. Just as we cross a river sitting on the boat but have absolutely no attachment for the boat; even so we must live in this world and continue to do all duties, but should not get attached. Just as we go on a pilgrimage by walking on the road but are not in the least attracted towards the road, even so, living in the world we should have no infatuation for the world, even as a pilgrim staying in a caravanserai mixes freely and lives with his fellow travellers, so also we have to maintain friendship with those who are our co-travellers. They do not belong to me nor do I belong to them. Brother, this is a hired ferry. Sometimes on this side, some times on that. So long as we do not see Him, our life is incomplete.

* * *

What is called birth? Understand this from the beginning. You are not yet born. You are still in the womb. In this world up till now only very few souls are born. The rest are still entombed in the womb of ignorance.

* * *

Were this world to follow the pattern of your desires, you would have no contentment.

* * *

For those who are full of desires, this life becomes an abode of discontent. For those people who are full of longings, this life is an abyss of despair. For devotees of God this life is the road leading to God. For the wise this life is a bundle of changing values. For those who are detached, this life is as dust. For those who have no self-control this life is a consuming fire, for the coward, it is a bundle of sins, and for the yogi, a means of purifying the mind.

* * *

Be it as it may, one should try to absorb oneself with his or her chosen ideal quickly according to one's ability.

* * *

Remember that gold becomes purer and purer by being put in the fire. Shiva is attained by penance; by continuous friction, life renews itself. Domestic discomforts make life strong.

* * *

The pupil was asleep. The teacher woke him up. As soon as the words of the teacher fell into the ears of the pupil, the divine sight in him was awakened. Since then he does not sleep. His eyes remain open day and night. The pupil makes ablutions with water of the feet of his teacher and his miseries and sins are destroyed instantly. He has put the dust of the teacher's feet on his head and wisdom has dawned upon him. He has drunk deep of the cup of love. Nothing attracts him. The pupil has entered the highest mansion and is sitting in the bower of nothingness. There neither sun, nor moon, nor lightening, nor stars, nothing can reach him. The one who moves on will reach his goal. The one who is exhausted will sit down. He will not be able to go without the instructions of the teacher. No one can reach that path by dragging his feet. None can reach Him sorrowing. A true disciple will reach that goal. A good disciple will go there. An undeserving and cunning disciple will be thrown down.

* * *

The master is the enjoyer of the body. Really he is not the master because the word master signifies the protector of modesty and prestige. He alone is the real husband who has protected you from life to life, who has given you this body, who has raised you high and who has protected you from anger, greed, restlessness and jealousy and who has made you strong. He is our master and yet we go on wandering.

* * *

Family life is the training ground for yoga sadhana, but what we see is a different picture altogether. If there is a difference between the minds of both it will be necessary to draw a parallel line, and both should be saved from contradictory situations. If the husband is religious and the wife given to pleasures, both these tendencies should be allowed full play. If the husband is active and the wife idle, it should be ensured that they do not cross each other at any point. In domestic life, where the tastes are common or contradictory, transgressing each other is dangerous. Both of them should complement each other.

* * *

If the whole world goes on a pilgrimage, let it go. These poor people seek comfort and change. But where will you go? Where are Dwaraka and Haridwar? Do they consist in buildings, or in temples, or in streets full of motor cars? Is it where your God resides? Go, Kailash lies on the banks of Mansarovar. There resides Lord Shiva. From there Ganga, Yamuna and Saraswati take their rise.

* * *

I repeat, do not go to a forest. Do not leave your house. Do not be a sannyasi. To meet your chosen ideal at least do not care for these things. Stay where you are and let your soul rise. Your soul itself is a place of pilgrimage when it is absorbed in the remembrance of God.

* * *

Oh disciple, you are holier than the Ganga. Your soul is a million times more real than Baidyanath. Badrinath is full of stones, Kedarnath is full of snow, Rameshwaram is full of sand, whereas within you reside the teacher and the God both. You reside in your own holy place.

* * *

Listen, "Oh Yudhishthira! Where life flows within the holy banks of self-control, where it is full of the waters of truth; where it runs between the banks of character and waves of compassion; wake up in that river of God-realization. Plunge yourself in it. Your atma will then be pure. And listen also what the *Mahabharata* says, "Bathing is not that which makes the body wet. That alone is called bathing by which the mind is brought under control. Therefore, he who bathes in the holy place of the mind and also in a place of pilgrimage secures identical fruits."

* * *

You are on a constant pilgrimage. This atma is the place of pilgrimage. By merging into it, the results of actions, good or bad, are destroyed. Sin and sinlessness and all the samskaras are the result of impurity, conflicts and darkness. Once the mind is devoid of all desires, then all previous impressions disappear. How will your past impressions be rendered sterile unless you bathe in this tirtha? Will the soul ever be able to cross the ocean of life without meeting God? This alone is the *tirtha*, the holy place of your pilgrimage.

* * *

That flame which is kindled to consume the impurities of the body and the organs of the action is called physical penance. To kindle this flame, one has to worship God, learned men, one's own teachers and continue to practise purity, straightforwardness, continence and non-violence. Once the flame is kindled, the impurities of this life vanish.

* * *

The flame that is kindled for purifying speech is called the penance of the speech. The first condition of kindling this flame is that we should not be restless. We should speak true and agreeable things and study scriptures. When this flame is kindled, all the impurities are consumed. The cheerfulness of the mind, goodness, silence, self-control and pure ideals are the attributes of mental penance. The performer of all these acts is the wider meaning of penance. This penance consumes the dross of life.

* * *

Each individual comes here with the accumulated treasure of his past actions and so long as these treasures are not exhausted, he remains engrossed in this world. Once the harvest is reaped and inward awareness dawns upon him, thereafter he treads the path of God.

* * *

Pray, not by moving the lips but pray from within. When prayer arises from within, the eyes will be full of tears and the voice full of emotion, and after prayers you will feel that the body is weightless. Remember that hesitation, shame and fraud will not work in the presence of God. He is always pleased to listen to your prayers. Displeased He never is. He likes straightforwardness, forthrightness and inwardness. Prayer means revealing before Him the innermost objects of one's being.

* * *

Destroy your association with worries, grief, sorrow and repentance. Learn to remain always engrossed in yourself. Let someone throw you into the fire, attack you with a sword, insult you, ignore you, nothing will happen to you. Only do not treat yourself as an insignificant creature, for, you are the form of Shiva, Brahma, the great bliss. Have you not been told that you are the repository of the all powerful and blissful atma? Just as oil is concealed in sesame, butter in curd, fire in wood, tree in the seed and life in the vital fluid, so also the bodiless One is concealed in this body, and just as oil is extracted by crushing, butter by churning, fire by friction, tree by sowing and life by conception, even so by an inward knowledge resulting from sadhana, the destroyer of three cities, *Tripurari*, comes out transcendent.

* * *

If you hear the slanders of the world or praise, keep them up to your ears and close the other gates. Who belongs to you and who does not? Who is a friend and who is a foe?

Rise above attachment and jealousy, a sense of my-ness and contempt. Know this in the mind but do not speak. Continue to play the part in this drama of maya and within you continue to see the sport of God. Remain like the jiva externally, but internally realize within you the Divine Brahman.

* * *

How long will this cycle of being and dying continue? In spite of my poverty, oh God, have I not surrendered everything to you? All that I have got is a material box which is full of rotten and old fruits. What shall I give you? I am on the horns of a dilemma. What do you want and what have I got? Whatever I have got is you. I do not want the delusions of this world. I long to see you day and night.

* * *

It has been said that if an individual wants love and exchange of love, he is a seller of love. His love is not love. It is mere self-interest. If instead of the love of God, you are after certain powers, that love will be interested or in other words it will be a sort of an activity to achieve a particular end. A real bhakta gives a wide berth to self-interest. He alone says, "I am your selfless devotee and let my love be disinterested. I am yours and you are mine. I want neither *moksha*, liberation, nor power, intellect, prosperity, abundance, greatness or anything. All I want is selfless devotion which day by day will grow from strength to strength at the feet of Lord Rama."

* * *

If a maidservant is raised to a level of a queen by a king, does she care for other powers? Then how does one who has been raised to the level of a devotee of God wander in the realms of selfishness? Fie be upon that devotee of the Lord who cannot even learn from an insignificant maidservant the lesson of self-surrender. She who surrenders the body for the sake of money, is a prostitute, and he who does the worship of God for self-interest is a hypocrite. Even when a maidservant of no consequence having attached herself to a king is able to share all his grace, how is it that a devotee of God is not able to achieve the grace of that great God? What sort of self-interest is this? How degenerate has our intellect become that leaving the truth we are attempting to catch the untruth?

* * *

We are in fact running after shadows. We have staked our life on an insignificant object. We are simply trying to steal diamonds only in imagination. What are we doing? Why are we doing that and for whom are we doing this? Child, return to your original self.

* * *

Whether flowers drop upon you or you see a light or smell a fragrance or hear melodious music, oh sadhaka, beware, do not for a moment be drawn away from the meditation of your chosen God.

* * *

Worries are a great nuisance. The life may be full of thorns or full of plenty, yet remain firm, wide awake and strong. Oh, traveller, look not behind or forward nor sideways, lest you be turned into a stone. Therefore, I tell you, look forward. He will be seen only in front.

* * *

Everybody is full of an activity to reform others but no one thinks of reforming himself and if he has an idea to reform himself, he comes out of that by pleading helplessness. Slander has been the mother of all activities for reforming others. It looks as if slander alone is the technique of correction.

* * *

Even if in a single day, each individual in the world does his duty and stops slandering others or trying to reform others, the very next day, the face of the world will change but this is not going to happen because in slandering others or trying to reform others, our ego is nurtured.

* * *

This world is a garden which is full of a variety of flowers, leaves, tress, creepers, plants, each one having a distinct fragrance and distinct feature. Some are thieves, some are generous, some are Brahmans, some vicious men, some are wanderers, some given to non-violence; all types are presented here. This is the museum of that Divine Government. It is for you only to observe this, not in a spirit of disgust, but in a spirit of wonder. Thank that God who is the creator of all such flowers. And say, "Oh God, since you have chosen to make them like this, who am I to look upon them with disgust?"

* * *

PART II

To achieve success in any great act, a great ideal is necessary.

* * *

Remember that he who has got a burning ideal before him will for ever and ever go forward on the path of life. He will never be able to return.

* * *

Thinking about the senses and their objects, shows the impurity of heart. Therefore, if you are able to prevent the senses' play, your heart will go above the sense objects and become pure. Only then you will be able to come face to face with your own soul, and for this company of the good is the first essential. By association with the wise, an individual is made aware of his shortcomings and through satsang he gets the awareness of the right way to cross this world.

* * *

This world is the battlefield of Kurukshetra. Like Arjuna, we are standing in the middle of the field. In this world we have to mix with all and live. It is inescapable for us to avoid living in a society which is neither good nor desirable. Therefore, in whatever sect one lives and conducts himself according to the mandates of such a sect, it is most essential that he should keep his soul pure.

* * *

It is quite true that it is not possible to please everybody, but it is always possible to talk casually in such a manner that people get pleased. This conduct is not against a religious code. If we are aware of the injustice perpetuated by an individual, we should adjust ourselves in such a manner that no greater reaction accrues. We may love a little, praise a little, agree a little and act accordingly. This is in consonance with religion.

* * *

Knowledge of the ways of the world is also a higher duty and in this iron age, it is a strong associate. Within it are concealed humility, politeness, cleverness, praise and blame; to yield at times, to laugh at times, to remain silent at times, to be mischievous at times, to just play the sycophant at times, all these are branches of worldly wisdom.

* * *

Ill feelings and jealousy are the destroyers of mental peace and according to popular opinion should be avoided. These are the leprosy of the mind and like cholera for the society. To be a good mixer in society, some solution has to be found out for these two. This is the chief aim of sadhana.

* * *

Daily poojas or recitations do not yield any greater results, neither ringing of bells nor going to temple. In order to raise the inner spiritual life within us, it is essential to cure mental deformities. Lust is the meanest of sin. Anger is the most consuming fire. Greed is the greatest whirlpool. Continence is the greatest friend; forgiveness and contentment of external life are ambrosia.

* * *

Peace will never be attained by recourse to karmas, by performing shraaddha, worshiping gods, going to pilgrimages, by studies of scriptures, endurance, penance or following the external elements of religion. The way of peace is not that long, that circuitous or troublesome. If the desires are reduced, sloth will disappear. If the thirst of the heart is quenched, if agonies disappear or if impotence is removed, peace will be obtained.

* * *

But how can nirvana be attained this way? Leave the confusion of life. Throw all the complications, all the conflicts of thought. Let life flow evenly. Do not raise any issues of conflict.

* * *

Tune yourself into a temple. Make yourself a tirtha. Make yourself a hermitage. This alone is the way to attain inexhaustible happiness. Keep your lamp ready. Light it yourself. You will get the light.

* * *

Iron when heated in a furnace and processed with a hammer; takes a new shape and a new life which is otherwise impossible. Absence of self-interest, contempt of society, discontent with the ways of life, disease of the body and political appeals, when handled by a clever artist create a new and full personality.

* * *

Man is unable to achieve anything by giving himself to worries. All efforts are being done conditioned by circumstances. The beautiful face of life is being marred by worries.

* * *

Worries are futile. We are all propelled on our way of life towards the highest perfection through the instrumentality of an imperceptible power and it is during this period that we have to migrate through a variety of experiences. We walk by day, get exhausted, sleep at night and experience happiness. This sleep, this happiness, this rest are only meant for cutting the next day. Miseries are for further struggles and forward progress. But a lazy pilgrim prefers to sleep even though he knows very well that in spite of fatigue, happiness and bliss lie in proceeding ahead. Brother! He who walks only gets tired. He who is immobile does not get tired. In his life, there is no possibility of progress. Therefore, do not be frightened by the exhaustion in this sojourn of life, for one day you have to reach the holy Gangotri. There the fatigue of the entire sojourn will be thrown out. Rest as much as you like.

* * *

Actions are a form of devotion to God. Take them to be the mantras. One should not get absorbed in anything while performing actions or desire to reap a reward. Instead of regarding yourself as the doer, inculcate this idea within you that God is making you the instrument to do some thing or the other. You are a mere instrument in the hands of the Almighty God.

* * *

Yoga is bringing about a balance in one's nature by cultivating equipoise in situations of joy and sorrow, gain or loss. Yoga is also the efficient performance of actions. Transcend joy and sorrow for the soul is above these dualities. He is yourself. Let the mind retain its equipoise during the state of dualism and then conquer it. You will then be able to go beyond this world of dualism and enjoy everlasting bliss.

*   *   *

True religion is sovereign. There is no dispute about it. Truth is one; the sages call it many. The same truth in different ages has been manifested by sages in different ways but this truth has been enveloped by men of circumscribed intellect by a plethora of different contradictory opinions.

*   *   *

Hindus, Muslims, Sikhs, and Christians are differences which are created by human society but in reality we are one; we are children of immortality, children of the same Father. The whole universe is one family and we are all members of that family. That is why I say, "Keep awake within you this universal spirit."

*   *   *

Only those, whose lives are disciplined, humble, rich with sterling character, can establish universal brotherhood, all-pervading peace and equality.

*   *   *

When a new road is being built, mounds of dust are raised. Thus in the first stages of sadhana there is mental trouble. Slowly it gets settled.

*   *   *

A sadhaka should not be disturbed by emotions, must transform all situations to his convenience, and must learn lessons for the future. Life is full of various types of situations. Many upheavals come and yet a sadhaka should not be troubled by these situations. In the midst of all turmoil, he must remain aware. He who is able to resolve all situations is a true sadhaka.

*   *   *

Carry out the mandates of your superiors. Learn to forgive those who are young. Cultivate affectionate contacts with your equals, restraint towards those friends who have gone astray, who have lost their character. Try to understand their situations, the raison-d'être of their conduct. Keep away from picking holes or trying to find faults. Look at the bright side of their life.

* * *

Those who are given to inner contemplation and carry on their activities with an inward awareness, for them all actions of life are acts of worship. Everything is a place of pilgrimage and for them every man is a satsangi.

* * *

He who is given to sense enjoyments, for him, family life is a sin, but for a saintly soul like you, such a life is a great instrument. Accept this thought as a sort of mantra. If you try to remain indifferent to the family life, you will go the wrong way.

* * *

Sannyasa is hollow like a drum. Devotion is like paper flowers. To leave the house and run to the forest is a sure way to a lunatic asylum.

* * *

He who has created all these karmas, he who is this prakriti, has already determined the course of karmas. One can attain Him who is all-pervading and an unknowable One by offering the worship through karmas and by performing one's duties as enjoined according to our prakriti. You and I and every one will again meet on the path of realization.

* * *

The most important thing in human life is peace of mind which is the direct result of mental poise. Life is a sort of battlefield where for the sake of lasting pleasures we are creating conflicts. One should not lose peace of mind because of anything of this world. Peace is one such thing without which life becomes dull and monotonous. Maybe one has plenty of wealth and everything, but it is all nothing if he has no peace of mind.

* * *

Live in the world as a witness. That alone is the one royal road to happiness. Do not try to identify yourself and establish relations with the changing insignificant things of this world. Perform all your duties. Rise above sentiments and do your duties.

* * *

Remember God. When ego disappears, feelings of attachment and envy are destroyed, longings and desires pass into nothingness, and the karmas are consumed; there is the descent of light. The universe becomes a smiling ocean where troubles do not rain, but on the contrary there is a constant rain of immeasurable religion. Seasons of peace come to flower. Flowers of happiness bloom and wavelets of enduring bliss rise in the ocean.

* * *

Everywhere there is a current of celestial light. Try to visualize that light and try to tell your children that you are looking forward to that light. Open the doors and open the windows, open your balconies and let that divine light enter every corner of your house.

* * *

It is raining. Sow the seeds of jnana. The heart is the field, sadhana is the water, satsang is the garden, the teacher is the watcher. It will be the season of God's grace. Let the field be saved from damage by cattle. Keep away the birds by clapping your hands. Put the manure of faith for even though the seed is small, the flower will be indescribable.

* * *

A sower of seeds started to sow seeds. While doing so, some fell on the road side; some were eaten by the birds in the sky, some fell in the soil, some dried up because of want of water. Some fell in regions full of shrubbery and though sprouted, could not grow. But those which fall on good soil, they yielded good harvest. Let those who have got common sense, grasp the meaning; let those who have ears hear this tale.

* * *

I am only sowing the seed. If you are a good soil, you will reap a good harvest. Be careful that the devil does not steal it. Be careful that they do not dry up, but after hearing my words, try to reap the fruits by patience. I repeat that those pure and noble minds, those with a mind full of pure and noble thoughts, derive a hundred times more benefit out of the seeds that I sow. The path is not even. There is darkness around. There is dust storm. This is not a world of imagination. It is a difficult path. Be steady and grow.

* * *

Remove the false ego and the base impulses of the mind and make yourself the centre of affection and love. We should not make anyone a target of our anger, jealousy or hatred. Human love is full of a multiplicity of errors. Why should we make them responsible for errors which are a part of their nature? Not only our relations but even those who are around us expect love and devotion from us, but unfortunately we fail to give it to them. They ask for love so that they can get us to sympathize with them, to forgive them for their mistakes, to be helpful to them. They ask for love so that we ignore the faults of their nature and forgive them. They ask for love because they did not get it from anybody else before. The world has yet to see a man or prophet who has been free from faults. Therefore, instead of ignoring an erring soul, one should sympathize with him. Most of the errors in life are due to one's nature. One should not consider them responsible for these errors.

* * *

Love is a sort of sadhana. Love is nectar. It is the very vitality of life. But how is it to be acquired? Contempt and disgust are found in plenty everywhere. We ignore the inner goodness very cleverly. We look askance at the efficiency for cleverness. We look with contempt on folly and ignorance. We continue to look with contempt and repeatedly do so. Thus this feeling of contempt reacts and comes back to us. Therefore, I say that man should really understand the implications of this thing and should remove from his heart, hatred, jealousy and other faults and believe that one truth, one God is concealed in every soul.

* * *

Look at the greatness of God who resides in you. He is your never failing and permanent teacher. He is your soul who directs and governs all your activities He is the power which makes your life flow. To have a vision of Him, you must destroy the veils of mind, senses and desires, and turn inwards.

* * *

This is sooner said than done but the process nobody knows. The teacher reminds us of it and the sadhaka has to follow up the process. Japa, kirtan and other sadhanas create new impressions and destroy old ones. Devotion, faith and confidence, these sadhanas transform the mind and the senses. This is the means by which you can have a vision of God within you.

* * *

He resides in everything. He is the essence of everything but the elements do not know it. The elements are his body. The immortal and governing monitor is you, yourself.

* * *

Oh friend, one who is a devotee towards good, never comes to grief. This is the never-failing support of the great Father to His children. For He forever continues to shower His grace upon His devotees and to destroy their afflictions. A little confidence, a little faith and a little surrender are enough to keep the devotee protected from many difficulties and future dangers. If with a humble heart he remembers God, even if he is a wicked man, he acquires grace. He is forever compassionate equally towards all. He loves those who love him. He is a greater friend for those who have been abandoned. He is the saviour for He saves us from the very powerful storms of maya and desires. He is the light on our path, for from untruth He leads us to truth, from darkness to light, from death to immortality. He is the most efficient navigator for He pilots the ship of our life from amidst the ocean towards the ultimate end.

* * *

In these days hardly a few enjoy a happy married life. To make life happy or miserable depends entirely upon oneself. Because of a disparity in conduct, thought, action and mental plane the domestic life does not remain happy. Marriage is a sort of yajna. It is an instrument for the expansion of life and yet none knows the trick to live it in a proper manner. If the husband is good then the wife is bad and vice versa. It is the duty of both husband and wife to attempt to raise each other mutually. They must be complements to each other. None of them should be an obstacle on the path but a help.

* * *

Two factors are most essential to make domestic life happy. The first is sincerity. The husband and wife must be true to each other and, secondly, both should render to each other true love.

* * *

Make the atmosphere of the house holy so as to nullify the influences of tamoguna. Let all members gather together in the evening and offer prayers. There should be no show, no vain exhibition. Sing His praises. Abundance of power resides in His name. Try to experience it and I can assure you that where there is mutual peace, where there is no conflict between husband and wife, where harsh words are forbidden, where husband and wife have mutual trust and respect for each other, there each act merges with the spiritual light and surely that house becomes the true heaven on earth.

* * *

The new year comes; the old one departs, new leaves come out and the old fall down. New life begins to throb and the old life disappears. New tendencies are acquired and old habits are given up. New activities are launched and the old ones are kept away. Therefore, this day is a day of self-analysis, self-development and self-surrender. Sit down, think new thoughts, make new resolutions and drive out the old ones.

* * *

If you wish to do great deeds, make humble beginnings. If you want to be great make yourself humble and small. If you want to be a siddha, begin to root out the minutest faults in you, and if you want to be something, be nothing. Efface yourself.

* * *

One who is given to anxiety is unable to do anything. We have a mission to perform in this world. Think such thoughts and live in the intoxication of that idea. Burden not the mind with anything at all.

* * *

He whose life is not progressive cannot go forward. Therefore, he who wishes to progress in life should remain attuned to that life. He should remove at once all worries and continue to make sustained efforts in life. We should not think too much of our faults and failings. We have to think again and again, more and more of the divine name.

* * *

You are anxious to see me. That alone is your sadhana. See me in you and yourself in me. Then alone will I be visualized in your meditation and you will be able to see me. We shall converse in that state, the fourth stage where divine consciousness remains. It is like the dreamworld but different from it. It is the plane of savikalpa samadhi. By transcendental love, you will reach this region and meet me.

* * *

The region in which my soul is moving is not the region of body consciousness. It is the region of truth. There only those lovers who are able to efface themselves and surrender, reach, because that path is narrow. There is no dualism there. It is beyond mind and speech.

* * *

Whether you are engrossed in some type of work, whether you are repairing in your workshop a lorry, a motor car or a tank, or whether you are doing physical training, at all times let the flow of mental japa go on incessantly. The hands may be working but the mind must remain engrossed in God.

* * *

By kirtan, your sinews will be thrilled and purified. That will result in the awakening of spiritual powers. After such a study for sometime, you will continue to remain in a state of God-intoxication. For ordinary men, this is the most easy, sure, sweet and best course for God-realization. There is nothing better than kirtan to make the heart mellow. The dry hearts of non-believers and the sinners of all types mellow by prayers. By kirtan the mind gets intoxicated with joy and merges in God. In that state of bliss, it loses its sense of ego and, in the acme of happiness, enjoys oneness.

* * *

The truth is that there is no difference between God and His name. The name and the repeater of the name are One.

They are not different. Where God's name is being recited, there God resides. God's name makes the mind, which is full of desires, pure and draws man towards universal consciousness or God-consciousness.

*　　*　　*

Of all the bad habits which destroy the ethical constitution of one's being wine, comes first. It destroys all your spiritual desires and your ideals. That creates confusion in the brain, destroys purity of thought and charity of heart, and it makes you lose even your sense of self-respect.

*　　*　　*

Even by staying in this world somehow or the other it is possible to keep oneself away from worldliness. See, this world does not belong to you or to me. It is God's creation. That which you consider belongs to you really belongs to God. You have to continue to live in the world with this thought in the background. The wife, the son, the parents, the friends, the relatives are all creatures of God. Whatever you do for them, do it with this attitude that through these diverse forms, you are serving Narayana. Then only your devotion for them will continue to grow.

*　　*　　*

Open your heart to Him. Then your success is certain. That is why I tell you to wake up and gird up your loins to reach the final goal. You will experience a strange sort of bliss. It will drown you in an ocean of bliss and you will get such intoxication which will keep you in a continued state of happiness till your last breath. Can such bliss be compared with the hollow happiness of this world? He who has even once had a taste of this divine happiness, to him all the happiness of the entire world is nothing. Mirabai, Narasimha, Tukaram, Ramakrishna Paramahamsa, each had attained to that state of bliss. Do not feel tired of family life. Family life is the guiding instrument for you. For you all the stages of life are holy places and all your actions are worship to God.

* * *

The essence of karma yoga lies in those acts by the performance of which one does not have a sense of being the doer or the desire for the fruits. Even if you give a glass of water to someone, you expect if nothing else, at least thanks from him. This is human nature. If we do something to someone and he does not reciprocate, then we complain that the person is arrogant and considers it below his dignity to reciprocate your actions. This is rajasic karma.

* * *

An ignorant man by performing his duties continues to think that he is doing them, whereas a yogi thinks that it is prakriti which is having all things done. The body, the senses, the mind and the intellect are all the instruments of prakriti. The moment you say that you are the seer you are bound down by the laws of karma. "The eyes see, I am merely a witness," that is the attitude of a wise man. The devotees always believe that God alone does everything and that they do nothing.

* * *

The impressions of all actions are recorded in the astral body. If you are angry, the impressions of anger will be recorded in your finer mind. If in the external world waves of anger rise, these waves do not die but they merge with the space and affect other people.

* * *

By the study of karma yoga, the impurities of the mind are destroyed and purity is achieved. What are the impurities of the mind? These are selfishness, vanity, desires, anger, greed, infatuation, envy, contempt and so on. By karma yoga the mind is made fit to receive the divine light.

* * *

Give good things to others always. Karma yoga makes your heart broad. It destroys the obstacles in the way of God-realization. It gives you inward awareness. The wise see themselves reflected in others when they serve them; whereas the devotees, when they serve others, see God in them. This is the difference between a bhakta and a jnani. The bhakta crosses the ocean of life by means of a boat. That boat is God-consciousness. A Vedantin crosses it by swimming.

* * *

Generally men of this world often speculate in this way that the wise men, the learned men, the Vedantins, also worship God as they do. Then how can they be called sannyasins? They should be dubbed worldly. Does it mean that from the standpoint of worldly-minded men, the man who becomes a sannyasin should not eat food? Does it follow that they should put on barks of trees instead of clothes or they should fly like birds instead of walking? Is it only in this way that you will believe that they are true sannyasins? Then what is the difference between a magician and a realized soul? No, no. This is not correct. Prakriti acts upon the body of a jnani and even though from an external point of view we see a similarity between the actions of a worldly man and an unworldly man, really it is not true. Between these two types of men there lies the difference that, while the man of the world has a superimposed sense of body consciousness and considers himself to be the body, the jnani does not think so; he does not identify himself with the body.

* * *

Lust is a blind desire. Just as in order to defeat a powerful enemy, you use rifles, machine guns, bombs and sharp weapons, so also in order to defeat this great enemy, lust residing in you, you will have to take recourse to different remedies.

* * *

Just as the elephant raises dust and throws it on his head so men, because of their folly and ignorance, invite themselves their miseries and difficulties.

*   *   *

Think of the body as something that is full of all impurities like excreta, cough, blood, flesh. Try to think of it in this way, that it is like a golden pot full of poison. Try to go away from these and live a life of pleasure, and believe them to be the be-all and end-all of existence and live accordingly.

*   *   *

Even when you are attacked by emotions, repeat your chosen mantra loudly. If you are resting, divert the body and mind into certain activities. Keep yourself forever engrossed in work. Let the mind be kept fully engrossed in the work. It is only when the mind has no work that it begins to think wicked things. An empty mind is the devil's workshop.

*   *   *

One should understand the significance of the ceremony of washing the feet of the teacher. The same applies to the ceremony of washing the palm of the guru and even though the importance according to the yogic thought of washing the palm is far superior to the other one, still the recognized and accepted practice of washing the feet has been in vogue only as an expression of a sense of humility.

*   *   *

Today, even though we have not understood the importance of these processes, the ceremony is performed merely as a matter of long-standing tradition. Yet that alone is one of the best methods by which one can have water surcharged with yogic power. The active spiritual waves of the yogic power make the water charged with that power. Don't you know the science of mesmerism? This power of yoga expresses itself through feet, hands, eyes and the forehead. By looking at the forehead, one can feel the impact of its power. Through the eyes that power reaches the devotee. By a touch of the palm also the power is transmitted to the devotee and similarly by the touching of the feet.

* * *

Water, offering flowers, sandal paste marks, touching the head and patting the back, diksha, instruction, gaze and faith are the media through which this current of yogic power is transmitted. In other words, through these media, the yogic power of the guru is received. According to the yogic tantras, these are the recognized media of that power. In vama tantra along with these, certain other media are accepted. Mesmerism is yet in its infancy.

* * *

Waves of spiritual power come out of the body of a yogi and these perform great deeds. These waves enter the body and start constructive and modifying processes. These waves do not affect the subtle body, but the causal body. These currents resulting from the power of yoga like the currents of electricity, charge water, prasad, flowers and so on. They are used for the removal of disease or sorrow or for sadhana or elevation. The influence of these currents is according to the qualification of the sadhaka of yoga. In other words, currents such as love, charity, blessings, peace, equanimity, and strength come out. Though these currents are more actively present in the cottage, the clothes or the articles of personal use of a yogi, they are not easily available, and therefore, they can be had through the media of water, prasad and flowers.

* * *

For this reason in all religions, different types of ceremonies are current to enable one to get charged with these currents. Here to sip the water of the feet, accept flowers, put a mark on the forehead, have the head touched, or the back patted, be initiated, hear the instructions, receive blessings, think in one's mind about clothes suggested by the guru – these are the paths commonly current to imbibe the power of yoga. The gurus also, in diverse ways transmit, their power and bless the sadhakas.

* * *

But it is not easy to wash the feet of the guru. There is a special process about it. What sort of water is to be used? What is the time for washing the feet? What feet are washed? How the water is to be used? How the water is being kept? Whether the yogi or guru should wear leather shoes? Does the guru see this science with his own eyes?

* * *

The first ablution of water of the guru's feet is normally thrown away, but this is a wrong procedure because it is the first washing which is activated and full of the current. First washings are a little dirty, and, therefore, the best time for washing the feet is when, after bath, the guru sits in sadhana. Then there will be no dirt and the first washing is available for sipping. The time of sunrise in the morning is best.

* * *

If the time is different then one need not wash the feet but receive the power through the media of other elements, or one can touch the feet for some time, or the process can be carried through the medium of the head or the palm. Try to follow this experiment according to the prescribed procedure, regard being made to the time and the media. The initiation into mantra should not be accepted in the months of Chaitra (April), Jyestha (June), Ashadha (July) and Posh (January). If it is the intention to sip the water of the feet immediately then this could be done by use of rose water, well water or river water, and if it is to be preserved then the water of the Ganges is the best.

The currents of the yogic power pass with greater force through the toes and, therefore, it has been enjoined that the toes and particularly the big toe should be washed, but there is no harm in washing the whole foot. It must be remembered that a small spoon should be kept for washing the feet. At least the time taken in reciting 108 mantras should be the time in washing the feet. This water should be kept in a copper vessel or in an air tight bottle. That is why it has been enjoined that the gurus should not use shoes because that will disturb the entire procedure of washing the feet. If they do use shoes, washing of feet should not be permitted. Only those gurus who have experience of receiving these currents of yogic power know these rules which are not being disclosed here.

* * *

Followers of other religions take the current through the medium of a kiss. This kiss is administered on the back of the thumb or the palm. For us, this procedure is not necessary. The sipping of the water of the feet of the guru should be done often enough at the time of a festival and also when there is a crisis in one's affairs or when one has long-standing sorrow or disease; or one is troubled by unseen beings. This is done after worshipping the family deities. In addition, kumkum used at the time of guru pooja should be applied to the forehead. If the guru has shown his secret remedy, it should be resorted to only at the end. If the guru is full of yogic power and the disciple is full of faith impossible things happen.

* * *

Lectures on Yoga

Swami Satyananda Saraswati

Yoga Publications Trust, Munger, Bihar, India

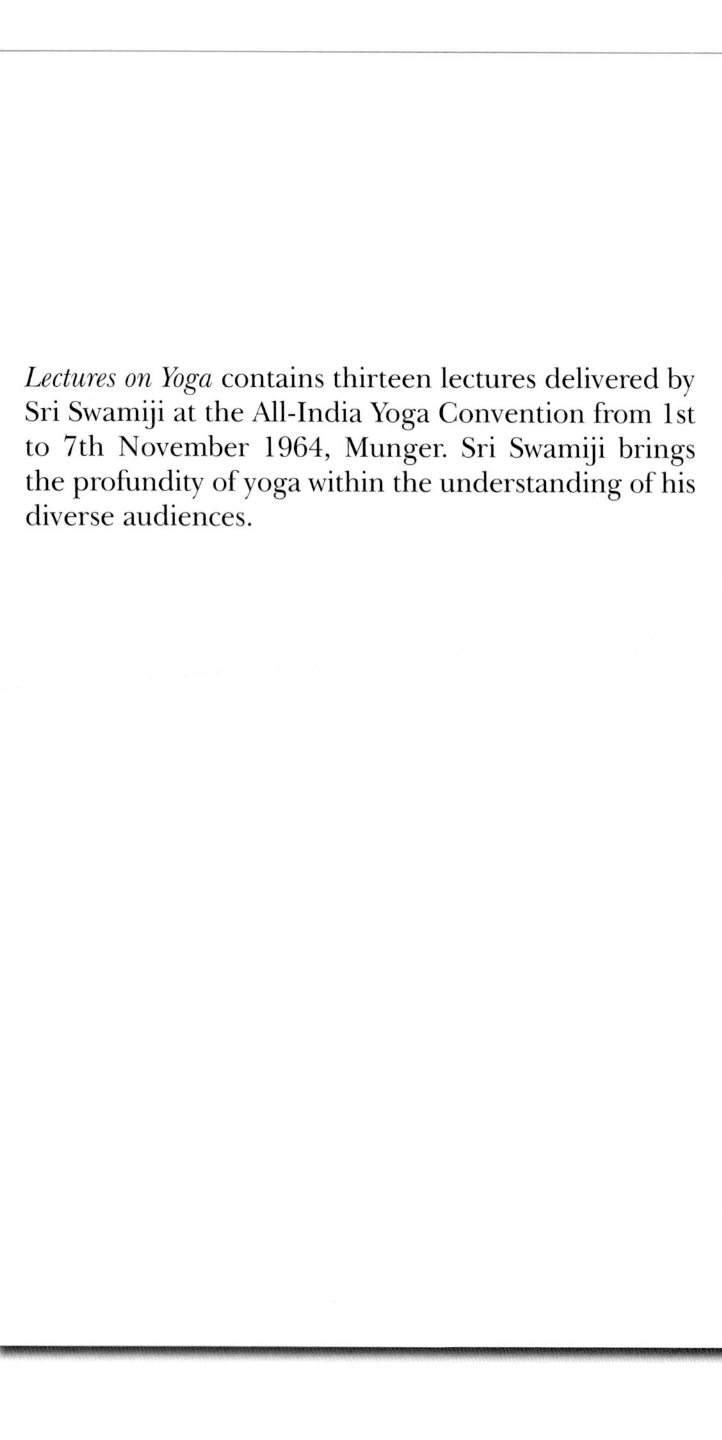

Lectures on Yoga contains thirteen lectures delivered by Sri Swamiji at the All-India Yoga Convention from 1st to 7th November 1964, Munger. Sri Swamiji brings the profundity of yoga within the understanding of his diverse audiences.

Publisher's Note

Bihar School of Yoga, Munger, celebrated its annual function by holding an All-India Yoga Convention from 1st to 7th November 1964. It was an epoch-making convention held for the first time in the history of yogic conventions.

Over seven hundred delegates from all over the country joined the convention and took part in its week-round deliberations.

Eminent speakers, acclaimed scholars, political personalities and mahatmas addressed the representative gathering on various topics of yoga for seven days.

Among twenty-one speakers who addressed the convention, there was one distinct and ringing tone, majestic, authoritative and unique, which arose from the dais and chanted its spell in the minds of the audience. Most eloquent, deeply inspiring and out and out dynamic in language, in delivery and in import the speech would emerge as if from the depth of an ancient cave and would end dramatically at the end of the tenth minute.

This voice was the heart-spoken and graceful speech of Paramahamsa Swami Satyananda Saraswati. His speeches left an abiding effect on the minds of all for the style, the novel approach and the captivating and smiling tone.

This is the collection of those speeches.

—K.K. Goenka, Publisher, Munger

Inaugural Speech

1 November 1964

The first convention of Bihar School of Yoga begins from today.

People have very strange notions about yoga. Some think that only sannyasis can practise yoga and that for householders it is taboo. This is a fallacy. In our religious lore there are many stories of householders who were yogis – King Janaka, for example. Again, some believe that yoga means a few asanas and pranayamas. Actually, yoga is much more than that. In the *Bhagavad Gita* mention is made of *Brahma vidya* and *yoga shastra*. These two interlink. The former relates to theory and the latter to practice.

Yoga is practical. Remember, the knowledge of yoga was imparted by Lord Krishna to Arjuna right in the midst of the battlefield. It was not given to a sannyasi, but to a person who was very much in the world, a warrior who was confused with the problem of right and wrong. Thus you will see that yoga does not mean performing a few asanas or pranayamas, although these are important, nor is it meant for sannyasis only. It is much more for the man of the world faced with day-to-day problems and the realities of life.

There are different branches of yoga. All these can help you in your individual and social life. Yoga is mental therapy. Asanas, pranayamas, ajapa japa, nada yoga and all other practices of yoga help in getting rid of the accumulated samskaras from your mind. Once these samskaras go, your neurosis, mental conflicts, complexes, frustrations, also depart. Children of exceptionally well-to-do parents are at times found stealing petty things. They leave well cooked, wholesome home food and run after unhygienic, dirty, ill cooked preparations available elsewhere. These and many such examples are met in daily life. They are a legacy of psychological problems. Man identifies himself too much with his body and then becomes a victim of all sorts of psychological neurosis. Even when there is no earthly cause for neurosis, he creates them like a fear complex, for example: fear of death, fear of ill health, fear of monetary loss, fear of this, fear of that. He has all these fears when there is not the slightest justification for harbouring them. He imagines all sorts of foreboding situations and worries without rhyme or reason.

If you want to change your personality, if you want to remove your complexes, then yoga is the answer. Believe me, liberation is not going into seclusion. Liberation means remaining steadfast where you are and overcoming your limitations. It means destroying the chains that bind you. It does not mean, as some people seem to imagine, going to some unknown regions, high up in the sky, from which there is no rebirth. It belongs very much to the world. It is a matter of here and now. If one cannot shake off his *vasanas*, the deep-rooted desires, which bind him in life, if one cannot overcome his personality deficiencies which are entrenched in his unconscious, how can he get happiness, bliss, liberation? Yoga will liberate him from the shackles that bind him. Through yoga he can fathom his unconscious and remove layers after layers of samskaras which hold him back and come in the way of his natural self-expression. When these samskaras go, power and wisdom begin to manifest in him which lay dormant within.

You may have heard about kundalini yoga. There is so much misconception about it. People think they will lose their life or go crazy if they learn and practise this yoga. Kundalini is a great psychic power lying dormant in mooladhara. There are various psychic centres in man which, if they open and begin to function, give different powers inherent in each one of these centres. The superpsychic centre is in the head. When the dormant kundalini is awakened and made to move upwards through the sushumna and join this centre, great power is released. There are various yoga practices for accomplishing this, like rotating your consciousness through the psychic centres, deep meditation, and so on. Awakening the kundalini power is not an easy process and calls for long and sustained practice.

In a research institute in a town in Rajasthan experiments have been carried out on people in meditation, and it was established that all mental, muscular and emotional tensions drop in meditation. In that state even high blood pressure comes down. People who practise meditation not only get rid of their tensions but acquire new power. Thus you will see that yoga is responsible for improving man's personality. A student of yoga can have a better personality by getting rid of his tensions and psychological complexes. This is how yoga helps the modern man.

Nowadays people know so much about doctors, diseases and their medicinal cure that they become disease-obsessed by constantly thinking on these matters. As such, mentally they become weaker and weaker. People should take to yoga to remain in robust health. In the final analysis, the cure has to be individual. That is why Communist countries which attempted to improve the lot of their population on a mass scale have failed.

In an ultramodern drawing room, furnished in the best taste, if there lies, hidden from the eye, a piece of some highly decomposed, stinking matter, no one would like to enter that room despite its elegance. The same applies to the human personality. If there is rot within, people will keep away from you. Yoga is the broom that makes a clean sweep of your inside rubbish. Our daily life is full of tensions. There are tensions between husband and wife, employer and employee, friend and friend and so forth. Nobody wants tensions but they are there, making life miserable. They are there because of our accumulated samskaras. Modern psychology does not believe in rebirth and karmas, but yoga does. The soul changes residence from one body to another from times immemorial and in the process accumulates samskaras. That is why a man acts as he acts, and is at times at a loss to know why he did a particular thing in a particular way.

From the standpoint of psychology, suppose somebody suffers from a deep-rooted neurosis, what do we do? We send him to a psychiatrist who puts him under 'deep meditation', and after a number of such sessions the patient begins to improve. Yoga does the same thing. When I started yoga practice, a time came when I began to know and understand more and more about my own personality.

Everyone wants peace and harmony in life. And in fact, even God-realization can be attained only after you have attained peace and harmony within yourself. Once you attain peace, tensions, complexes, frustrations, all these vanish. You become the master of your mind, and when you become the master of your mind, you will know God. Mind-realization and God-realization go hand in hand. Therefore, first try to understand your mind. A yogi never overlooks his mind. He synchronizes his psychic consciousness with his mind. He withdraws his senses from their objects and joins them with his consciousness, his *atma*, self. This is yoga. When your mind becomes introvert and begins to meditate then you get supreme peace, *paramananda*. You become one with your self. This is meditation on your self. There are various methods whereby you can attain this state. To mention a few: nada yoga, meditating on one of the psychic centres, trataka, meditating on the question, 'Who am I', and so on. All this is yoga.

Some say yoga is too complicated for them to understand. They find it easier to practise bhakti. That, too, is yoga. Saints have laid down that bhakti, karma, and *jnana,* the path of knowledge, are all yoga. Raja yoga, of course, is common to all these three yogas as salt is to food preparations. Ultimately, all the above three yogas become one with raja yoga. Without raja yoga you cannot control the dissipations of your mind. Karma yoga is difficult because you have to act treating alike pleasure and pain, gain and loss, victory and defeat in your daily life. Jnana yoga is easier, and bhakti yoga is the easiest to practise.

You will thus see how all-embracing our scriptural concept of yoga is. The practice of yoga transforms a rank pessimist into a robust optimist; one becomes a king unto himself. The science of yoga can no longer be kept away from humanity. We have to propagate it. It can do tremendous good to a wearied world.

Sri Ramakrishna Paramahamsa was a great believer in bhakti yoga. All surplus emotions, uncontrolled and unfulfilled desires get exhausted when you practise bhakti yoga. Man is an emotional being. He tries to channel his emotions in his love for his wife, relatives, friends, and so on, but love for worldly objects cannot give fulfilment, and unfulfilled love creates complexes. Instead of controlling his emotions, his emotions control him. This results in all sorts of social maladjustments and evils. Bhakti yoga can take care of all your surplus emotions. It can transform your mundane neurosis into sublime neurosis. But along with bhakti yoga, also practise karma and jnana yoga. Then only can you have an integrated personality. This is poorna yoga. Having established yourself in poorna yoga, go into meditation and by and by you will attain samadhi. You don't have to take sannyasa for that. Stay where you are and practise it.

In this convention you will be told of various methods of doing meditation and attaining samadhi. But for all practical purposes, you will have to seek answers to two questions. One is, whether yoga can help you to improve your everyday social life. The second is, whether man can overcome his personality deficiencies by the practice of yoga. As you will soon realize, the answer to both these questions is in the affirmative.

I sincerely hope that the tradition of having yearly Yoga Conventions will be established and that every year each convention will cover new ground.

Yoga is a philosophy of balance. When you expose yourself to yoga, you learn how to be simple in every aspect of your lifestyle and being. Where there is simplicity there is relaxation, where there is complication there is tension. When you expose yourself to the influences of yoga, the light of spirituality has to shine. Yoga is a way of life. It is concerned with man's personal life and how he can improve it.

Yoga should be introduced into every stratum of society to enable everyone to restructure their mind and personality. The most important task is to expose more and more people to the benign influence of yoga. They are striving for peace of mind and happiness, but this will only come when they expose themselves to yoga and begin to know a little more about the person within.

Yoga is the greatest gift that can be given to man today. If anyone asks me what I have given to humankind in my role as a spiritual teacher, I can definitely say that I have given yoga – the gift of peace.

—Swami Satyananda Saraswati

Ajapa Japa

2 November 1964, Evening session

Today, on the second day of our convention, I shall speak on one of the most simple yoga techniques, ajapa japa. I have already told you that yoga can cure present day frustrations and abnormalities. The utility of yoga as a mental therapy has been widely recognized abroad, so much so that in Germany attempts are being made to use yoga methods not only for the cure of common diseases, but, believe it or not, for the cure of malignant diseases like cancer.

Let us forget for the moment that yoga is a means to God-realization. Instead, let us talk of yoga as a means to self-improvement. For this, certain techniques such as meditation on nada, bindu, prana, and so on, are very useful. Of these, meditation on *prana*, the breath, is the easiest and most effective. The goal of each one of these techniques is to attain peace and power. Just as a farmer sows seeds and reaps the harvest when it is ripe, so also you meditate and, in the course of time, reap the harvest of peace and power. But, as we all know, seeds can yield harvest only if favourable conditions exist. The soil should be fertile; there should be no undergrowth of weeds. Similarly, peace and power follow meditation practices only after the correct receptivity has been created. Such receptivity is created by what we know as pratyahara. After this, the exploration of your unconscious becomes easier. And when you go deep into your unconscious, you get rid of the samskaras that lie embedded there. When the samskaras go, mental tensions and agitations also depart. Then you get peace, *shanti*. Once peace is attained, the stage is set for the manifestation of *shakti*, power, through the practice of kriya yoga. With shakti, you attain *jnana*, knowledge.

So long as you do not acquire mental, emotional and muscular tranquillity, you cannot have favourable conditions for the manifestation of power. Power can manifest only when the dissipations of the mind stop. As long as the mind is not steady, it is weak. When mental turbulences vanish, power manifests. This power is called *atma shakti*. It takes various forms in its external manifestation. Great men in history realized this power and used it to advantage in their respective fields of activity.

Our scriptures have laid down various methods for the realization of this power. First of all, by pratyahara practices such as asanas, pranayamas, japa, you introvert your outgoing senses. Thus the pratyahara sadhana is a prerequisite for acquiring power. When you hear a melodious song, your mind is en rapport with the song. When you watch an absorbingly interesting game, your mind withdraws itself from surrounding distractions and becomes one-pointed. Similarly, by pratyahara you make your mind one-pointed and go inside. Ordinarily, we are awake to the external world and asleep within. In spiritual terminology this is called *ajnana*, ignorance. When you are awake within and asleep to the outside world, it is jnana, knowledge. When you are awake both within and without, it is samadhi. In samadhi the line of demarcation does not exist. When this happens the mind becomes very powerful and acquires creative power. What it thinks and says, does take place. It becomes the doer.

Why are there frustrations in the world? Because the mind has not acquired the creative power, it is lying dormant. This dormant power has been named variously. Some call it kundalini, others call it purusha. How to awaken it? Inner peace is the first essential, and ajapa japa is the best means for obtaining inner peace. Then comes the practice of kriya yoga. When the sadhaka becomes proficient in kriya yoga, then the door to further advancement opens out for him. The technique of kriya yoga is taught by the guru in the traditional way only. The instructions are personal. They cannot be committed to paper and have to be kept secret. A veiled reference to kriya yoga is made in the *Bhagavad Gita* (4:29):

> Some offer the prana into the apana. Others the apana into the prana. There are still others given to the practice of pranayama who having regulated their diet and controlled the course or both the prana and apana airs pour their prana into prana.

Similarly, ajapa japa is also mentioned in the *Bhagavad Gita*. The ujjayi pranayama is part of the ajapa japa technique. In this pranayama you rotate your consciousness along your breath in the sushumna nerve. Kabir has described this process very graphically in one of his mystic songs.

Every time you lose your mental equipoise, it has a lowering effect on your blood circulation. This process produces toxins in the physical system which in turn has an adverse effect on mental operations. Thus a vicious circle is formed. Mind affects body and body affects mind. Our sages declare that mind alone binds or liberates. This, as you now know, is literally true. It logically follows that if the mind improves, your over-all personality also improves. How to overcome this body-mind morbid state? With ujjayi pranayama you start a process of decarbonization of the system and throw out the accumulation of toxins. By khechari kriya you retard the ageing process. You reabsorb the saliva. Yogis call it *amrit*, nectar, which is produced by khechari kriya and prolongs your youthfulness. But khechari is beneficial to those only who lead a moral life, do not go in for excessive physical labour and conserve vitality. For them it is amrit, for others it is poison, it harms. Our mystic poets have sung songs in praise of khechari kriya. The vicissitudes of life run you down. These yoga techniques will again put you on the top, and you will face challenges of life with courage and equanimity. This, in brief, is the technique of ajapa japa.

Kriya Yoga in the Bhagavad Gita

4 November 1964, Afternoon session

Nowadays, it has become very common for people to give talks on the *Bhagavad Gita*, but as these speakers have borrowed their ideas from various books, their knowledge is mostly academic and quite often inaccurate. If you have to undertake a long and complicated rail journey you must consult a railway guide and you cannot, of course, afford to refer to an inaccurate guide. The same applies to commentaries on the *Bhagavad Gita*. After all, the *Bhagavad Gita* is our guide, our book of knowledge, for the tortuous journey through life and misleading talks or commentaries can lead you nowhere.

There are, of course, excellent commentaries on the *Bhagavad Gita* by various learned men down the ages, but each one of them wrote purely from the standpoint of the school of thought he represented. These writers, as a rule, have remained silent on the yoga techniques described in the *Bhagavad Gita*. However, I must say that Saint Jnaneshwar, and, in modern times, the followers of Sri Yukteshwar, have written to some extent on this aspect of the *Bhagavad Gita*. As traditionally the guru instructs his disciple in kriya yoga by word of mouth only, we can easily understand why the great commentators have maintained a veil of secrecy over this subject when it occurs in the *Bhagavad Gita*.

In deference to our tradition, I too cannot speak very openly on the actual technique of kriya yoga, although a good number of those present here have already been initiated in it. Suffice it to say that it is a very advanced and powerful technique which both householders and sannyasis can practise. Patanjali has defined kriya yoga as constituting tapas, swadhyaya and Ishwara pranidhana, but I can assure those of you who have read this aphorism, that the real meaning of these words is quite different from what they have understood. *Tapas* here does not mean penance, *swadhyaya* does not mean the study of scriptures, nor do the words *Ishwara pranidhana* mean total surrender to God in the commonly accepted sense of this term. As you advance in practice, their real meaning will become clear to you.

There are cryptic sentences in the Bible to suggest that Jesus Christ was familiar with kriya yoga. There were occasions when he 'went to heaven' to contact his Father. And when he 'returned to earth', he would tell his followers that he went 'by a ladder, first with eyes open and then with eyes closed'. Clearly, this refers to kriya yoga. Kabir, too, has sung of kriya yoga in mystical language. In recent times, Lahiri Mahasaya, followed by Sri Yukteshwar, Paramahamsa Yogananda and the present Daya Mata have kept up the tradition of kriya yoga.

Kriya Yoga is a scientific technique. It is described thus in the *Bhagavad Gita* (4:29):

> Some offer the prana into the apana. Others the apana into the prana. There are still others given to the practice of pranayama who having regulated their diet and controlled the course or both the prana and apana airs pour their prana into prana.

There is a widespread belief that you attain yogic powers only after you have mastered the art of meditation culminating in absolute concentration. I can say from experience that this theory is not correct. In my early life, I too believed in this theory and even experimented with intoxicants like bhang and ganja in order to attain the laya condition of mind and body. I knew that out of the numerous *chakras*, psychic centres, in the body, a few were very important, and one nerve, in particular, acted as a channel for awakening the yoga shakti, the kundalini, within us. I also believed at that time that the laya condition of body and mind was a sine qua non to make any progress in this direction. Now I know that although to get into the laya condition is very good for householders for relief from their worldly tensions, but for attainment of yoga shakti it is not absolutely necessary. The mind may wander when in meditation, but it should retain awareness of the yogic chakra concerned. People believe that without absolute concentration one cannot get samadhi. But this is not so. There is an important chakra in us, when it is 'touched' samadhi occurs. The state of samadhi is somewhat similar to the unconsciousness of a drunkard or an epileptic whose eyes are open but the mind is vacant. We cannot say that their minds had become totally concentrated before they fell into that state of unconsciousness.

The prana and apana yoga is the yoga of consciousness. Prana here does not mean the physical prana. Prana and apana are the two streams of consciousness. Prana flows down and apana flows up. These have to be united. Continuity is to be created in the same way as you keep the sacrificial fire going by throwing oblations, *samidha*, in it. This is kriya yoga. The jivatma-paramatma yoga, uniting the individual soul with the Cosmic Spirit is different; it is the yoga of the scriptures and has nothing to do with kriya yoga. Real sadhakas whether householders or sannyasis who wish to advance in the spiritual path should put implicit faith in the teaching of the guru even if it differs from scriptural teaching. The guru speaks from personal knowledge, and as far as scriptures are concerned, sadhakas are not always competent to understand their hidden, esoteric meaning.

In the *Bhagavad Gita* all the different systems of yoga are mentioned, but I have specifically told you about kriya yoga because commentators are always silent about it. The *Bhagavad Gita* can lead you to liberation, but only the guru can show you how. If you take the *Bhagavad Gita* merely as a book of moral precepts for right or wrong action, then the *Bhagavad Gita* loses much of its importance, because there are many other books available which teach you such science of success.

Yoga Education in Schools and Colleges

5 November 1964, Morning session

It is a general belief that yoga vidya is only for householders who have always had a spiritual leaning, or those who have renounced the world. As you know, it is our mission to bring knowledge of yoga to every home, and we should not be surprised if in time to come it also becomes part of the curriculum in every school.

There is no reason why this should not be so. Yoga promises all-round development of our personality, it gives physical and mental power, and that is the reason why everyone should learn this *vidya*, science. Not only yoga does this, but it also teaches us how to harness our mental and spiritual forces and use them to tackle the challenges of life, how to remain serene and undaunted under adverse circumstances, nor to get elated when fortune smiles on us. It is because yoga teaches all this that it could have a place in our children's school and college education. They should have intellectual development, physical development and yogic development. The last-named includes moral and spiritual development, and has a wholesome influence on the entire personality.

Psychologists declare that when you go into deep meditation, the layers of samskaras which cause abnormal behaviour are uprooted and destroyed. The personality then becomes normal. To put this in scriptural parlance, *satyam*, *shivam* and *sundaram*, truth, auspiciousness and beauty, within you begin to express trough you, and your true personality blossoms. A positive attitude towards life develops. Social obligations are no longer shirked, worries, fears, anxieties go, and a quiet confidence takes over. Yoga can do all this, and if the individual gains in stature, in the final analysis the nation, too, gains in stature.

A time may come in our mission for the propagation of yoga when our voice will be raised to such a pitch, that our leaders will have to take notice and begin seriously to give yoga its rightful place in our national life. Even the man in the street has begun to realize the importance of yoga. Each according to his needs can gain from this wonderful science and overcome his deficiencies.

We shall have to devise yoga textbooks to suit elementary, high school and college students. There are many religious books, but there is a singular lack of books on yoga. Practice of yoga nidra which is so simple can remove our children's neurosis. It also reduces the normal hours of sleep and thus increases our active life. Khechari mudra, ujjayi pranayama, trataka, all these being so simple and yet so effective, increase mental powers tremendously.

People have false notions about yoga. Yoga is not a fad. Yoga is not charlatanry. Stopping heartbeats or lying buried underground is not yoga. Yoga is a rational science. It makes you a useful member of society. The curse of the modern age is on us and it threatens to make our children more and more irreligious and abnormal. Let yoga bring back a spirit of religion and good behaviour in them. Then when they grow up, they will lead a purposeful life and play their individual role for the greater glory of our nation.

Rasa Lila in Bhagavata

5 November 1964, Afternoon session

Our Bhagavata mentions *rasa lila*. It is commonly understood as the cosmic dance of Purusha and Prakriti or Ishwara and Shakti. Between these two a constant dance, rasa lila, goes on, and that is our samsara. Learned men have interpreted this rasa lila variously. I shall try to interpret it from the standpoint of yoga. It will necessarily differ from other interpretations.

In our body there is Purusha, call him divine Krishna. Purusha also means the kundalini power. You must have seen the illustration of Bhagavan Vishnu on the eternal Shesha Naga. This is based on our Puranas, but believe me, this illustration is not merely a figment of someone's imagination. Very few know that it is an actual reproduction of what is there. The Purusha gets up on the *Sharada Poornima*, the autumn full moon night. Sharada Poornima, a great favourite of our poets, here means spiritual illumination. Our senses, which constantly run after external objects, and which you can call Gopis, give up their objectives when spiritual illumination, Sharada Poornima, comes, and unite with the Purusha or Krishna within. At that moment occurs the ecstatic dance, the rasa lila of Krishna and the Gopis, of Purusha and the senses. This phenomenon is described in the *Bhagavad Gita* also – as going from *dhumah ratri*, from the dark night to moonlight, in other words, attaining *chitta laya*, dissolution of the mind. Our commentators have given various meanings to these words in the *Bhagavad Gita*, but with all apologies to them, I must say that these terms mean chitta laya and nothing else.

When the full moon stage for the Krishna-Gopi love sport is set, at that time there is the call of the divine flute. This is nothing but the nada emanating from the sushumna when the chitta laya is complete. Remember the song of Saint Dariya Sahib:

> Who plays the flute under the canopy of the sky, at Trikuti, where the confluence of the Ganga and Jamuna occurs?

These lines refer to the ida, pingala and sushumna, and the entire song describes the union of the senses with the Purusha, or, in the language of the bhakti marga, the Krishna-Gopi rasa lila.

The dance has begun and it pervades every fibre of one's being. It is bliss supreme. It cannot be seen by the eyes. It can only be felt. When it occurs, "The blind sees it and the armless plays the mridanga."

The Gopis, the senses, wake up, that is, become aware of their true function, forget their clothes, meaning the habits they had fallen into; forget their homes, meaning their inherent tendencies of external perception of smell, form, taste, and so on, and hark within to the call of the divine flute. Here is a paradox. Sadhakas will see this rasa lila even if they don't understand what I say, and non-sadhakas will not see it even if they understand what I say.

The laya condition of the senses does not mean a state of complete inertia. It is like the electric wire. It is not alive when electricity is not passing through it but it is full of energy when charged. Similarly, our senses because of their dissipations are inert and impotent, but when they become introvert, return to their source and unite with Purusha, they are charged. There is tremendous power.

The floods in the Yamuna river, the removal of vestments of the Gopis by Krishna, all this did not happen in actual life.

And still, those with ecstatic experiences will maintain that it did happen, and they are right. This is the mysticism of the bhakti marga.

It is called rasa lila for the followers of the bhakti path or *yoga milan*, union, identification, for yogis. Names differ, the experience is same. When you are too much with the world, it is viyoga. When you withdraw yourself and go in, it is yoga. Here again is a paradox. You get attachment through detachment and detachment through attachment. When you are attached with the inner Purusha, you are detached from the world and vice versa.

This is the mystical rasa lila of our scripture. And remember, listening to didactic discourses is dry, but going in and listening to the divine flute within is pleasant.

Rasalila is a part of consciousness. The dance of Radha and Krishna with the gopis is eternal, it is universal and it is ever present. In this universe which is material, mental and spiritual – and maybe something else also – everything is dancing. Nuclear scientists say that atoms and molecules and electrons are dancing all the time. This dance of atoms is the bedrock of the entire creation. Speech, action, feeling, experience, creation and dissolution of each and every aspect of matter is nothing but a play. Sri Krishna brought dance to the level of the masses, to the cowherd boys and girls, who graze and milk the cows. That dance has become immortal in Indian history and is called the rasalila, the cosmic dance, the celestial dance, the divine dance.

—Swami Satyananda Saraswati

Yoga Therapy

5 November 1964, Evening session

For most people yoga stands for miracles, for superhuman feats of endurance and so forth. If that were yoga, then it could be of no use to humanity. But yoga is a science, and like all other sciences it has a benevolent role to play for the wellbeing of mankind. This benevolent role of yoga is known as yoga therapy.

An average man is far from perfect, and his faults make life miserable for him as well as for others near and dear to him. Can he improve by precepts or moral platitudes? Moralists and religious teachers have tried to improve him without success. Moral precepts reach the intellect, but they cannot penetrate the subconscious, the region where the samskaras of the past and present lives. They lie buried. Therefore, leave aside your books of morals and try a different method, the method of self-cure through yoga. Remember, mind and body act and react on each other. Mental ailments cause physical ailments and vice versa. We allow our senses to run hither and thither to hunt physical satiety. We identify ourselves too much with the body, and it results in neurosis and frustrations. Yoga offers a remedy for the reconstruction of our personality. Withdraw the senses from their objectives and go within to the 'middle chamber', the subconscious of the psychologists. When we contact our subconscious through regular meditation, one by one our deep-rooted samskaras come to the surface and slowly but surely depart from us. This process is entirely in accord with modern psychiatric practices, with the difference, however, that here you are your own psychiatrist.

Can you visualize the benefits of this therapy for our modern students with their outbursts from time to time of indiscipline and misbehaviour? We cannot blame the atmosphere or society. We give them physical and intellectual training and neglect their mental training. Religion cannot give mental training. Not that I am against religious training, but as we all know, regardless of moral precepts against wrong-doing, stealing, telling lies, and so on, children continue to do so, and their personality in the course of time gets stunted.

Thus you will see that yoga is much more for the man in the world. A sannyasi has no need to improve his personality. He does not have to face challenges of life and he has no tensions to overcome. Yoga gives you a psychosomatic treatment for present-day ills. Depth meditation, depth psychology, all this is going deep within and contacting your subconscious. Remember the prayer, 'Lead kindly light amidst the encircling gloom'. It is the inner light which when contacted removes the outside sorrows.

Scientific experiments should be conducted in various yoga kriyas so that they are adapted to our present-day needs. Yoga nidra is beneficial for various neuroses. Trataka is good for insomnia. Ajapa japa reduces hypertension. In ujjayi pranayama the blood pressure gradually comes down. Kapalbhati removes impurities of the system. Jalandhara bandha improves functional as well as heart disorders. Shankhaprakshalana improves the pancreatic glands and tones up the entire system. I am a visionary and I want these hatha yoga kriyas, which are now practised by our sadhus, to get an honoured place in every home. The science of psychotherapy was known to our yogis centuries ago before it became a cult in the West. Our yogis paid great attention to the mind. They knew that lust, anger, avarice, and so on are nothing but *chitta vrittis*, fluctuations of the mind.

Thus, I have put before you my concept of psychosomatic yoga. I am a sadhu, you are all men of the world. It is up to you to derive maximum benefit from this science. If I can derive benefit from yoga, you need it all the more with all your worldly tensions. Teach your children these yoga practices, and their maladjustments will go. Yoga is our priceless heritage. If efforts are not made to preserve this heritage, it will be lost for ever.

The present civilization has made man abnormal. He is sick physically and mentally. He hugs pain and broods over melancholic thoughts. If this is so now, what will happen to the coming generation? Medicines offer no cure. By deep meditation alone can we overcome mental, physical and emotional tensions and rid the world of its besetting maladies.

Yoga and Psychoanalysis

6 November 1964, Morning session

The only book on yoga down the ages is Patanjali's *Yoga Sutras*, but it is also one of the smallest books. All aphorisms of Patanjali would hardly occupy four pages of octavo size note paper. The reason why there are not many text books on yoga is because yoga cannot be learnt by study of books. It can only be learnt by practice. Since ancient times the guru instructs promising disciples by word of mouth, and therefore there are no text books on yoga.

You have probably heard that by the practice of yoga an individual can attain various siddhis, such as clairvoyance, thought transference and levitation. You also know that, for a sadhaka, yoga is a means to God-realization. However, you may not know that for a householder yoga is a powerful therapy, a therapy for body, mind, and all-round self-development.

In my boyhood days I was abnormal in many ways, but I was not conscious that I was so. I don't know why, but at that time I had a strong impulse to learn hypnotism and I did make some progress with it. Subsequently, I tried the vama marga of tantra, went to cremation grounds and carried out a few practices, but I did not go very far and my enthusiasm for the vama marga ended there.

Then I had darshan of Anandamayi Mataji. At that time I was unwell and naturally quite unhappy. A relative of mine advised me to learn asanas and I followed his advice. The result was that my mind became very receptive and I became fond of satsang. After some years it suddenly struck me that there was a considerable change in my outlook on life. A slow but sure transformation had taken place and my thoughts had changed out of recognition. No more fears of death or disease, no more ill will or malice for others. I was still developing mentally but the development now was of a different order. My fancy for yoga had transformed my life. This is not an isolated case. I know many people who took to yoga merely to keep good health and were transformed mentally as well as spiritually as a side result. Have you ever tried to fathom this mystery?

The blood circulates all over the body, and if there is impurity in the blood, the centres in the head governing our emotions also get affected, and so our actions are no longer pure and abnormalities result. By asanas and pranayamas we improve the quality of our blood, our actions become pure and we become masters of our circumstances.

People say yoga is for sannyasis. This is not true. A sannyasi has no family, no problems, no attachments and his wants are few. For this reason he does not develop any aberrations, but the life of the worldly man is different; it is complex. He is bowed down with the weight of his problems and when he suffers those dear and near to him also suffer. Therefore he needs yoga. But instead of trying out simple yet effective yoga practices for self-improvement, he tries to drown his sorrows in clubs, cinema shows, and cigarette smoking. The remedy he employs is worse than the disease.

My original leaning was for the path of knowledge and my energies were directed to that end. I learnt yoga for a different reason altogether. I soon discovered that it is an immutable law of life that pain is inherent in pleasure. People run after happiness and become full of miseries. I knew yoga could improve their lot and that is why I learnt yoga. Life has become competitive. This is the age of the survival of the fittest. The *Bhagavad Gita* tells us (2:50): "Efficiency in actions is yoga."

The sannyasi has detached himself from life. He does not need efficiency in actions – you need it. But how can you have efficiency in actions with a mind that is restless and fluctuates from moment to moment? You are agitated when in sorrow and you are agitated when in joy. Either way, you have no serenity. You should learn the art of remaining steadfast under all circumstances of life. This art is known as yoga.

German psychologists got yoga from the East. They are now working on it and will return it to us as a therapy. They will call it yoga therapy. We had yoga since the time of the Vedas, but we never bothered about its practical use. Another discovery of these scientists, psychotherapy, has been hailed by the world. It is based on the removal by psychoanalysis of latent complexes and fixations formed in early life when these make a man's life miserable. This is no new discovery for us. What the psychologists call complexes, our ancestors called *samskaras*. They, too, know that as soon as your samskara, that is complex, is brought to the surface it vanishes. In psychology a mentally healthy man is called normal. We call him yogi, one who is not affected by good or bad influences of life. In its broad sense, the term yogi does not mean a sannyasi. It means a mental condition, and therefore, everyone can become a yogi.

Western psychologists have not concerned themselves with man's spiritual salvation. They are content with curing mental disorders. In their study of human mind they stumbled upon the discovery that man is endowed with extra sensory perception power and that it is dormant in all of us. Those fortunate few in whom it has awakened perform superhuman tasks. All of you must have heard about the mathematical feats of the South Indian girl Shakuntala, to give one example. Again, this is no new discovery. Our yogis all along knew about this power. They could see with eyes closed, walk without moving and hear with ears plugged. They practised the art of awakening our superpsychic centres by deep meditation. The ESP of the modern psychologists was the yoga shakti of our yogis.

It is my belief that all our great scientists were raja yogis. They searched and searched within, and gave us their findings in the form of great discoveries.

I referred to psychotherapy not because I am enamoured with it. Psychotherapy is a child before yoga. A modern author, Hans Jakob, has written an excellent book called *Psychology and Hindu Sadhana*. He commends our practice of meditation on form. He maintains that when we meditate on form, as it becomes clearer and clearer, our samskaras, the root cause of all our troubles, begin to leave us. When this happens inner purity takes over, and the individual manifests power. That is why religions declare that so long as you do not have the vision of God, lust, greed, jealousy, and so on will not leave you. When God-realization comes, lower instincts go. Your actions become pure and unselfish. Thus when we practise meditation for God-realization, a change for the better occurs in our personality, and our gain is ultimately the gain of society!

Research into meditation and brain chemistry has revealed that we hold the key to healing within ourselves. Scientists are searching for methods to turn on the switches to increase or decrease the secretions at will, in order to balance the metabolism and nervous system. Research indicates that yoga possesses the techniques required to do this. We cannot emphasize enough the need for more study and research into the uses of yogic techniques. This will bring us one step closer to a life which is free from disease.

—Swami Satyananda Saraswati

The Art of Meditation

6 November 1964, Afternoon session

When you leave your room and go out, you are in the external world, *samsara*, but when you shut yourself in your room, the world ceases to influence you. In the same way, in meditation you go within having withdrawn your senses from external objects. Your meditation gets deeper and deeper as your senses become weaker and weaker to their external perceptions. It is like this. When you become sleepy, the sounds you hear within become less distinct; when you are half asleep they are faint; and when you are fast asleep, you hear them no more. The analogy goes further. In sleep you see dreams; in meditation you see images, scenes, but in sleep the dream is a vague affair, in meditation whatever you see, you see with full awareness.

If you meditate on Rama, you will ultimately see the form of Rama. If you meditate on the form of your guru, his form will come before you. Whatever the object of meditation it will manifest provided your meditation becomes sufficiently deep. However, before you master the art of meditation, you have to cross some hurdles.

When you go into meditation you see images, all sorts of unintelligible images. In order not to get stuck, you must use your imagination when you encounter these images.

Suppose you are meditating on the form of Rama. Suddenly you see a cave. Go inside. The cave rises and goes up. Mentally take a ladder and reach the cave. But the entrance is closed. Again, mentally carve a passage and go in. You find a deep well inside. Although it is suffocating, go inside with determination. At this stage, without knowing it, you have entered deep meditation.

You are meditating on Lord Krishna. Suddenly you see a winding path. You walk on and on until it leads you to an isolated house with the main gate closed. You open it and go inside. The hall leads to a closed room. You open it. Another closed room. This time you are not sure. Does the door open inside or outside? Anyway, you manage to open it. Pitch darkness. You try to find your way about and come up against a door. This time it is locked. Somehow you feel that you have got the key, but where is it? If you delay you will 'come out' and lose meditation. However, you do find the key and unlock the door. And then you see brilliant light all around.

I have given you only two examples, but there is, of course, no limit to them. The important point is, whether you should try to bring back the form of Rama or Krishna, your object of meditation, or go on exploring the scenes as they project on your mental screen. The opinions are divided. Some advocate the first course, others the second. I consider the second course to be of real importance in your sadhana. You must explore the images that emerge at your subconscious level. These subconscious patterns stand for your samskaras. You must bring them out before you can have God-realization. It may take months or years but these images, which rise up in all sorts of weird shapes representing your samskaras, must get exhausted in this manner and liberate you from their shackles.

As meditation progresses, the sadhaka goes in one of the two paths known as uttarayana and dakshinayana. Our commentators say *uttarayana* stands for liberation and *dakshinayana* for bondage. But their interpretations are wrong. As we go in deep meditation the consciousness of some of us goes into the laya state, of others into the samadhi state. Those who go into the laya state, remain suspended in that state. For them there is no further progress without the help of the guru. Those who go into this condition of 'this far and no further' are said to have proceeded in the dakshinayana path of meditation. The other path, in which you see fire, then the hazy light of early morn, and finally daylight, is the uttarayana path of meditation.

When you meditate in the chidakasha, first there is darkness, then stars appear, dim light, more light, and then the whole chidakasha is suffused with light. This is the uttarayana path. Those on this path must continue with it. Their onward journey is safe and assured.

You go into meditation. See darkness. It goes on increasing till a thick black veil is formed. Then suddenly moonlight spreads over the firmament. This is the path of the *dhumah*, smoke, Krishna, *ratri*, the night of Krishna, *chandrama jyoti*, light of the moon, the dakshinayana path wherein you go into the laya state and go no further. To overcome the stalemate, practise meditation on *sakara*, form. Then samadhi is assured. But those practising meditation on *nirakara*, formless, will not attain samadhi here, because it is very difficult to achieve the preparatory state of concentration culminating in samadhi in nirakara meditation.

Yoga Nidra

6 November 1964, Evening session

Today I shall speak on psychic sleep, yoga nidra. Sleep rests your body, but yoga nidra rests both your mind and body. When you are asleep your consciousness sleeps in your astral body, but in yoga nidra your consciousness is awake within.

Yoga nidra performs two beneficial functions. It removes fatigue and invigorates the body. The stresses and strains of daily life create tensions and these rob the mind of its serenity. Yoga nidra removes tensions and restores the elasticity of your mind. Evils of day-to-day life are deposited in our subconscious and in due course exert a deleterious influence on our mental make-up. Just as our houses must be swept daily to keep them tidy, similarly for a normal personality, we must remove these samskaras, the mental dirt, that accumulate daily in our subconscious. Yoga nidra performs this essential service for us. It removes our mental abnormalities and clears the way to spiritual progress.

How to practise yoga nidra? Do a few asanas and pranayamas first and follow them with yoga nidra. The technique is best learnt from the guru. Not that it will harm you if you practise it without his help, but if you do it on your own, the chances are that every time you begin it, you will end up falling asleep. Then your samskaras will not get destroyed, with the result that you will not make any progress. Yoga nidra, to be absolutely successful, presupposes a spirit of communion between the guru and the disciple.

Only that disciple who has complete reverence for his guru can appropriate the benefits of yoga nidra. Yoga nidra should not be practised immediately after meals. Mentally sick persons should practise it thrice a day and for longer durations, say for an hour each time, after a preparatory round of asanas and pranayamas. Trataka will increase the efficacy if practised during yoga nidra, but if it is found difficult, then shambhavi mudra or gazing at the nose tip should be done. If these preliminaries are gone through, the guru is in a better position to help the disciple. Yoga nidra is a psychophysiological therapy.

What is yoga nidra? It is a state in which you are neither asleep nor awake. If you fall asleep it is not yoga nidra. If you remain awake then too it is not yoga nidra. If dreams overtake you it is not yoga nidra. Yoga nidra is a state in which there is awareness of the conscious, subconscious and unconscious fields of your mind, all at one time. It is a perfect therapy. It removes all psychological abnormalities, samskaras, and helps you to become your normal natural self.

Patanjali has defined yoga as the control of chitta vrittis. Good behaviour is the outcome of chitta vrittis. Similarly, bad behaviour also is the outcome of chitta vrittis. Our conscious, subconscious and unconscious fields are our *chitta*. Simultaneous awareness of these three fields is, 'Aham Asmi – I Am'. The state in which you are aware, but are not aware that you are aware comes in yoga nidra. Thereafter, a process of sure but imperceptible sublimation takes place within.

I have read somewhere that meditation creates a fire which burns away our sins. What is sin? Actions which create uneasiness and abnormal feelings in the mind are sins. Cynics dismiss the word 'sin' with a smile of derision. Whenever your conscience pricks you for any action of yours, that action is sin. And cynics are no exception to this rule, sin is there whether they admit it or not. In meditation your consciousness penetrates the various layers of your inner self. This is the fire that burns away the dross of samskaras within. Thereafter the yogic state of supreme peace and tranquillity of mind comes as described in the second chapter of the *Bhagavad Gita*. There are many yoga techniques of meditation for the attainment of this Brahmic bliss, such as yoga nidra, nadanusandhana, ajapa japa, rotating of consciousness by ujjayi pranayama in sushumna.

The all-important point in meditation is that you must not allow yourself to fall asleep, because in yoga nidra as well as other meditation practices, sleep tries to overpower you. If you can overcome this weakness, you will gain in willpower, and willpower can do great things in life. If sleep comes, do asanas, or meditate on your body, or on the sleep itself as if it is trying to possess you and you are watching it. If images rise before your mind, go on watching them. In yoga nidra when you feel that you are unconscious, it actually means that you are conscious of being unconscious.

Those who follow implicitly the guru's instructions are assured of success. Circumstances or worldly ties are no hindrances to spiritual progress. The only hindrances are your own ignorance and sloth.

We must make the blessings of yoga nidra known as widely as possible. Many mental and physical disorders of both young and old are cured by yoga nidra. It is a psychosomatic technique and could do immense good to our children if our educational institutes were to include it in their curriculum.

Ajapa Japa

7 November 1964, Morning session

The other day, in my speech, I omitted to tell you that the easiest method of awakening your sushumna nerve is to practise ajapa japa. 'Do your work simultaneously with japa' is not a wrong principle, but it cannot suit everyone. Ajapa japa definitely does not mean that you go on chanting the name when driving a car. If you do that, it may prove disastrous.

The real ajapa japa is that which goes on within in silent rhythm all the time and still there is no loss of concentration in your external activities. To acquire this art you have to master the technique of pranayama through the sushumna, a subtle motor nerve in our spinal column which transmits our consciousness. Of the three, ida, pingala and sushumna, which comprise our central nervous system, sushumna is the most vital nerve, and our aim is to awaken it and to make it fully operative. There are, of course, other techniques to awaken this nerve, but the process of ajapa japa in ujjayi pranayama is the one we are concerned with at the moment.

Let us first consider ujjayi pranayama. Have you heard the sound of the waterless hookah which old village ladies blow? Can you recall the breathing of an asthmatic or a man in deep slumber? Or the last faint puffs of a railway engine just brought in the yard? These sounds resemble the vibrations of the ujjayi pranayama. As you will see, the ujjayi pranayama is perceptibly different from other varieties of pranayamas.

Rotation of breath by ujjayi pranayama, in descending and ascending the spine through the sushumna, eventually materializes our consciousness. When the subtle power of our consciousness moves upwards, it penetrates, one after the other, the psychic centres located on the path of sushumna. Each of these centres has its special attributes which become operative as the centres unfold and get switched on. This does not, of course, mean that all this happens straightaway. It is a very slow process. You get stuck for a long time at each centre, and in many cases there is no further progress without the help of the guru. As these centres begin to function, our mental and spiritual development is vastly accelerated.

It happens with most of us that when our concentration becomes one-pointed, a time comes when our breathing is suspended, and feeling uncomfortable, we come out of meditation. To overcome this difficulty, as our concentration becomes more and more intense, the pranayama should become more and more subtle. This is a knack which can be acquired by practice and does not call for strong lung capacity.

You have to achieve three things in sushumna. First, the creation of *nada*, vibration. Second, the rotation of the breath. When the breath comes in, the consciousness comes up, and when the breath goes out, the consciousness goes down. The consciousness performs, as it were, a rhythmic dance. Third, the synchronization of the *Soham* mantra. Mentally join *So* with the ingoing breath and *Ham* with the outgoing breath.

After having practised these three kriyas, the next stage is to meditate on the form of your chosen deity in chidakasha. Remember in sadhana, those with impure minds should practise mantra anushthana. Those who lapse into the laya condition should practise hatha yoga. Those whose minds flit hither and thither should participate in congregational bhajans and kirtans. When you are able to visualize the form of your deity clearly in the chidakasha, you are ready for the higher technique of kriya yoga.

International Yoga Fellowship: Aims and Objects

7 November 1964, Delegates meeting

The International Yoga Fellowship has been in existence for the last two years. It is doing good work and will continue to do so. I have no doubts about it.

Let me give you the background of this movement. In 1961 I had given sannyasa diksha to Mataji and I was proceeding to Rishikesh to obtain formal blessings from my guru, Swami Sivananda, as deemed by our traditions. I took advantage of this opportunity to visit Badrinath. Ma Yoga Shakti, Mahendra Babu and Sunil were with me. At Badrinath, suddenly Mataji's body became ice cold and soon there appeared a glow all over it. This was an unusual phenomenon, but later we realized that she had received, at that moment, a divine mandate for the propagation of yoga to the world. Subsequently, on our return, a few of us met at Raigirh to discuss ways and means of carrying out this mandate. Thus was born the International Yoga Fellowship.

In Rajnandgaon we opened our first centre. From there I went on a tour of various provinces of India. There was great enthusiasm for the idea in Bombay and our most active centre was established there. That was the time when the fight on our borders had been called off and a cease fire declared. The Mayor of Bombay in his inaugural speech said, "There is never a cease fire in the war of thoughts. We can build up defences against the Red aggression, but we have to build up an intellectual defence against the enemy in our mind. Only yoga can do this." Soon there were centres in other cities.

What are the objectives of the International Yoga Fellowship?

1. *Establishment of yoga training centres*
   The first of these, Bihar School of Yoga, has already started functioning.
2. *Dissemination of knowledge of yoga through publications*
   We now own a press. Books and periodicals are coming out at regular intervals.
3. *Establishment of yoga clinics*
   A beginning has been made. A section of Bihar School of Yoga has been converted into Yoga Nidra Vihar. I am looking forward to a unique type of hospital, a hospital with only one doctor, many patients, no equipment, no assistants, no nurses, no sweepers. This is the sort of yoga clinic I have in mind.
4. *Yoga Research*
   For the advancement of any science, research is of primary importance. We shall have to establish a central library with thousands of books on yoga in various languages because at present literature on yoga lies scattered. Students can do research under our guidance and go back to their universities with a thesis on yoga. They will receive all encouragement, and we shall not hesitate to give them free boarding and lodging.
   We are busy with this project and hope to see it functioning very soon.
5. *Introduction of yoga in schools and colleges*
   For sadhakas there are ashrams. Those who want God-realization there are institutes like Bihar School of Yoga. But when you want to teach yoga to the millions, the best way to go about it is to teach them when they are young in schools and colleges. For this, suitable textbooks will have to be devised. If Sanskrit, which has ceased to have any utility, can find a place

in our education, there is no reason why yoga, with its usefulness in our day-to-day life, should not find a similar place in our education.

This is the vision of the International Yoga Fellowship.

In the last quarter of every century, a movement begins and comes to fruition in the first quarter of the next century. This is a historical process. At the end of the last century we had a movement for revival of Hinduism under Sri Ramakrishna Paramahamsa, Swami Vivekananda and Dayananda Saraswati. This movement found its fulfilment in the first quarter of this century.

With the changing times, life has become more and more complex. The powers of darkness are once more stalking the world. There is, however, a compensatory law. When satanic forces are abroad, divine forces come forward to ward them off. That is why you find a revival of religion everywhere.

The primitive man was a caveman. He was followed by the intelligent man who ushered in the age of philosophy. Now the age of the intuitional man is dawning near, in the coming age man will be supramental. Sri Aurobindo prophezied the same thing. This is laid down in our scriptures also.

We have started our movement in the third quarter of this century, and it will take some time to gather momentum. Already people are coming forward, some with money, others with brains and still others with offers of fieldwork. Each according to his capacity is eager to give a hand to it.

It will not be long before scientists will acclaim yoga and give it a place of honour along with other sciences which serve humanity. Already well-known writers, thinkers, musicians, painters and cinema stars, all over the world, have agreed that yoga can do wonders for the promotion of mental and physical wellbeing. There was a time when to believe in yoga was to belong to a bygone age. It was considered the weakness of the credulous, the superstition of the uneducated. Nowadays ignorance of yoga is considered a lack of culture, lack of scientific spirit and lack of modernity.

God willing, in another ten years time, if only the mystery and miracle mongering that is still being associated with yoga is done away with, it will become a natural habit with people, and their lives will be incomplete without it.

Once the true meaning and significance of samadhi, which is considered very mysterious and beyond the average person, are understood, everyone will practise it to maintain a vigorous mind. Just as men go to cinema shows for relaxation, people will turn to yoga for relaxation. These are not flights of imagination. In the short span of twenty years ideas on yoga have undergone great changes. People talked differently about yoga then. People talk differently about yoga now. So you see the climate for yoga is there, and our movement, the International Yoga Fellowship, is not out of time.

Although I am against orthodox methods of approach, I do not like modern publicity methods of leaflets, advertisements and loudspeaker propaganda for the furtherance of yoga. Yoga is not a ballet; it is not a dance show. It is a *vidya,* science. You cannot apply the methods of the market place to revive yoga. Therefore, our present propaganda will have to be confined to select gatherings of intelligent people.

There are people who bring gifts for me and think that it will give me happiness. Such acts may give them a feeling of self-gratification, but how can these things please me? I am a sadhu and I do not mean anything to you. I am here for a mission. When my work is done, I will not be here. The best gift you can bring me is to try and realize what this mission is and how best you can serve it.

The International Yoga Fellowship has no constitution. It has no accounts. It is my brainwave, my vision, translated into thought, into language, into action.

Kundalini Yoga

7 November 1964, Afternoon session

Today I will speak on kundalini yoga. This is a subject on which people have very hazy ideas. Most of them think that to dabble in kundalini yoga is to play with fire – it is dangerous.

The first book on kundalini yoga that I came across was *Devatma Shakti – Kundalini* by Swami Vishnu Tirtha. Next I read Sir John Woodroff's *The Serpent Power*. He has written very exhaustively on kundalini yoga. No other writer, not even any of our own religious writers, has written so well on this subject. Sir John Woodroffe is considered a great authority on Tantra Shastras. In the beginning, before I came to yoga, I was interested in tantra, and therefore I had gone through his works on Tantra Shastras and found them of absorbing interest.

After reading Sir John Woodroffe's book on kundalini yoga I concluded that this serpentine power resides in each one of us and that it is dormant. So far so good. But where does it reside? We know where our heart is and we know where our lungs are. Similarly, can we pinpoint, with certitude, the abode of this great power? Again, without sight our eyes are useless. Without hearing, our ears are useless. Likewise, we have kundalini, but if it is passive, what use can it be to us?

I soon embarked on a serious study of kundalini yoga, but it led me nowhere. I realized, to my dismay, that no two writers held the same opinion on this important subject. During this period, one day I happened to be reading Penfield's book on biology. Penfield is considered an eminent scientist, he challenged Darwin's theory, and he is a great authority on biology. In that book he relates an interesting experiment. The skull of a demented criminal was being cut open and in the process the instrument touched a particular gland. Immediately the man exclaimed, "I see mother coming. I see mother coming." Penfield maintains that the instrument touched the gland that materializes forms in our mind and makes us conscious of sensations. This must be so. Surgeons doing operations for brain tumour tell us that if a particular nerve is removed the patient has no sensations even if a block of ice is kept on his head. One tiny gland with such important performance! It occurred to me that although we know quite a lot about organs and glands which govern functions in our body, there are, without doubt, nerves and centres, equally important, whose functions we know not, and to that extent remain poorer in the development of our latent powers.

An infant cannot walk. After a few years he walks with ease. He grows into manhood. Now if we slap him, he is sufficiently strong to fight back. From childhood to manhood his strength developed from within. In other words, all our powers, physical, mental and spiritual, are within. They have to be kindled so that in the course of time they shine in full splendour. Another thing that struck me was if our eyes and ears are our centres of sight and hearing, if our brain is our centre of intellect, surely there must be a centre in us for spiritual powers?

In my study of kundalini yoga I found that some authors maintained that kundalini is a nerve in the spinal column, but those who had dissected human bodies refused to agree with them. Others declared that it is spiritually something, physically nothing. But this definition did not impress me. I was convinced that not only it is spiritually something but it is also physically something.

Slowly and slowly, I came to the conclusion that from the cerebrum down to the perineum in our spinal column there is a passage with several centres, *chakras*, which if awakened can release spiritual powers and that the most important chakra is in the cerebrum. This chakra, known variously as the golden egg of Brahma, cosmic egg or hiranyagarbha, is protected from all sides by grey matter just as the white pulp in a coconut is protected by the shell. It is a very small gland and is called bindu. Yogis declare that if by some method, some sadhana, you can throb it you will get the spiritual vision of the entire universe. But to manipulate such throbbing is not easy, for it is said that the mind cannot reach it, speech cannot go there, sensations cannot affect it. How to reach it? There is a way. All you have to do is to activate mooladhara, the abode of the dormant kundalini in the perineum.

At the end of the spinal column, there is a small nadi, red in colour, resembling the infinitely small newborn snake. Physicians and biologists know nothing of the true function of this nadi. All that they are prepared to concede is the existence of some such inactive gland. This nadi lies dormant, asleep, one end fitting snugly to the small cavity in the terminus of the spinal column. If this coiled nadi could be suffused with an extra supply of blood by hatha yoga, meditation or similar practices it straightens. This chokes the entrance to the sushumna, creating a feeling of suffocation in the spinal column. The subtle flow of prana becomes heated, and if the sadhaka has taken care to close the nine gates of the body by naumukhi mudra, it moves upward in the direction of the tenth gate in the cerebrum. In this upward thrust, it pierces, one by one, all the chakras in its way, and when this happens, their powers which were dormant begin to function.

When the first chakra, swadhisthana, at the bottom end of the spinal column, is pierced and becomes active, the sadhaka has to be vigilant against his animal propensities breaking out. Lethargy and drowsiness will also sneak in.

When the next chakra, manipura, behind the navel, is pierced, it bestows the gift of speech and power of literary expression. When anahata chakra, situated behind the heart, opens, the power of right thinking comes and your judgment is never wrong. This is a difficult chakra, but once it opens, you move on to the next chakra with ease. Vishuddhi chakra is situated in the region of the throat at the junction of the spinal column. Ajna chakra is situated between the eyebrows at the back of the skull, bindu visarga at the place where our pandits have the tuft of hair on their heads. Just in front, in the cerebrum, is sahasrara.

To awaken these chakras, one has to study kundalini yoga with particular reference to the location and characteristics of these centres. If the sadhaka is able to concentrate well, he can see the counterpart sign of the chakra concerned. What is a counterpart sign? If you look at the sun, and then close your eyes, immediately a small disc of light will play before your mind. This is the counterpart sign of the sun. If you concentrate on mooladhara, the counterpart sign of kundalini will appear which is a snake with three and a half coils in an inverted triangle, tail up and face down. Concentration on swadhisthana will make you sleepy. In manipura you will see a golden lotus. Remember the Tibetan invocation, *Om mani padme hum*. In anahata, first you will see a faint gleam of light. Once that light becomes steady and constant in meditation, it is said that sorrow keeps away from the sadhaka. In vishuddhi, you have the sensation of drops of nectar trickling down your throat.

In ajna chakra, the sadhaka sees his own form like in the mirror. He may see it dead, alive or in some other way, but it is certain that he will see it. First you get a feeling of drowsiness, awake neither to the external world or within, and then you see the form. Self-realization is not very far when this happens. Ramana Maharshi had this experience. When he was twelve, he felt he was dead. He said, "Here I see my body, but who sees whom through whom?" In ajna chakra the sadhaka will see his consciousness by his own consciousness, his self by his own self. Followers of Ananda Marga and of tantra call this guru chakra. It is also known as the third eye. Ajna chakra opens out by the practice of trataka or by shaktipat medium of a powerful guru; but if the disciple is not fit to receive shaktipat, he will come to harm. In homely language, if the guru possesses AC current and the disciple has DC current then shaktipat will not work. Also, if the disciple's voltage is poor, he cannot stand the high spiritual voltage of the guru. To open the ajna chakra, shaktipat is the best method, concentration between the eyebrows comes second, trataka third and concentration on the forehead comes fourth.

In an island of gems surrounded by an ocean of nectar, with groves of celestial trees on all sides, in the house of *chintamani*, jewels, rests Lord Vishnu. This refers to bindu visarga. This is a very important chakra, and it is why our pandits sport a tuft of hair at this spot. When the sadhaka concentrates on this chakra, he sees the vast canopy of the sky. Beyond, he sees land with mountains of stupendous height. There is also a placid lake with ambrosial waters in the centre of which Lord Narayana rests on a hooded snake with Goddess Lakshmi massaging His legs. This is the vision you have when, with sheer thought power, you touch this centre in your brain. You touch it by concentrated thought, materialized thought, solidified, unified thought. Only such intense concentration can awaken this chakra. Go on hammering this chakra, the strangest possible visions will be the result.

Now move on to sahasrara. You will see a thousand petalled red lotus with a shivalinga in the centre. Over it a hooded cobra, the waters of mother Ganges pouring down and a half moon.

These important chakras are awakened by kundalini. Every chakra has its own letters and the whole alphabet is represented by them. Speech starts from these chakras, but the main station, the source of *nada*, vibration, is in the head.

How to awaken kundalini? Three things are essential: purity of chitta, deep meditation and hatha yoga practices.

By merely doing hatha yoga you cannot awaken kundalini. Deep meditation practices and purity of chitta must go hand in hand. To a very limited extent, everyone's kundalini is awakened, and much more so in child prodigies.

All our faculties, intellectual, instinctive and intuitional, originate from our mind. Animals and infants have instinctive faculties. Adults can develop intuitional faculty, *prajna*, if they master the art of meditation. Prajna awakens when chitta becomes one-pointed. Along with hatha yoga practices and purity of chitta, practise deep meditation every morning for half an hour on any object, with or without form, your ishta devata, guru, or whatever you like, but meditate, meditate, meditate, so that you become oblivious to everything and only the object of meditation abides. When you get such non-dual experience, your kundalini will begin to be detached. Your body will become hot, you will perspire. Suddenly, you will feel in your spinal column a sensation as of a sinuous worm wriggling upwards. That will be the awakening of your kundalini.

After the awakening of kundalini, the mind becomes calm, sorrows cannot disturb it. The sadhaka comes in possession of superlative powers, and if he does not become a virtuous man, he will surely become a notorious criminal.

New Horizons of Yoga

7 November 1964, Concluding session

This is the last day of our convention. I have no doubt that you will go back with the inspiring message of yoga. Let this message wing its way to every nook and corner of India and beyond.

Laymen have very vague ideas on yoga, but even you, who are not laymen, will find it difficult to appreciate the obvious truth of what I am going to say now. It will uproot many of your pet theories on yoga. What are these new ideas of mine? Firstly, no one need leave his home and go into oblivion to practise yoga. It is about time that we scotched the belief that sannyasis only are fit to practise yoga. Secondly, marital relations do not stand in the way of yoga. Thirdly, meat eaters are not required to go all out for vegetarianism just because they have taken to yoga. The real aim of yoga is to attain peace and tranquillity within. For this, you need not give up any of your normal ways of living.

Let me put it more bluntly. Running away from life is not the way to deliverance. Samsara is not *maya*, illusion. It may be maya to the philosopher because he lives in a world of imagination and his feet are not solidly on the ground. Yoga is different, it is practical. It has nothing to do with philosophic flights of fancy. Never believe for a moment that the householder's life is low, and renunciation is superior. Let no woman think that her status in life is inferior to that of man. Those who hold these orthodox views are not fit to live in this world. This is not the sort of yoga that we are out to propagate. We believe that yoga has a special role to play in the world of today. It can remove our mental and physical afflictions. It can bring joy to our hearths and homes. The yoga of our concept does not lay down extraordinary rules and regulations of self-discipline and behaviour. You can continue enjoying good things of life and still be a yogi.

One more idea that will give you a jolt, but I must remove the cobwebs of your mind, don't give up your worldly ambitions, your material aspirations. If you do so, it will do you no good. It will bring harm to society and ruin our country. But don't become slaves of your desires. Be like the ocean which remains undisturbed as the turbulent rushing waters of rivers come to it. Enjoy sense-gratifications but don't let them overpower you. Don't despise life. There is no virtue in retiring to the woods and sitting enchanted in the solitary grandeur of samadhi. Heroism lies in remaining steadfast in the tumult of life when the scales are heavily loaded against you, and in attaining the samadhi of self-equilibrium.

That physician who wants only healthy persons for his patients is no physician. Likewise, if yoga could work its wonders on normal, healthy people only, then the scope of yoga becomes limited. Yoga can benefit all people under all circumstances of life. After your daily round of mental and physical toil, if yoga cannot bring back your resilience and vigour, then you have learnt yoga in vain.

Your life is karma yoga. Sannyasis do not do karma, and therefore they cannot realize the duties and obligations of householders. Life for you, as worldly family men, is a continuous yajna. All your labours to keep your home fires burning, the activities to discharge your social and national obligations, are oblations. Once you understand this truth, you can keep undimmed your vision of self-realization in the midst of unremitting hard work that your station in life enjoins upon you.

But ceaseless activity, in the rough and tumble of life, takes its own toil. Anxieties, frustrations, exhaustion of mind and body, all these accelerate the ageing process. Yoga is a powerful remedy against these forces of destruction. Why hug the belief that the road to the Himalayas is the royal road that ends all your worldly troubles? The *Bhagavad Gita* does not teach you escapism. When the magic moment of his crowning achievement had arrived, Arjuna faltered and began to talk of sin, salvation and retreat to the Himalayas. The Lord brought him back to sanity by preaching the excellence of karma yoga.

Do you wish to pursue the soul-lifting science of yoga? If so, life-long celibacy is not a sine qua non, notwithstanding what our wise men of old have declared. Age does not come in your way. Whether you are on the threshold of life, or whether the spring of youthfulness in you has yielded to venerable old age, you can learn yoga. There are no limiting factors.

Yoga does not mean solely the ashtanga yoga of our scriptures. Such simple practices as likhit japa, nada yoga, trataka, mantra anushthana, are also yoga. Karma yoga, bhakti, jnana yoga, and raja yoga are all different facets of yoga. Because music is an integral part of it, bhakti yoga has a soothing effect on your bottled up and fevered mind. Trataka is a form of pratyahara. But why go far? Life itself is yoga. Religion is yoga. Your day-to-day work is yoga. The field is vast and inviting. Let the thrill and quiver of yoga transform all your activities in life.

In the snares and pitfalls of life, you cannot allow yourself to be divorced from reality. Satya, ahimsa, brahmacharya, and so on, are wonderful words, but I have yet to see the individual who can claim that he has not departed one iota from their practice. Not even our greatest saints can lay such claim. Patanjali's yama and niyama were formulated for an age that is gone and done with, and the simple adamantine fact is that they have no place in the world of today. In the good old days the very air that our ancestors breathed was full of these virtues. The vitiated air that we breathe now is full of falsehood, violence and countless other imperfections. Admittedly satya, ahimsa, and so on are forces of great potency, but they are so only if one practises them to perfection in obedience to an inner compulsion. Yoga is not concerned with the cultivation of impossible virtues. We leave them to moralists. Yoga is a system, a technique for stilling the turbulence of mind, for harnessing it and maintaining its resilience. Aim at developing an integrated personality. The best way to achieve this is a synthesis of bhakti, karma, jnana and raja yoga. Man should not be all intellect; he should not be all emotions. There should be a happy blending of both. Otherwise he will have no peace in life.

When I was in Swami Sivananda's ashram, I kept no money on me or in my room. This, I thought, was aparigraha, but Swamiji thought differently. He saw no harm in my keeping money and giving it away to whosoever needed it. The real meaning of aparigraha then became clear to me. If you have money and can use it, when necessary, to help others, seeing no difference between any man, then it is aparigraha. What is the use of developing virtues in the solitary confinement of your room entirely for your own spiritual progress with no benefit to society as a whole? The basis of Hindu sadhana being individualistic has done enough harm to our nation. If you practise aparigraha in its strict scriptural sense, individually it may bring you spiritual gain, but collectively it can only bring poverty and starvation for your entire family.

The householder takes one path and the sannyasi another. Paths differ but the destination is the same. One has a small family, the other adopts an infinitely large number as his family. Whether one is a householder or a sannyasi, a single test applies to both, how far your attainments, your siddhis, will benefit others? Remember, any religion which aims at improvement of man in isolation cannot be a good religion.

Unless we make root-and-branch changes in our traditional concepts of yoga, we cannot fully bring the blessings of this wonderful science to humanity. The word yoga is of great significance. It is derived from *yuj* to unite. It means *milan*, union, identification. Identify yourself with the joys and sorrows of everyone, extend your horizons, rise above the pettiness of life. This is yoga. If you take it in this sense, it ceases to be individual. Mother and son have emotional identification. If the son is unwell, the mother does not feel well either. Another such relationship is that of husband and wife; if one is unhappy the other is unhappy too. Have such emotional integration with all around you. That is the sort of yoga my master, Swami Sivananda, taught me. He wanted me to identify myself with the mind of a thief, that of a liar or one who spoke ill of me. "Put yourself into their position, that is how you can understand them," this was his advice to me. If you can develop such an attitude in life, you are not very far from yoga siddhi. To attain siddhi is easy but to understand yoga is very difficult.

It is my business to explain the meaning of yoga to you and I will do so in a language that leaves no doubts in your minds. First of all, understand what it stands for. Yoga stands for your physical wellbeing, it stands for your mental wellbeing. It comes as a blessing to suffering humanity as psychosomatic treatment. It comes as the shortest cut to God-realization for seekers of truth. It does not stand for magic-mongering or mystifying the unwary.

Half-truths and untruths have been propagated in the name of yoga and religion. People have been taught to look down upon *grihastha ashram*, the life of householders, but my guru, Swami Sivananda, was wont to give it a lofty status. He used to call it 'yogashram'. Householders are the real yogis. They have great duties and responsibilities. We sannyasis have kept ourselves away from the stormy seas of life; how can we treat grihastha ashram lightly? He used to say, "Grihastha ashram is the crucible which burns the dross of past samskaras and tempers the steel in you, so that your personality may blossom out in full fragrance. The householder's life is a long, continuous sadhana. He has to stand firm and hold on to his duties, *dharma*, when storms and tempests of life try to sweep him off his feet."

Why, why should you consider your station in life less worthy than mine? You have the capacity to earn, to feed yourself and others, to acquire wealth and throw it away. I am a penniless, vagrant sadhu. I have nothing to give, I can only take. Like the wick in the lamp, you burn yourselves away, so that others may live. Those who say that grihastha ashram is inferior do not know what they are saying. They speak from a mental perch so remote that they cannot see the glory and grandeur of life around.

Having said so much in praise of grihastha ashram, I must also tell you that it is up to you to uphold its sanctity. Live in the world but abjure all that is vulgar and petty. Perform all your actions in a spirit of detachment that is how you can have renunciation in samsara. Strive for perfection in every action of yours, that will be the yoga of efficiency mentioned in the *Bhagavad Gita*.

People make high and noble resolves, they want self-realization, they wish to follow the great ideals of the *Bhagavad Gita,* but there is a catch – they have no willpower. There is no progress, spiritual or material, without willpower. So first of all, increase your willpower. Once you take a decision, stand by it, right or wrong. See that you don't develop a split personality: show of willpower in public, pandering to weaknesses in secrecy; a conflict between ego and superego.

In this convention you have heard speeches by learned men on different aspects of yoga. I have my own ideas on yoga; they often differ widely from what has all along been taken for granted. I have put these convictions of mine before you. It would have been a denial of truth in me if I had not done so. I do not like borrowed ideas. I do not allow myself to be swept off my feet by other people's convictions. I do not believe in making prim and proper speeches. I have no time for goody-goody talks. What I have to say, I say it with all the force at my command. I have a mission to fulfil.

A few more words and I shall have done. Do you enjoy a happy, harmonious home life? Are you afire with enthusiasm in your day-to-day activities? When adverse circumstances squash and suppress you, do you rise above them with a cool head and easy assurance? If so, you are a yogi.

Strive and put your house in order. Strive for the betterment of society. Strive, strive with every fibre of your being, for the welfare of humanity. Let caste, creed and sex be no barriers to you.

Hari Om Tat Sat

Discussions on Yoga

Swami Satyananda Saraswati

Yoga Publications Trust, Munger, Bihar, India

Discussions on Yoga is a souvenir publication of the Coalfield Yoga Convention, held from 1st to 3rd November 1974 in Dhanbad, India. Talks and answers to questions on religion, society, health and, of course, on yoga are proof of Sri Swamiji's deep understanding of an immensely wide area of topics.

Contents

Yoga and Hinduism

Even laymen of the Hindu faith have very casual impressions about yoga. They feel that yogic practices are hollow pursuits and that simple, but potent, techniques like japa are adopted in yoga merely because the Hindus repeat the Lord's name in japa. It is often held by such persons that yoga has a very limited scope for adoption and that it is not to be practised by householders or persons burdened with worldly responsibilities.

There are those who hold that practising yoga is embracing the Hindu faith and some who feel that yoga can be practised by Hindus alone, or that yoga is a monopoly of Hinduism.

The following questions and answers should clarify the real position.

Why is it necessary to do so many yogic practices and sadhanas, such as asanas, pranayama, concentration or dharana? As a layman of the Hindu faith, when I love the Lord all I have to do is to fall at His feet and cry! Why can't you do it?

First show me where His feet are and then I'll cry! Our body and mind are invaluable instruments, and therefore, we should not misuse them in drinking, overeating and abuse. We should take care of the body and keep it in the best condition by practising pranayama and asanas. One cannot get food from a cookbook, only cooking can satisfy our stomach. By reading a book on electricity no light can be brought into the house. Likewise, by reading books on yoga theory one cannot attain samadhi. One needs to practise. Yoga increases the mental, physical and psychic capacities of the personality. Even if we are to dedicate our life in the service of the Lord, what use is it to offer a diseased, sickly flower unto Him? In the ancient scriptures it is said:

> *Shariramadyam khalu dharma sadhanam.*
>
> This body is only a means for the sadhana of dharma.

This means that the body is a means to great virtues, great attainment, spiritual or otherwise.

But what about japa? It is practised by Hindus to remember the Lord. How does that help in yoga? You are just repeating the name of the Lord over and over. Is it only to keep you busy or to prevent you from doing anything worldly for a period of time before you commence your regular activities? How does it improve the mind?

Japa is practised in all faiths, but maybe without understanding its psychological importance. The emotional energy should be sublimated and properly channelled for constructive work. Bhakti is the best method for sublimation. Japa is the easiest and safest way by which a person can elevate the state of consciousness, by reciting the name in a particular manner, either alone or in a group.

What happens in japa is that you slowly create a rhythm, and then a momentum in your brain is produced. After a while the mind loses touch with external objects, and the consciousness is withdrawn and elevated. A blissful state is reached and eventually it brings you to a state that is higher than pratyahara. Sometimes it gives a glimpse of meditation also. You will thus see that japa is not repetition of the Lord's name for the sake of repetition and that it is not a prerogative of the Hindus.

Well then, you mean to say that japa is primarily intended to concentrate the mind. If that is true, then why can I not say, "Kitchen, kitchen, kitchen" instead of the Lord's name? Any word or name will have the same effect.

The origin of the sacred syllables, *mantras*, can be traced back to the time of ancient sages who received these sacred syllables through higher states of consciousness in meditation. Every mantra has a deep meaning, according to the arrangement of letters and sounds. When we do japa of a certain mantra we simultaneously meditate on it. For example, the mantra *Om*, by doing japa and meditating on it, we reach a certain cosmic realization which is not possible in repeating, "kitchen, kitchen, kitchen."

Even though I am a Hindu, I do not believe in the name of the Lord and I am not emotional but intellectual. Why should I do japa?

Man possesses all the three qualities of intellect, emotion and spirit, although they appear in different degrees in each individual. There are many situations in life when one is not only intellectual but emotional. Even too much intellectualism is actually suppression of emotions. The question is how to employ emotions for spiritual development.

A certain amount of emotional energy should be sublimated through divine love, *bhakti*, and by using emotions for constructive purposes, such as maternal love or social service. If this is not done there will be emotional imbalance, and that has taken place in many cases. Even those who have faith in God are also sometimes found to be imbalanced, because the whole emotional energy is not let out but is suppressed inside. When the emotions are suppressed they have to come out in some form or other. Even an intellectual person, on hearing good music, can be moved deeply. At that moment, he forgets his intellectual personality. In the same way, by seeing a lonely house in a forest, even an intellectual person can be moved. He becomes calm and relaxed. The happiness in such instances is an expression of his elevated emotion. He is separated for some time from his intellectual personality. Even a hard-boiled intellectual becomes emotional from time to time.

Why are we not happy at times when the most beautiful vibrations are present?

Because the intellectual lock is very strong at such moments.

Yes, I can understand the value of japa and some of the other yogic practices, but let's be practical. What will happen to our social structure if everyone practises yoga all day long? No one works, no one earns money, no one is concerned with family and friends. Should you be only concerned with your sadhana and forget that there is a society and a world besides your own self? As a Hindu, I cannot contribute to such a lethargic attitude to life.

Yoga is not asking you to cut yourself off from your day-to-day activities. In this context you have completely misunderstood the role of yoga. For instance, when we ask you to go to the hospital, we do not ask you to remain there forever. You just go there for a certain period to rest, take medicine, recuperate and then you return home. You do not stay in the hospital forever. No one asks you to take medicine for twenty-four hours a day. A yoga student does his sadhana for one or two hours in the morning or at night. For the rest of the day he can fulfil his worldly and social duties. We will actually find him more capable and energetic due to yogic sadhanas. There are certain students of yoga who seek higher spiritual attainments. Indeed, in their case, they keep themselves completely away from worldly struggles and responsibilities, but you must know that, after their spiritual illumination, they return to society and serve mankind on the social, cultural and spiritual planes. Thus, they prove themselves more valuable and certainly not useless. Moreover, when you say that the social structure will be disturbed by the practice of yoga, we would like to know which yoga practice is disturbing the social structure.

It is obvious there are certain practices that seem to have nothing to do with spirituality, but rather they create ill feelings and disturbances, for example, walking on fire, sleeping on nails, walking naked in the freezing cold, stopping the heartbeat and doing kumbhaka for two to three hours. If everyone begins doing these things what will happen to society?

You should study yoga from its very beginning because you are not talking about yoga at all. Walking on fire is not yoga. Have you not read Swami Sivananda's books and have you not read Swami Vivekananda's books? Yoga is certainly not concerned with performances of impossible feats, witchcraft and the like. Its objective is physical welfare, mental equanimity and spiritual progress. This is the most invaluable promise of yoga and assigning any other attributes to yoga is only being unfair and mean.

Then what is yoga after all?

Just as the water of the river flows to the ocean and becomes one with the ocean, in the same way the human mind wants to become one with the Supreme Consciousness. Why do the rivers run to the ocean? Because the ocean is their origin. Water comes from the ocean as vapour, clouds, rain and snow. In the same way we all have come from the eternal reality – that reality where we find eternal bliss and not the temporary happiness created by worldly objects and enjoyments. Through the practice of asanas, pranayama and meditation we realize the higher truth and that is called yoga.

What does tantra have to do with yoga? There are many tantric sadhus who do some kind of worship whereby they attain psychic powers with certain mantras. You can see them doing their sadhana in the cremation grounds.

These people are so awkward, inhuman and hideous that it is impossible for our modern society to tolerate that sort of thing. If that is the approach of yoga, in order to have some psychic powers, I certainly do not believe in it.

It is true that there are certain tantrics who practise their sadhana in the cremation grounds, but that is not all about tantra; it is a very small part of tantra called leftist tantra. Besides this there is a vast field of tantric science known as rightist tantra, which is a very powerful means to conduct the psychic forces for higher spiritual realization. In yoga, as in tantra, the fundamental belief is the spiritual, mental, physical and social development of the individual in relation to society.

One should remember that in both yoga and tantra psychic powers are only a by-product, they are not the goal. Though the methods of tantra may seem strange, they are based on a wide and scientific understanding of the mind and how it can be harmonized and harnessed for spiritual aims. There are sixty-four tantras in which a number of methods of self-evolvement have been given and there are many aspects of yoga included in the body of tantra.

Summary

Yoga is not only asanas and pranayama or the isolation of oneself from society. It is not only a code of ethics and morality adopted by Hinduism, but it should be understood as an all-round method of perfection of the individual in relation to society. At best we may say that the science of yoga is an offering, the finest contribution of ancient Hindu rishis, seers and yogis for the welfare of humanity. In yoga we do not at all encourage individual isolation from society. However, we feel that the individual should expand his individuality to such an extent that he ceases to be an individual for the time being in order to serve the social cause. If you think that this is not yoga, you should find out for yourself. We recommend that you study yoga from the very beginning.

Communism and Atheism

A lot of questions have been answered, but still yoga has to answer to communism and atheism. Atheism throughout the world is always challenging the utility and validity of yoga.

In ancient days, Charvaka did not believe in something which could not be ascertained or proved by the senses. In the same way, today there are many people who are atheists, sceptics, agnostics or whatever you like to call them. They do not feel like taking to yoga. There is also a classical branch of atheism dedicated to the economic and political welfare of all mankind. The political and economic convictions of these thinkers are to bring in a classless society and nationalize every economic, social, political and cultural activity. They do not believe in spirituality. Their method of propagating their philosophy is to exploit the sentiments of economically suppressed masses by inducing them to demand bread, clothing, shelter, employment and other benefits. They decry higher thoughts as religion. Therefore, they do not want yoga to flourish.

There are yet other people who think that everybody has spiritually evolved and become ethically perfect. There are also some who hold communism to be an interim arrangement which is followed by socialism, in which a healthy society springs up out of the strict body of communism, and where yoga is of no use. Yoga talks of something which means to control the individual self and that is exactly what is done by communism.

"Religion is opium for the people" said the great Karl Marx, and how right he was! The fact that, despite the ever-growing temples, churches and mosques, the hatred and wars between the people and the exploitation of economically weaker sections of society are continuing, is the best proof that religions have failed to solve the problems of human suffering. Now you come and preach another religion under the name of yoga.

We are very sorry for the complete lack of respect that you are showing towards religions. They have been the source of many great cultures throughout all times and have served as powerful channels for directing the emotions of the individuals. Religions have helped to check the anarchical actions. It is most ungrateful not to recognize the contribution of the different religions in the history of mankind. But coming back to yoga, it is not at all a religion. It is mistaken for religion because its final aim is to realize the supreme reality.

Yes, but isn't that just another name for what the different religions call God, Christ, Krishna or Buddha?

People have a natural thirst to know the secrets of life and the world, and life is a continuous search for these secrets. It is the beauty and purpose of life to seek the absolute truth about them. Through this continuous search man is realizing that he is not only flesh, blood and bones, but he has also the capacity to feel, understand and be conscious. Also, that these are the things which can help him to a higher subtlety and the more this subtlety is developed, the nearer he comes to his aim, which is to find out the mysteries of life.

The path of evolution to this subtle state or higher consciousness is called the spiritual path, and its aim is to realize the Supreme, the absolute reality. The consciousness through which their reality is perceived is what the different religions call soul or spirit, and the reality is called God.

Don't come and tell me that all these hypocrites who are called religious and who talk about God have all developed

this supreme subtlety and have realized what they call God, and what you call reality.

They may or they may not. Whatever the case, at least some of them share the unreserved desire to find the way to reality. It should be the birthright of every human being to search the truth about himself, about the world, and about the relation between the two, whether it is called cosmic consciousness, supreme reality, or God.

This is then your way to admit that yoga is a religion!

No. Yoga is not a religion. It is a science, as are engineering, physics, physiology or chemistry. It is only much more perfect than these others. Yoga is the practical method for the realization of the cosmic consciousness. It is suitable for everybody, as it does not require any higher state of intelligence, physical strength or psychic development and everybody is absolutely sure to draw the greatest physical, mental and psychic benefit out of its practice.

What do you mean by everybody? What benefit can an atheist or communist, for example, draw from yoga?

Infinite benefits! For even an atheist must, unless he is a fool, believe in his own body and mind, its limitations when neglected, and its limitless capacities. This is all he has to be convinced of in order to get the wonderful advantages of the practice of yoga. You might be surprised, but yoga does not put faith in God, or even desire for spiritual evolution as conditions necessary for its practice.

As to communism, it needs yoga perhaps more than anything else and we are confident that the communists are intelligent enough to realize it. The communists are the most ambitious technicians and scientists in the world and according to all the signs, they certainly wish to keep this honourable position and defend their prestige against other developed countries. We remember them as the first country to launch a spaceship, the famous Sputnik, into orbit. They claim to have the most advanced technique for the use of atomic energy. Of all the electric brains or robots that have been invented of late, the most refined is said to be produced in one of the communist countries.

With such an outstanding sense for technical equipment and instruments, it should be only a question of time to realize that the most perfect machine in the world is the human body. Everything else is gross and terribly limited in comparison. The human body and the development of its full potentialities must come as a natural step forward in the course of development in civilization. Moreover, in the communist system the harmonious relation and cooperation between the individuals is of even more importance than in other societies, and therefore, the welfare and balanced personality of each individual is of extreme importance. After all, individuals make society! The sense of efficiency of the communists must make them realize that of all systems of inducing efficiency, yoga is unquestionably the best.

Summary

There is no end to arguments because it seems that people have different views, but if you make a comparative study of a yogi and a communist, you will find they have the same code of conduct as the yamas and niyamas, the same spirit of dedication and other qualities. There are many people in the communist countries who have been practising yoga, and moreover, yoga has nothing to do with religion, and you know it very well.

It should be also borne in mind that yoga is a science which deals with the deeper states of consciousness. It is also a science which takes care of the welfare of your physical body. Well, instead of discussing physical gymnastics, it is better to discuss yoga, which is a superior method. Instead of discussing psychology, it is better to discuss yoga, which is higher psychology. Those who may not agree with the spiritual importance or significance of yoga may ignore this aspect.

In conclusion, a communist can practise a few asanas and pranayama every morning, and practise techniques of relaxation like yoga nidra.

Yoga and Christianity

Some devout Christians are opposed to the very word 'yoga'. They may be right, because one should be true to one's religion, but it seems worthwhile to discuss Christianity contra yoga.

Has Christianity anything in common with yoga?

To quote the Jesuit Professor Fr. Nauner, "Yoga is the name by which Indian spirituality is best known. Primarily, it means a technique of spiritual training by which all bodily and psychic energies of man are controlled and unified in such a way as to serve to the attainment of man's highest destiny. Yoga is also understood as the art of attaining superhuman powers or bodily achievements such as remaining without breathing or food for a long time. However, the yogis consider such achievements mere by-products of yogic practices, which in itself has no spiritual meaning. Yoga tells us that man's highest aim is the isolation of the spiritual element in man. Yoga is primarily a system of training which may be connected with a deeper philosophy and with truly religious aspirations."

Is he considered as a great authority in the Catholic church?

Oh yes, Nauner is a great Catholic authority in Indian and theological problems, Professor and Dean of the Faculty of Theology, De Nobili College and Pontifical Athenaeum

Poona, and the theological expert called from India to the Second Vatican Council.

Has this person anything to say about the fundamental thesis of yoga?

Yes, in the book *Religious Hinduism*, a presentation and appraisal written by ten known Jesuit scholars (European translations in German and French), edited just after the Second Vatican Council for a dialogue *In Depth and Sympathy* between Christianity and Hinduism, Chapter 17.

Speaking about the fundamental thesis of yoga, sub-chapter B, 'Patanjali's System', Nauner says, "Yoga is the organized effort of self-deliverance." Referring to the yogic postures as the third of the eight stages of the raja yoga of Patanjali, he writes, "The purpose of such injunctions is to secure the best possible bodily disposition for the process of meditation. Calmness, equally distant from drowsiness and forceful efforts, is required for mental concentration."

Coming to the fourth stage of the same system, pranayama or the control of breath, he says, "The direct influence of deep and smooth breathing on the mental attitude is easy to trace for any one. The particular stress of yoga on the control of breath is connected also with the idea of breath as manifestation of individual vitality."

So he is only concerned about the exoteric part of yoga?

No, he is also dealing with questions that are called esoteric in yoga. About dharana he says, "The purpose of this exercise is mental control." Further, he adds, "Coming to the highest stages of self-realization through yoga, the mystic experiences samadhi, the eighth and last stage in the Patanjali yoga system." Nauner quotes the Jesuit psychologist and theologian J. Marschal (*Etudes sur la Psychologie des Mystiques*, p. 148) who says, "The more or less complete ecstasy, which crowns the prolonged application of these means of yoga consists in the silence of the soul, disengaged from the phenomenal knowledge of the world and the self, and thus placed face to face with its own subsisting ground, which is nothing else but the universal spirit." Nauner adds, "This means that man truly may succeed in cutting through the layers of phenomenal experience and touch the spiritual ground of his being."

What is the general opinion of Nauner about yoga?

Nauner underlines that modern interpretation tends to give yoga a more positive outlook and quotes S. Radhakrishnan, who describes it as leading towards the highest fulfilment of man's religious aspirations, and who further says, "The yoga discipline is nothing more than the purification of the body, mind and soul." (*Indian Philosophy II*, p. 373). Nauner quotes and underlines also N. K. Brahma's view that, "Regulation and control in yoga do not suppress but expand, and these are the only ways of expansion and development."

Do you see any chance that Catholics will accept yoga in their education and asceticism?

Nauner says in his book, "What has Christianity to say about yoga? Remarkable attempts have been made to integrate the psychophysical technique of yoga into the Christian way of perfection in the Book of Benediction, Fr. J.M. Dechanet OSB (Descles de Brouver 1956) *Christian Yoga*. Such attempts are based on the assumption that a truly Christian life means the total consecration of man to God and consequently demands the integration of all faculties of body and soul into God's service.

Asceticism is not the suppression of the body nor a merely negative struggle against inordinate passion, but the attempt to control the entire structure of our psychophysical nature and to offer it to God's service. We must try to find the best possible disposition of a calmed body, quiet nerves, a balanced mind, an atmosphere of silence, for our time of prayer and contemplation and, in fact, for our whole life. Yoga with its experience and its studied technique may help much. The Christian may learn much from the yogi:

his calmness, perseverance and systematic approach to his task."

Are there any other authorities who are in favour of yoga?

The Polish professor Stefan Swiciawski, from the Catholic University in Lublin, Poland, late auditor of the Second Vatican Council, says in an article, " . . . a problem is more and more actual especially before pedagogues of the young generation, namely the right sort of physical education, resulting in a harmonious personality, not necessarily the training of sport champions, and it is here that the integration of yoga in the education system may be the answer in the future."

Also, the Indian Jesuit Fathers, in their monthly *Ignatiana* (No. 9, Feb. 1961), write in this context, "It is very important for us to assimilate every possible element of the yoga technique for our life and Christianity."

Are there any reports from any reliable Catholic authority regarding the results obtained by yogic exercises?

We are also quoting, with the official permission of the author, part of a private letter from Prof. Dr. George Kalinowski from France, late Professor of Philosophy, Lublin, Poland, (English translation) "I am very happy that I have taken to the yoga system and I am practising it. I am thanking God for this as a great grace. My prayer and religious life changed very much since six years, the time when I began yoga exercises. My prayer and religious experiences are greater and richer. Moreover yoga exercises are giving me great physical, mental and psychic energy. Now I can work for a longer time, better and easier. Yoga gives me relaxation, regeneration, calmness of mind and self-control . . . As a philosopher I am influenced by the philosophy of St. Thomas. I find his conception of human personality as especially pertinent. It is the conception of an integral personality. The yoga system as an educational system agrees with it mainly because yoga exercises are giving me this full personal integration."

Are there any restrictions on yoga by Catholicism?

Yes, but only from a philosophical point of view. The above-quoted Nauner says in the subchapter 'Yoga and Christian Asceticism', "The Christian lives a life of grace, which is the gift of God. The supernatural life is not hidden in man's heart to be discovered and developed by the technique of yoga. Many natural possibilities may be hidden in the depth of man and may be brought to light, but the life of personal union with God can be given by God alone."

Here we would like to add that according to Hindu and yoga philosophy, we are all Brahma, God, and this highest state of consciousness obtained by yoga practices called samadhi is the awareness of this fact or the communion with God. According to Christian teaching, as says Nauner, "Only God can awaken man to the supernatural understanding of things divine. Only He can stir man to the response of love by which man is able to offer himself to God. Man cannot produce grace, he can only, with the help of God, dispose himself to receive God's grace more deeply and in richer measure . . . Spiritual self-discipline among Christians will not develop into self-concentration, but into greater readiness to hear God's word, to meditate on it, to be silent in His presence, to surrender to God a body and mind which are truly controlled and prepared to be spent in His service."

Summary

If various branches of science such as physics, chemistry, physiology, anatomy cannot be divided as Hindu chemistry and Christian biology, being universal truth, yoga with its profound influence on the body, nerves, glands and different dimensions of consciousness can be adopted by Christians as by Hindus alike.

Yoga and Vedanta

Vedanta is the highest philosophy ever conceived by the human mind. It is complete in itself. According to Vedanta, man is eternally liberated and is ever united with Brahman. He has only to become aware of this unity through inner awareness and by self-enquiry. Should it then be necessary to subject oneself to yogic discipline? This is the question some Vedantins are apt to pose to a yogi.

The yogi does not question the vedantic conclusions, but being fully aware of the intellectual and physical limitations, is convinced that in order to reach the heightened state of inner awareness, to realize the vedantic conclusions, a physical, mental and spiritual discipline is essential. While Vedanta is the conclusion, yoga is the means to arrive at that conclusion.

In the following discussion the vedantic viewpoint and the standpoint of yoga have been brought forward.

In my opinion, Vedanta is the highest form of philosophy ever treated by the human mind and it is sufficient in itself – without yoga. According to Vedanta, man is eternally liberated. He is ever united with Brahman. He has only to become aware of this unity by inner awareness and self-enquiry. Why is it necessary to subject oneself to yogic disciplines such as japa, asana, pranayama, and so on?

"Man is eternally liberated in Brahman; I am Brahman. Oh yes, this is the truth, it is the highest philosophy and it is the aim of human life. But please say whether you are aware of the fact that there is a great distance between our relative states of existence and awareness and the state of consciousness attained by the rishis, from where they revealed to mankind the truth of the Upanishads?

The path of evolution leads us to a gradual conquest of body and mind. According to Samkhya philosophy and according to our experience, there are two birds that live on the same tree of life; one is sitting in peace and is only aware of all the events and the other is all the time active – it is flying, searching for food, eating, enjoying life, and so on. The natural law reigns supreme for this bird. To become conscious of this unity is what the human being is searching for. Our whole history is a continuous struggle to reach this goal.

When people try to comprehend the truth with the intellect and do not become one with the inner self, the result is that one's actual life is in contradiction with the assertion, "I am Brahman," or "I am eternally liberated in Brahman." It is something like the parrot that has been taught by the housewife to repeat "Ram, Ram, Ram . . ." He keeps on repeating "Ram, Ram, Ram . . ." day and night, but when a cat appears and tries to bite him, the parrot forgets this mantra and shouts simply, "pip, pip, pip."

Similarly, there are two types of Vedantins – pseudo-Vedantins or Vedantins who repeat like a parrot, "I am Brahman" without having realized the meaning, and the others, the real ones, who actually practise it. The following story illustrates both kinds.

Indra, the god of gods, and Duryodhana, the god of demons, went to Brahman, the creator, and asked him for spiritual instructions. He said to both, "*Tat Twam Asi* – That Thou Art"; that is to say, 'I am Brahman.' Indra went to his heaven and Duryodhana to his land. They became full of this idea, but Duryodhana told himself, "I am Brahman, this moustache is Brahman, these cheeks are Brahman, Brahman has one thousand wives." He went on this way repeating, "Thou art That – Brahman."

But Indra said, "I know that Brahman is immortal and without form and that this body is mortal and perishable." Through this kind of introspection of the senses and the mind, Indra became concentrated and one-pointed. Thus the real knowledge came to him, the realization of Brahman. It is for this type of person who is pure in heart, who can think deeply and is capable of introspection, that jnana yoga is suitable. For other people, raja yoga, bhakti yoga and karma yoga might be needed as a supplement. It means that before starting higher practices of Vedanta, one must go through pranayama, pratyahara, and so on, as it is written in the *Brahma Sutras*.

Yes, but you will admit that the aim of evolution is freedom, moksha, and that this freedom is attained only by self-realization. How can a system of fixed and rigid practices give freedom? If freedom is the end, the means must also be free but yogic exercises are, on the contrary, a mere mechanical formula which other people have been blindly practising for centuries. Why not take a pill instead? We cannot attain liberty by imitating!

As an answer to this I will give you a parable. Once a king was annoyed with his prime minister and put him into prison. One evening the prisoner's wife came to see him. He asked her to bring one beetle, one silken thread, one cotton thread and a rope. Next evening she brought the beetle and the other articles. She tied the silken thread on to the beetle which then climbed up to the prison cell. On the end of the silken thread she tied the cotton thread and on this was fastened the rope. Then the husband was able to pull up these different threads until he had the rope in his hands, which he tied inside the prison cell and climbed down from the prison.

The process of freedom for every man is like this. It is not possible to become free from the bondage of the body and from *avidya*, ignorance, without first having prepared the body and mind through asanas, pranayama, pratyahara, concentration, and so on. Of course, we agree that moksha is the ultimate aim; yoga is to be adopted as a means and not as an end. *Veda* means knowledge and *anta* means the end or culmination, therefore *Vedanta* means the culmination of knowledge.

About Shiva, the representative of cosmic transformation, it is said that he himself is the creator of yoga who created the postures called asanas. They include all the natural gestures of man. Everything that exists is all the time in a posture of some kind. All the yogic postures also signify a moment of tranquillity, awareness of existence. It is the awareness of 'I am the cosmic dancer and the creator of my own history'.

Do you know the nature of your own mind, its divine and demonical tendencies? Do you know how the stream of the mind runs towards freedom and knowledge? It is said that it flows towards the goal, but if it flows in the whirl of existence downwards towards indiscrimination, it is said to be flowing towards evil. Man becomes that with which he identifies himself. From this point of view, belief and faith are most important in human life. How can the ordinary man living in the family, society, the modern atomic age, attain the higher state of self-realization and create peace without yoga practices?

Nevertheless the fact remains that the highest state is self-awareness and that the direct way to the self is through jnana, viveka and vichara. So why waste people's time with asanas and pratyahara, which give only relative results, when you can put them directly on the path of self-realization by teaching them how to discriminate and do self-enquiry?

Even a Vedantin has a body and his physical limitations, and can also catch cold, get stomach ache, and his kidneys might secrete a lot of uric acid. After all, his body is governed by physical laws and this body has to be kept in good condition.

I still hold that it is not possible to free man from his psychological problems, fears and complexes by using a fixed system of techniques. On the contrary, routine

exercises only enslave man's mind, we cling to our exercises for security and for fear of losing our little personality. Thus, all these yogic disciplines are rather an obstacle towards peace, freedom and self-knowledge.

Oh no! By practising asanas one maintains good health and exterminates the fear of disease. This point of view is very significant so far as education is concerned. Also, for spiritual realization a perfectly healthy body is indispensable. Self-awareness, self-observation is the end of the way. Before this victory we must conquer our body and mind. A confused mind creates confused thoughts and the actions are likewise confused. It is said in a Buddhist scripture, "As clear water when poured into clear water does not change, so also the self or the seer of truth does not change, oh Gautam!"

The ultimate truth is that I am not the body or the mind but the Supreme Being. However, the practice of asanas, mudras, bandhas and kriyas only serve to exaggerate the awareness of mind and body. What, then, is the use of practising them?

Awareness of the body is only maintained while the practices are actually going on. After that, you can be sure the body is functioning perfectly all by itself and you can contemplate on your mental or spiritual activities. It is when you neglect your physical body that you are in constant danger of falling ill, in which case even the most wise and illumined person is disturbed and unable to think of anything but his body.

You yogis talk of controlling the senses by means of pranayama and pratyahara, but this is impossible because it is the very nature of the senses to be restless. It is also unnecessary, because Brahman can be worshipped everywhere and at all times, in the world and in the domain of the senses. He is infinite.

This is a good argument. It is certainly the dharma of the *indriyas*, the senses, to see, hear, taste, smell, and so on, but the Supreme Being within you is different from this dharma.

By the practice of pratyahara you do not withdraw your senses but separate yourself from them. It is like pouring clear water into a yellow-coloured and a green-coloured jug. The water appears to be yellow and green, but if you wish to know the real nature of the water you will have to pour it into a colourless jug. In the same manner, the practice of pratyahara is not meant to control the senses but rather to separate the self from the senses. The senses continue their activities. Even after jivanmukti the eyes continue to see, the ears go on hearing and the mind continues to think.

But if Brahman is transcendental, both in the universe and beyond it, what is the use of worshipping idols, symbols, a shivalinga? God is not limited to these things but is in the heart of all.

Yes, you are right, but always remember that yoga is an absolute science. The exponent of Samkhya philosophy was Kapila, who was atheist and agnostic. He did not believe in God. Patanjali has written in his *Yoga Sutras* that idol worship only serves as a basis for the mind to become more and more subtle. Ultimately, it is not the form which is important, but the consciousness.

Summary

Vedanta is not different from yoga, and yoga is not different from Vedanta. They are only two different approaches to the same problem. A man, intellectual by temperament, takes to Vedanta while another, mystic by temperament, will practise raja yoga. The predominantly emotional man will choose bhakti yoga, while the active, dynamic person by temperament should practise karma yoga.

Of course, it is true that all Vedantins cannot tread this path without the help of yoga, because for most people physical, mental and spiritual discipline is necessary. They cannot assert that Vedanta is the only way, nor can a yogi affirm that yoga is the end of everything. Yoga is the means, while Vedanta is the culmination. Through the path of yoga we can attain Vedanta.

Yoga and Hedonism

Men of the world engage themselves in ceaseless pursuit of transient pleasures which they interpret as happiness. They condition their mental attitude to consequential losses resulting from the pursuit of pleasure as taking life as it comes. While lost in ignorance they shun the path of enlightenment, under the pretext of independence.

We will now hear a hedonist defending his pursuit of pleasure and independence and a yogi explaining the path of everlasting peace, joy, enlightenment and freedom from bondage that is the path of yoga.

The aim of all of us, yogis or hedonists, is happiness, and I am quite happy after my third glass of whisky. So why should I take to more complicated means like yoga in order to attain the same happiness?

It is not a question of the same happiness, for the happiness of a yogi is a lasting one, but can you remember yourself happy any morning after a whisky party?

That depends on what you call happiness. The morning after my whisky party I am dull, have a headache and feel miserable, but that's what I call to live life fully. Life consists of pain as well as pleasure and after enjoying its extreme pleasure I also accept its dark side as a consequence. The equal state of mind of the yogi doesn't

appeal to me, as it seems to be an escape from both the good and bad and must therefore be monotonous.

Isn't it rather the alcohol which is a means to escape from reality? Is anything real in the eyes of a drunken man?

Reality or illusion, call it whatever you like, as long as it gives me pleasure, I don't pretend to give any exact scientific definition to good food, marvellous landscapes, nights of moonlight and beautiful girls. All I want is to enjoy it all!

You are the slave of your own lower passions. Do you know what passions are? They are born out of the *triguna,* the three qualities, as Lord Krishna describes them in the fourteenth chapter of the *Bhagavad Gita*, "So long as man is a natural medium of the triguna, there is neither gain nor loss of his own. He is as good as an animal, because his behaviour is more or less on the instinctive plane."

The way you are analyzing things, everything loses its natural charm. It reminds me of the story of a soldier who was a passionate admirer of Brigitte Bardot. He used to keep a big picture of her as a decoration in his shabby military quarters. She, rather the picture, used to comfort him in all his sorrows and difficulties with her beauty and charm, and she was his only point of light in his life full of darkness until one day another soldier arrived, who happened to be a biochemist. He said, "What is this thing called B.B. in reality? 90% water and the rest some solid matter." If I happen to live happily, then what right has any philosopher, scientist or theologian to come and destroy it with any reasoning, under the pretext of bringing me enlightenment or salvation? All he does is destroy my joy and appetite for life.

What you do, in other words, is to offer a toast to this happiness of fools. You lift your glass of whisky, shouting, "Long live ignorance."

You keep calling me a fool, but what have all those gained who have climbed up to the intellectual level by adopting

the laws of the so-called civilized society, or the austerities of the different religions, except complexes as a result of suppression of their passions and emotions?

Complexes are also a result of *avidya* or ignorance. When you, instead of running away from yourself, try to understand yourself and your nature, including the passions, then you don't suppress them but on the contrary gain mastery over them. One of the most efficient ways to do this is the method of the *Yoga Sutras*.

Why the *Yoga Sutras*, and why not the *Kama Sutra*, which has been perhaps the most popular literature for several centuries and which has proved to be the most efficient guide to the mastery of passions?

Remember that passions, when uncontrolled, lead to degeneration, which was the reason for the fall of the Roman Empire, for example.

Who cares for empires and power in general, for that matter? Just leave us alone with the benedictions of God, which are many. We have no ambitions; all we want is to be free.

To be free is not a modest desire. In order to defend one's freedom one must be strong indeed and in order to be strong one must have the courage to know. One is closely connected with the other. The enlightened one is master of himself as well as master of the ignorant; consequently, the ignorant is not only the slave of his own passions but also the slave of the enlightened. Thus the freedom that you, the hedonists, appreciate and worship most of all is lost for you. To want to remain ignorant and to want to be free is to want to eat the cake and have it.

Summary

Pleasures are not happiness. The former are temporary, the latter is everlasting. Freedom is not ignorance or avidya; it is certainly not slavery to lower passions. Freedom is enlightenment. Yoga promises peace, happiness and freedom.

Modern Medicine and Yoga

For many people allopathic medicine and yoga seem to be in contradiction with each other. "Let us laugh at yoga in order to cure illnesses," the doctors say. "We have plenty of drugs to treat all the sufferings of humanity and if you have a headache, it is better to take aspirin than to stand on your head." To this the yogi exclaims, "Don't take aspirin at any cost. Drugs are poison for your body. It is better to do asanas and pranayama every day, then you will never get a headache." Who is right and who is wrong? It is this question that we are going to decide. We present for you a doctor and a yogi. Let us listen to them.

Your yoga is not at all a panacea. For instance, what can you do in the case of patients suffering from an agitated mind? Nothing! We have many helpful drugs like tranquillizers, or even exciting drugs, according to the case.

In extreme special cases your drugs are very useful, for example in the case of operated patients when they start being agitated and anxious, or happen to suffer too much. It is then necessary to give a tranquillizing drug, for these patients are not in a position to control themselves. But this should be an exception. Do not forget that drugs are toxic. Permanently taken, they slowly but surely poison the organism, and this does not solve the problem. An exciting or tranquillizing drug given to the soldier who is afraid will never make him courageous. With your drug you will only excite or abolish his nervous or volatile reflexes for a time, but when the effects of the drug are over, the soldier will remain the same fearful person as before with a certain amount of toxins in addition in his body!

In contradiction to the effects of drugs, yoga makes a man consciously command his nervous reflexes without the intervention of any external factor like drugs. Since we have chosen the example of the soldier, let us go on with it. If in the case of war he is afraid, as is natural, and if at the same time he is an experienced yoga practitioner, he will know what kind of pranayama to take to his rescue to regulate the speed of his heartbeats and bring calm and control to his mind. When he has to perform some very hard or even cruel duty, he will know how to find strength in his manipura chakra, or if he is a swara yogi he will know when and how to make use of pingala or sushumna flows. If he has understood the meaning of the *Bhagavad Gita*, he will then be a perfect kshatriya, able to assume the defence of his country without anger, passion or hatred.

But why take such an extreme case? Everybody is not a soldier and fortunately we are not always in a state of war.

What we said about the anxious soldier can be applied in all cases of anxiety in society: students passing examinations, artists before their audience, businessmen and technicians. Who was never anxious in his life? The yogis or students of yoga can tell you that a lot of nervous or psychosomatic disorders can be treated by yoga. Its methods have been successful not only in India but also in the West. By certain techniques of pranayama and concentration or meditation, patients suffering from insomnia or nightmares have been cured.

So, you assert that yoga can help in cases of nervous disturbance but what about tuberculosis, cancer, leprosy, or the less harmful illnesses that we meet in our life?

In France there is a proverb which says, "When the wine is drawn, it should be drunk." When you come across some extreme cases such as those you have mentioned, when the body is not able to respond anymore to the mind and obey it, then the use of drugs is necessary. However, we make an exception concerning the very advanced yogi. He will never take drugs, even in the case of a very acute illness because, unless, of course, he is dying, he will be able to cure himself with the help of yoga. By certain techniques of hatha yoga, according to the case, he is capable of getting rid of the toxins in his body. Proper rest, fasting or special diet will be added whereby the agitations of the brain are spontaneously calmed. A proper massage to the internal organs will bring about order in the metabolism, and thereby the depressions that are due to a lack of oxygen in the brain and in the system will be eliminated.

This advanced yogi will use also his science of breathing. With the ingoing breath and antar kumbhaka he will be able to distribute the prana in his body. With expiration he will consciously throw out the accumulated toxins. Even if it makes you smile, we should add that if this yogi is a highly spiritual person he will remain conscious of 'He who is within'. In this unexplainable inner atmosphere of complete surrender to and confidence in God, and a positive way of thinking, he will realize what is said in another of the French proverbs, "Help yourself and heaven will help you."

What a nice discourse, which makes me full of joy and victory! You recognize that even a yogi can fall ill, which is proof that yoga does not protect against illnesses.

Please do not confuse yoga and yogi. Yoga is a perfect technique worked out for centuries and experimented upon by thousands of people, some of whom have become mahatmas, saints, gurus and jivanmuktas known to the whole world, and especially to Indians, since almost all of them are the sons of India. The yogi, at least in the beginning, is an ordinary man like you and me, walking on the path of self-realization. As long as he has not reached emancipation he can fail. If he falls ill, he knows that it is due to some mistake, either conscious or unconscious, but the more he advances in yoga the less he is likely to fail, and his health is always perfect. The body is equipped with its own living chemical laboratories, such as the secretions of the various glands.

But don't you know that in our laboratories we also produce the same substances? When you have a lack of some of them, you are only too glad to use our drugs!

We know you have, but let us tell you about that. First, they are only similar and not the same as the substances produced in the human body. Secondly, they are dead substances. Suppose you want to give follicle or lutein to a lady who has menstrual disorders, it is a good intention. But then we ask you, "Out of what will you produce your medicine?" Generally it is done out of the ovaries of a cow. And again we ask, "Are the follicle cells of the cow's ovaries the same as those of the human body and are the general endocrine cycles of ovulation, the time of pregnancy, and so on, the same for a lady and a cow?"

Another point is, suppose there is a patient whose bones get broken easily due to lack of calcium. You are a good and helpful man and give some daily doses of calcium produced in your laboratory. If you then analyze the stool of your patient, you will find in them the calcium you gave for bones. Why? Because the thyroid and parathyroid glands do not secrete their hormones in a right proportion, and therefore, the metabolism of calcium, for which they are responsible, cannot take place. In this case, as in the case of the lady patient mentioned previously, some particular asanas which have a special influence on the thyroid and pituitary glands make them do their duty and the natural chemistry of the body is restored. In addition, we insist on the point that your drugs are most of the time only dead substances and therefore have nothing to do with this wonder that is life in us.

Some great scientists of our times assert that life is but the result of balance and metabolism between different chemical substances, and they have determined the proportions of these chemical substances in a human body. Now, if we take the same amount and proportion of calcium, phosphorus, carbon, and so on, which compose a human body and put these substances in a heap all together on this table, this will certainly not create a human being.

We also want to point out the importance and relationship of the mind with all living phenomena. The glandular secretions depend very much on the mental and psychic state. Fear, for instance, releases an important secretion from the suprarenal glands. It is a well known fact that a stomach ulcer is the illness of an anxious man, and modern psychology is on the way to demonstrate that almost all illnesses have their origin in the mind and not in the body. There is indeed a connection between the mind and the body. When the thyroid is overworked it can cause some pre-pubertal excitement and as a result the thyroid, which normally starts working at the age of fifteen or sixteen, starts working at the age of twelve, and when the thyroid is malfunctioning one feels like an old person. As long as your thyroid is working normally, you always feel that you are young. If you continually feel tired then it is possible that your thyroid is not working properly.

The thyroid is an important gland and many asanas have a direct influence on it. It is also the gland which commands the reproductive system. The thalamus, hypothalamus, mammary bodies, pituitary gland, pineal body, and so on, are intimately connected and interdependent in their structure, circulatory system, hormonal secretions. All the balance of your body depends on what is happening in this tremendous factory, more delicate and complicated than the delicate and complicated system of the wheels of a small watch. If we put a grain of dust in a watch, you know what will happen, and if you introduce the poison of a drug in this hormonal system, the functions of your body will be more or less disturbed, whereas yoga introduces no poisonous factor in the body.

By special asanas or bandhas that methodically press or expand some particular part of the body you can, at will and consciously, either stimulate the function of some definite exocrine or endocrine gland, or reduce their secretions. The medical men want to be helpful and it is good of course. They think that a man can be helped physically and mentally by introducing some poisonous or semi-poisonous drugs in the system. On the other hand, it should be kept in mind that every drug introduced in the body brings about a temporary state of immunity by which also a certain amount of resistance is lost. You will always find that a medicated body has less resistance, while an unmedicated body has a higher resistance.

So, according to you all our drugs are poisonous, or if they are not, they are dead substances and therefore not efficient. You want our death! In such conditions only one thing would remain to be done by the medical men if the world was full of yogis: to close the doors of our laboratories and become beggars.

We are sorry but we cannot change the facts. You know very well, for instance, that the dose of a drug necessary to kill intestinal worms is the same that is necessary to kill a man. You know very well that the drug you give to cure a headache is at the same time harmful for the kidneys. You know very well that the antibiotics act only because they destroy the intestinal microbial flora, and when these are destroyed the fungal intestinal flora can develop without a break, creating other illnesses in place of the previous one. You know very well that the daily dose of insulin for diabetes gradually destroys the defensive power of the pancreas, and so on.

Even vegetables cannot escape your chemical science. The farmers are provided with potassium fertilizers. The result is wonderful regarding money because the vegetables are bigger and plentiful, but you know that potassium expels magnesium and when the human organism has not the correct proportion of magnesium cancer starts. We are really sorry, but we cannot help! But rather than become a beggar, why not become a yogi?

Summary

Even if one is a yogi, when fire is burning one's house one does not go into meditation, one calls the fireman. By spreading water everywhere in the house the fireman will spoil the furniture, but at least the walls and roof will be saved. If one breaks a leg, one does not do sirshasana, one goes to the hospital. It is said in ayurveda that when a man has failed to understand and follow the true laws of nature and has become weak, the duty of the wise people is to bring help in the form of medicines. But the use of drugs should come last. It should be recognized that modern medicine has its own contribution in helping mankind in certain acute cases.

Yoga is not at all against modern medicine but it is very essential that doctors understand yoga as a science which is not inimical or antagonistic to their own science. Understanding and recognizing that yoga can bring physical and mental welfare to humanity, they should start working in harmony with yogis and with their scientific means try to do some research on yoga. Yogis will not avoid these investigations because they know their science is a true one.

On the other side, the doctors should take into consideration the difference between an ordinary patient and a yogic patient who may some day have to take drugs. The ordinary patient is a passive man, he expects that the drug will do everything for him and he does nothing in the way of personal effort. He has chosen the easiest solution but in appearance only! The yogi patient is a conscious, positive and cooperative man and is able to help the effects of the drug by his inner mental state and his well disciplined mind. In spite of an accidental state of illness, his body has been well-trained and all his organs are functioning in perfect order, so the illness will be easily overcome with the help of some natural medicine. Natural is better than chemical, and the doctors have also some good natural medicines. Lastly, the yogi is conscious of the powers of shakti which is in every natural drug that can be given to him and better than anyone else, he will be able to make the effects of the drug stronger and more efficient.

Yoga in Society

The welfare of society has become the prime duty of the government. In a democracy the welfare of the people is taken care of by various institutions such as educational institutions and different types of hospitals. The welfare activities also include insurance policies and old age grants. A government has to be alive to the importance of wars, social psychology and varied aspects of public security such as crime, subversion in the national sphere and aggression against the borders. In this context it is difficult to conceive of yoga as having any place at all in serving a constructive purpose in patterns of government.

Please tell me, how old you are and what you are doing these days?

I am fifty one and practising yoga to be able to teach this great science.

I think you are aware of the great changes that have taken place in the world. Great activity in many countries is directed towards individual and social welfare. Could you tell me how yoga relates to this subject?

We have heard that some of the state governments of India are likely to introduce yoga teaching in education. In fact, Maharashtra has already done so. We are deeply concerned because in other states nothing seems to be done along these lines. Yoga should be introduced everywhere so that the health, mind and personality of the children may be properly developed.

But why worry about health? We insure each individual's life and we give them medical aid through the government, and for maintenance of law and order we have the police and army.

Yes, very well, but then you are in fact making the body a hospital! Haven't you forgotten the ancient adage, an ounce of prevention is worth a pound of cure? Moreover, you are taking away the self-confidence of the individual and leaving every sphere of social activity to the Government.

You have a good point but if nobody takes medicines, what is going to happen to the national economy?

It is not a question of national economy. Don't misunderstand. We must create conditions in educational institutions and elsewhere so that people do not fall ill. We mean to adopt preventive measures.

You advocate preventative measures, but what about the many thousands of doctors, nurses and pharmacies?

In olden days there were few doctors, nurses or pharmacies.

And no population either! By the way, tell me, how is your health?

Oh, I am in excellent health!

I happen to know that you have diabetes. Please do not lie to me!

I do not lie. I am completely cured of diabetes through yoga.

It is very hard for me to believe this – yoga curing diabetes! Diabetes comes from a deficiency in the secretions of the pancreas. Lack of insulin causes diabetes and you tell me yoga can cause an increase in insulin!

Exactly so. By the practice of bhujangasana, shalabhasana, dhanurasana and halasana, the pancreas is directly stimulated and the pancreatic secretions produce insulin in the blood stream and change glucose to glycogen in the liver.

These are very high claims you are making. Give me exact proof through clinical data, perhaps then I can believe these things.

You are after scientific data regarding the curative value of yoga in diabetes. You will have to go through various papers published on the studies carried out at the yoga institutes in Rajasthan and elsewhere. Yogic bandhas, kriyas and mudras can actually work upon internal organs causing hormone secretions, and in such a manner diabetes can be cured.

Well, perhaps I can accept the introduction of yogic asanas into our modern culture but I cannot comprehend the use of meditation. In this pattern of society I see no relevance or usefulness in meditation.

Then you have not seen much of the world. The minds of people are not at rest, either in the East or the West. The great psychoanalyst Freud has stated that 80% of all diseases originate in the mind. Through meditation we learn about the mind, its mysteries and its control, and through the control of the mind one is able to control one's entire personality. Then there will emerge an integrated personality, there will be no mental or physical disease and each individual will become a disciplined entity of his own society and of the nation.

Can you cite some examples of the far-reaching effects of yoga? You are dreaming of a utopian yoga culture, but has anything concrete been done so far?

Of course, yes. The Punjab government has introduced yoga in its educational system and in jails yogic asanas and pranayama are taught. In the Sagar University in Madhya Pradesh, a Department of Yogic Studies has been started.

In Rajasthan we have a centre for yogic diabetes cure, to say nothing of the widespread acceptance and practice of yoga in foreign countries.

Yes, in Holland we have the 'Stitching Yoga Netherlands', under the direct guidance of Dr Rama Polderman. All yogic practices and teachings are under careful medical guidance. However, I am very much aware of the fact that crime, juvenile delinquency, suicide and murder are increasing rapidly in many countries. As you are so enthusiastic about yoga, tell me – can yoga help counteract the criminal attitude of an individual?

Yes. Without a doubt, yoga is instrumental in the total rehabilitation of the criminal mind. Let me tell you of a very important experiment conducted in London under perfect scientific control. One hundred criminals were taken as subject matter. During sleep, when they were totally unconscious, a tape recorder with biblical sermons and quotations was played over and over for them throughout the night without interruption. This experiment continued for fifteen days, when the hundred criminals were released into their respective communities once again. The results were highly optimistic. Sixty criminals gave up crime entirely and some of these sixty joined the police force.

The psychology of this treatment is as follows. When a man is unconscious he is most receptive for at this time the intellect does not function or oppose, and the impressions given are spontaneously carried to the unconscious mind, returning as in a record to play back to the conscious level of thinking and action at a later time. In spite of prosperity, in spite of all modern methods of welfare and education, crimes are increasing every day. Why? Because the unconscious mind is not properly trained. It is only the unconscious mind of man which should be trained and the training of the innermost mind of a person is only possible through the deep states of yogic meditation such as yoga nidra, prana vidya and antar mouna. A lasting effect is greatest when introduced into the unconscious mind and in yoga we introduce everything through the unconscious. Errors in personality are errors of the individual mind. Therefore, instead of correcting errors you have to correct the mind itself – the entire pattern of thinking, not merely the intellect. If yoga is introduced in jails in a correct manner through asanas and pranayama, yoga nidra, trataka and autosuggestion, it will in time produce a good group of rehabilitated people when they conclude their jail sentences. Do you understand how yoga can cure even the criminal mind?

Summary

This has been a very important discussion and we think, looking at the present restless condition in our country in particular and other countries in general, it is the immediate and urgent duty of political thinkers in every country and especially educationalists, to sit together and form a group of advisers so that we can introduce yoga properly into those institutions where we want our students, adults and even criminals to improve and become better citizens of a new and healthy world.

Physiology, Psychology and Yoga

The effects of yogic techniques on the physiology and mind offer a challenging field for investigation by physiologists and psychologists. The field of psychological investigation presents a multitude of difficulties in the absence of an apparatus to study the unconscious mind. How then to prove the effects of yoga on the body and mind? Is simplification of the ultimate yogic aims desirable? Should yoga be simplified to propagate it on a mass scale? These are the questions to be discussed now.

The science of yoga offers a novel field for research by physiologists. By devising more precise techniques to examine the effects of yoga therapy, useful data could be collected for convincing the modern mind.

Sorry, but we venture to disagree with the two expressed ideas. Firstly, yoga is not only therapy but something more. It is a means to prevent disease and the method of complete integration of the personality. Secondly, yoga deals with all aspects of the personality by the subjective, introspective method. Therefore, it is impossible to investigate the phenomena of yoga by objective scientific methods which approach only one aspect.

We agree that research on yoga must he done in all scientific fields, but do not forget that ultimately the influence of yoga practice is manifested on a physical level in the human

body. The physiological and biological changes in the body are only secondary events occurring in addition to the main process of evolution of personality through yoga. But don't you think that perfect health of the body, by ensuring physiological balance, is an undeniable indication of proper bodily functioning?

You are right. Yoga doesn't deal with human relations directly. Don't forget that yoga was devised as an integral part of an ancient spiritual culture which dealt with all aspects of human life. People were well settled in those times; the life of society was running according to well formulated rules. There were no serious disturbances from abroad, there were no problems of food or other economic problems. Indian culture was at its peak at that time, therefore the thinkers were dealing with discoveries of all the hidden faculties of man. Today it is the task of the social psychologists, sociologists, educationalists and others dealing with society to introduce yoga in modern life to those people who are prepared to pick it up and use it in their daily routine.

Oh, but yoga should be modified for each individual. It is not possible for everybody to do the same sadhana.

The means of yoga can be modified but the aim, the integration of personality and reunion with the self should always remain, otherwise we cannot speak of yoga. To employ yogic techniques in different spheres of human functioning can help us introduce yoga, but there is one danger. When yoga is practised without proper understanding it can be misused by those people who are not able to live in society. They use something that they call yoga in order to escape from life and from their duties, and society is then harmed and disgusted by such things. All of us are witnesses and some of us are aware of similar situations in another context in India today. Some aspects of western civilization, which can be of great help to the Indian people, are spoiling Indian life. Why? Is it because they are bad? No, because they are introduced without proper understanding to people who are not sufficiently prepared to accept them as an aid.

Summary

Yoga is a science as far as method is concerned but the truth of yoga goes beyond the realm of science. Science always refers to something in order to prove something. On the other hand, the ultimate point of yoga is unconditioned reality. Yoga is dealing with subjective reality, but this psychological reality is not less real than physical reality. This subjective reality can be understood by each individual according to his maturity, but ultimately each person must live and experience himself, in order to know himself. To memorize scientific theory, rules of life or sacred scriptures without experiencing the expressed notions means nothing. That is why the verity of yoga on the highest planes cannot be proved generally. It must be solved for each individual separately and everybody must solve it for himself if the solution is to have personal value. The only criterion here is progress in all aspects of life, and to be able to judge it one must be honest, honest to others and especially honest to oneself.

The science of yoga has great physiological and psychological potentialities and can be effectively practised as a therapy. The effect of yogic techniques on the human physiology is an inviting field for investigation and research, and so also is the scientific investigation of yoga psychology a challenge to the modern psychologist.

Yoga is being reduced to a few asanas and pranayama under the plea of simplification and being propagated in the East and West. This is hardly being fair. It is essential to explain in unambiguous terms the theory and practice of yoga to one and all, and then leave it to every individual to adopt what is possible for him. In this way yoga can be assimilated by the different intellectual levels of society.

The impression that yoga is useful only for the individual and has no social utility is erroneous because society is constituted of individuals. The welfare of society is determined by the wellbeing of the individuals, and yoga is surely the blueprint of perfection.

Materialism and Yoga

The rapid progress of science and technology has made life competitive and materialistic. The urge to possess wealth, property and conveniences is ever increasing. Every individual aspires to be wealthy and pursues a path of pleasure. The accumulation of wealth is beset with maladies such as anxiety, mental strain, neurosis and such other mental afflictions, and lowered physical standards.

While the onward march of science and technology cannot be halted, acquisition of serenity, mental equipoise, and mental and physical welfare are prerequisites for living a life of plenty. Yoga offers these mental and physical capacities, as will be brought out during the ensuing discussion.

I think that yoga is only good for masochists. Just look at that posture. Not only is he entangling his limbs in the most complicated way but in this fantastic position he is supposed to rest. For heaven's sake! Don't you think that to buy yourself a nice and comfortable easy-chair to rest in is more practical?

It might be more practical for an American millionaire, but yoga is not only dealing with people in that part of the world and not uniquely with the upper class of society. Also, this is not the point. The point is: have you ever compared a man of, let us say, forty years of age who has been spending most of his life in an easy chair with a yogi of about seventy, who has been resting in this posture?

I don't know any yoga except from these funny books, but what's wrong with the gentleman who prefers an easy-chair?

We would rather like to ask what is not wrong with him. He is likely to look about twenty years older than he is, fat and unattractive, mostly bald and flat-footed. The question is if he is at all able to sit in his beautiful easy-chair when spending his best years in hospital treating his heart disease, indigestion, ulcers and over strained mind.

What does all this have to do with an easy-chair?

Modern civilized man is destroying his mind by his obsession for possession and the more possessions he has, the less he is capable of enjoying them.

What do you mean, don't enjoy my possessions? What about my ultramodern home equipped with the latest innovations like colour TV, superautomatic dishwasher, and my latest model cars? Are they not giving me pleasure by giving me more time to relax?

Do you remember the last time you relaxed?

Well, it is too early for me to relax. At my age I have still to devote most of my time to my interests, but the more I work and earn now the more I shall be able to take it easy in the future and also afford, I hope, all the luxuries that make life comfortable.

This is always the case with you materialists. First you spend half of your life hunting after money with the hope of enjoying the fruits of your labours later, and then, if at all you have the chance to survive this period and not die of a heart attack, you spend the remaining part of it by trying to treat all the ailments that you have gathered through an unhealthy way of living. It is about your type of man that it is said, "Man spends his life in ruminating over the past, complaining about the present and shivering over the future."

Is it the opinion of yogis that material things have absolutely no value?

Oh no, certainly not! The pure materialist knows the price of everything and the value of nothing, and when you don't know the value of small things, then no matter how many treasures you accumulate, you are not capable of enjoying anything of it. Have you heard the proverb: 'To live in the present is the aim of life and everybody is doing his best to reach it'. But half the people live the moments that have passed and the other half imagine the moments that are yet to come.

Well, there is some truth in this, but has anyone found the solution to this problem?

Oh yes, yoga has. You see, yoga is not only limited to some funny postures as seen in some yoga books. It is said that the difference between a worldly man and a yogi is that the worldly man is controlled by his senses, whereas the yogi is their master. Yoga practices first of all help you to keep your body and mind in perfect shape, and you must agree that a healthy body is the first condition to enjoy anything in life, as well as to accomplish tasks efficiently. Secondly, by continuous yoga practices you become a subtle instrument, capable of perceiving a vast richness of your own personality that is absolutely priceless and which can never be shattered by any economic crisis or devaluation. It is in this state that you are able to appreciate the present. The only pleasure, which is the true basis for all other pleasures, is the delight to be, the delight to sense this moment of existence, the delight to breathe, the delight of sparkling sunshine, the delight to rest – and without an easy-chair – the nearness of sleep, the pleasure of feeling the presence of two people sitting in the room. Unless you are able to achieve this state of permanent happiness and to see the charm of every small thing, you can never expect to be satisfied with anything in life, no matter how much wealth you possess.

In other words, you want me to renounce all my fortune and start to be satisfied just with the idea that I am?

Quite the contrary. We want that through yoga you realize you are even richer than you think. You possess a whole cosmos within yourself, a microcosmos, which is just the same as the macrocosmos. To assess your fortune only according to your bank account is an underestimation of your own personality. Could you ever dream that to obtain such richness only about one hour's practice a day is enough?

Summary

We do not decry material pursuits. We certainly do not oppose material progress. We do not wish to deny society the conveniences brought to its door by the advancement of science and technology. We do not hold that one should not answer the calling of one's station in life. On the contrary, we assert that one should attend to worldly duties with maximum concentration, imagination, care and efficiency. While engrossed in material pursuits one should not fall prey to one's senses, tensions or frustrations. This serenity is offered by the sincere and regular practice of yoga. Higher powers of concentration, efficiency in action, mental and physical strength and above all, the ability to emerge as the master of situations rather than a victim of circumstances, are certainly attributes which every individual, whether materialist or not, should aspire for. Yoga can give these very attributes to those who practise it seriously.

Yoga and Fatalism

Throughout the world there is the widespread conviction that all events are determined by fate. What is the use of worrying when everything is being controlled by a vast cosmic law? In astrology and palmistry it is said that the future of man is already cast and if one is to suffer or enjoy, prosper or fall; all such things have been predetermined. In this context, therefore, if any change is to take place, how far is such a change logical? Or is it not possible at all?

We fatalists believe that everything we do is predestined, every action that takes place has been decided beforehand, every event in life has been planned in advance, therefore, nothing can be changed by our actions, deeds or thinking. No matter what we do, the world has been planned by a higher cosmic intelligence. It is not in our hands to change. You cannot alter what is already planned and predestined. This is the fatalistic approach held by many people and I am a fatalist. Therefore, with this view, I cannot understand why we should do asanas, pranayama and meditation. Why should we waste our energy in these pursuits, when no matter what we do we cannot alter anything? To me it is unintelligible that you should spend your time in these pursuits.

You see, we yogis believe that we can direct our destiny by our conscious efforts and thus we become the controllers and designers of our actions and our future.

But can't you see that you have a very egoistic approach to this question in that you say your own individual self can alter the higher intelligence, the cosmic mind, by which our destiny is designed? I do not think that you have the right to disrespect this higher force.

We do not disrespect it but we know this higher cosmic power is within ourselves, within every individual and yoga enables us to become aware of this truth within.

But according to the law of karma one is born with samskaras, impressions from former incarnations. These samskaras are guiding and determining your desires, tastes, will, ambitions, and this corresponds exactly with the philosophy of fatalism.

No, not exactly, because there are three types of karma: *kriyamana karma*, the current karma which can be controlled and directed by proper associations, satsang and viveka; *prarabdha karma* the accumulated samskaras from past impressions coming to fruition and thirdly, *sanchita karma*, those karmas still in the unconscious and not coming into operation for perhaps months or even years.

Please let me explain and illustrate to you how we understand the law of karma. A man at the beginning of the wheel of incarnations is heavily charged with a large amount of accumulated karma. At the end of his evolution he has exhausted that karma and is free from them. This liberated state is called moksha. Between these two extreme stages he is taking many incarnations and gradually, at each incarnation, he exhausts some of this karma. Let us suppose that this birth of mine is at the stage of evolution when half of my karma is exhausted; therefore, whatever I do I will have to suffer to a certain degree in order to get rid of the remaining karma that I am supposed to exhaust in this incarnation. In this case what difference do my efforts, yogic or otherwise, make in the long run?

Of course it makes a difference, because through sadhana you are speeding up the process of exhausting the karma. Sanchita karma gives you free choice to exhaust any amount of karma, and therefore, brings you nearer to the state of moksha.

But you cannot eliminate suffering, can you?

It is not a question of eliminating the sufferings or changing them. Our prarabdha karma has brought these sufferings. It is our attitude towards the sufferings that can be altered through vairagya.

But all this still does not release me from the bondage of destiny!

You must remember that, in addition to prarabdha karma, or the compulsory sufferings of our destiny, there is a free will given to each individual and it is this free will which makes all the difference. With this freedom to choose one can accelerate the process of one's evolution.

But isn't it one's very own karma that also decides the speed of evolution, whether it be an encounter with yoga or anything else?

No, no, no. In the doctrine of karma there are two other things to remember: prarabdha and purushartha and there is a clear-cut distinction between the two. With purushartha the individual has free will, whereas prarabdha karma is compulsory with all the sufferings and enjoyments, successes and failures. In the course of evolution one gains more mastery over the purushartha and is less a slave of prarabdha. At one's highest stage of evolution, one is finally free from prarabdha and achieves emancipation and salvation.

Summary

One can release oneself from the slavery of destiny by one's own effort. We must accept both prarabdha and purushartha. Prarabdha is a great force and it is very difficult for an ordinary man to remove himself from the clutches of destiny. Only those few people who are strong and relentless can go beyond the confines of destiny or become the *muktas,* liberated ones. Therefore, we must acknowledge yoga as a means to inform us about the possibility of total liberation and complete freedom, yet at the same time, we must accept the basic tenets of the fatalistic viewpoint which say that destiny has to be undergone, must be accepted and undertaken. Both are true. Every yogi believes that prarabdha must be undergone, but at the same time he shows us a small spark of light which reveals the way to the possibility of freedom from this great force of destiny. Somehow or other we can escape, we can get out of it. What is this way out? It is the aim of yoga to show the way and it is the responsibility of people to understand it.

Yoga and Education

The world today is highly technical and functional to such a degree that idealistic and spiritual values are often subdued by an ever-growing materialistic outlook. Day by day humanity receives new scientific inventions which ameliorate living conditions, but at the same time we observe that humanity is losing its sound contact with life. Mental disorders are on the increase, the sense of life is being lost; life is becoming shallow and purposeless. World statistics show how juvenile delinquency is on the increase, as are divorce and suicide. While some educationists feel that the introduction of a scheme for inculcating discipline should suffice, there are others who feel that religious education in schools is the need of the hour. There are yet others who say that unless yogic techniques are skilfully introduced with modern education, we cannot expect children to develop and maintain an integrated personality. In the discussion that follows we will hear the different points of view on education in relation to yogic claims.

These days it has become the practice of some persons who style themselves as yoga teachers to prescribe yoga for all problems, including education, but I feel that what we need at present is a change to a more unified and complete system of education for the development of not

only knowledge or intellect, but the whole personality. What contribution can yoga make to ideal education?

Well, you have been very cunning though diplomatic. At the very outset you have decried the science of yoga and then said things which are very general but not leading closer to the answer. Before we answer your question we request you to enlighten us with your viewpoint, "What do you think is the remedy for our educational problems as they are today?"

You are being evasive by putting the ball in my court. I think that something on the pattern of a national discipline scheme or compulsory physical training may be the answer.

We are sorry to say that you are talking about schemes which have already ended in failure. Everything that is forced on students has invariably ended in failure. Do you have any other scheme to recommend?

I am inclined to agree with the great thinkers and educationists when they urge the inclusion of religious instruction in our schools and universities.

How are you oblivious to the fact that India is avowed to secularism, and rightly so, with the complex distribution of various faiths in this country? For that matter, in all those nations where more than one religion is practised, the introduction of religious education will always meet with justified opposition. Do you have any alternative suggestion?

No, but I would now like to have your views. Please be reasonable and not say things in the name of yoga which enter the realm of impossibility.

Our first suggestion is to introduce references to yoga in the books on history and literature, introduce a few yogic exercises in the physical training classes, and teach the students techniques of proper breathing and concentration through demonstrations and audio-visual aids such as slides and movie films.

In the nursery stage children may be taught very simple breathing techniques only. Then teachers should be trained so that the students are prepared to receive further lessons in yoga.

In the primary stage children should be taught surya namaskara, a powerful exercise which is beneficial for the muscles, nerves, glands and mind. They may also be taught some breathing exercises. In the secondary stage they may be taught asanas, pranayama, techniques of concentration and yoga nidra. To these should be added the study of the *Bhagavad Gita* and Upanishads.

In colleges the above courses should include deep meditation and the study of the *Bhagavad Gita*, Upanishads, *Brahma Sutras* and *Yoga Vasishtha*, along with some lessons in psychology. Given the chance, we would scrap the present faulty syllabi and give them a yoga bias. What is your opinion? Are not these syllabi useless?

I agree with you in respect of what you said about yogic training, but I cannot subscribe to your views on scrapping the syllabi and introducing new ones. The present courses have been evolved in the course of time and are backed by a fund of experience. What we should strive for is to blend yoga training with the present courses.

Of course! It is only a matter of a few years for you to be fully convinced.

Summary

We do not advocate discarding the present syllabi or the systems of education in vogue. We plead for early and skilful amalgamation of yoga techniques with the existing teaching, from the kindergarten to university levels. We are convinced that yogic practices can develop powers of concentration, mental balance and sound physique in the students. Yoga can help to give a new outlook to the children, to be alive to the beatitude of life.

General Questions and Answers on Practical Yoga

ASANA

What is the definition and purpose of yoga?

Yoga means union of human consciousness with the universal consciousness. It also means rediscovery of the inner bliss in man, which he has lost due to the lack of introversion, self-enquiry, and inner and outer purity.

The purpose of yogic practices is to achieve peace, power and spiritual wisdom, as well as perfect health, a sound mind and balanced personality. Yoga also cures many physical, mental and psychic diseases and abnormalities. It awakens all the dormant potential faculties in man. Yoga gives spiritual realization and destroys all kinds of ignorance, thus establishing brotherhood and unity between man and man.

What is the history of the origin of yoga?

The history of yoga can be traced back to the oldest literature of human culture such as the Vedas, Upanishads and Tantras. The Vedas are full of the deepest spiritual wisdom, which proves that its composers were living in an era of great spiritual culture, so the science of yoga should be much older than the Vedas.

What are the different yogas and why this difference?

The important yogas are raja yoga, jnana yoga, bhakti yoga, hatha yoga. They are designed to suit different varieties of persons and tendencies. For example, raja yoga is for psychic persons, jnana yoga for rational minds, bhakti yoga for the emotional temperaments and karma yoga for dynamic persons. There are certain other special yogic techniques which are suitable only for selected and qualified people. Some of these techniques are kundalini yoga, tantra yoga, laya yoga, nada yoga, swara yoga, kriya yoga and other such higher spiritual and occult sadhanas.

What is the meaning of yoga asanas and in which way are they different from physical exercises?

Asana in Sanskrit means 'posture of body', and *yoga* means the 'science of deep and subtle phenomenon of human awareness and organic functions'. *Yogasanas* mean different bodily postures by which we can control, conduct, regularize and stimulate different organic and glandular functions of the human body, and its magnetic and cosmic forces.

Yoga asanas are far superior to physical exercises because they are based on the detailed and all-round study of the human body as well as human awareness. Thus they affect the glandular and pranic functions of the body and result in the inner transformation of human personality.

What are the spiritual contributions of yogasana?

As already mentioned, yogasanas awaken and regulate the glandular secretions and pranic forces, resulting in physical, mental and spiritual efficiency.

The awakening of pranic forces in the body intensifies awareness and thus the higher unexplored centres of the brain are being harnessed, therefore yogasanas, if scientifically done with full precautions, give astonishing results.

What are the most important asanas for the common man?

Shavasana, yogamudra, shashankasana, bhujangasana, shalabhasana, dhanurasana, paschimottanasana, supta vajrasana, halasana, sarvangasana, matsyasana, ardha matsyendrasana and sirshasana.

We have heard that there are static as well as dynamic asanas. Would you please clarify these two varieties and explain their therapeutic values?

Although, according to the classical point of view, all asanas are supposed to be calm and steady postures, later on they were physiologically divided into two. Asanas such as padmasana, siddhasana, yogamudra, shavasana, shashankasana, dhanurasana, matsyasana, which require less bodily movements, are termed static asanas. Asanas with quick and frequent body movements such as surya namaskara, paschimottanasana, trikonasana are termed dynamic asanas.

Static asanas are beneficial either in activating or slowing down abnormal glandular secretions and making the blood circulation efficient. They vitalize the organs and give spiritual strength. Dynamic asanas make the body warm, quicken the blood circulation, tighten the skin and muscles, strengthen the lungs and stimulate the digestive functions.

All asanas have their own special curative values. They are systematically and scientifically classified according to different abnormal body functions or diseases. Different asanas are prescribed for the diseases of lungs, digestive system, blood circulation, metabolism, eyesight, glandular functions and excretory system.

What are the general rules and precautions for asanas?

Some of the general rules and important precautions for practising yogasanas are:

1. Asanas should be selected and practised according to the individual state of health and ability.
2. One should consult a yoga teacher who has knowledge of physiology, anatomy, the flow of prana and also psychology.
3. Number and duration of asanas should be gradually and slowly increased.
4. Asanas should preferably be practised in the morning before taking food.

5. Diet, sleep and rest should be adjusted to avoid constipation.
6. The room for asanas should be clean and ventilated but without draughts.
7. To avoid accidents, practise away from fire, instruments, fan, table or chair.
8. The stage or base for asanas should not be too soft.
9. Asanas should not be practised on the bare ground or floor; a thick blanket or mat should be used.
10. After asanas sufficient rest should be taken. One may lie down in shavasana between asanas when one feels tired.
11. Don't take a bath immediately after asanas; bath should be taken at least fifteen minutes before asanas or half an hour thereafter.
12. Half an hour after asanas one may take milk, fruits, or some light and natural food.
13. For spiritual benefits each posture should be done slowly and for a longer time.
14. Beginners should do inverted postures like sirshasana at the end of the practice, average and advanced practitioners first.

MUDRA AND BANDHA

What are the different bandhas? Please explain definition, technique and benefits of each bandha.

Bandha literally means 'to hold or tighten'. Yogic bandhas are contraction or tightening of different body organs and glands. There are four main bandhas: they are termed moola bandha, jalandhara bandha, uddiyana bandha and maha bandha.

1. Moola Bandha

Moola bandha is the contraction and holding of mooladhara or the anus.

Sit in padmasana, siddhasana or any comfortable asana in which the knees touch the ground.

Keeping the arms straight, place the palms over the knees and hold the breath inside or outside.

Then contract the anus or mooladhara upwards, press the chin against the chest and at the same time raise the shoulders and press the knees down.

Concentrate in mooladhara or vishuddhi chakra.

If you cannot do this bandha then you can do agnisara kriya instead, which is contraction and expansion of the sphincter muscle.

2. Jalandhara Bandha

Jalandhara bandha is the chin lock which presses the windpipe or trachea.

Sit in a steady asana.

Inhale deeply.

Holding the breath, press the chin against the chest.

Press the knees down and raise shoulders.

Concentrate on vishuddhi chakra.

3. Uddiyana Bandha

Uddiyana literally means 'flight', but it is the contraction of the abdomen with outer breath retention.

Sit in a steady asana.

Exhale deeply.

Holding the breath outside, press the chin against the chest and place the palms on the knees.

Then contract the abdomen so that it goes close to the backbone. Hold the position for a comfortable time.

Release the contraction of the abdomen, then the contraction of the throat, and inhale.

4. Maha Bandha

When the three bandhas – moola, jalandhara and uddiyana are practised together, it becomes maha bandha.

Sit in a steady asana.

Exhale deeply.

Press the chin against the chest, contract the anus and draw the abdomen back.
Press the knees down with the palms and raise the shoulders.
Hold the position as long as is comfortable and concentrate on mooladhara, manipura and vishuddhi chakras.
Then release moola, uddiyana and jalandhara bandhas.

Bandhas give wonderful results. They cure diseases related to the anus, throat and lungs, increase the digestive fire and remove constipation. Moola bandha cures haemorrhoids and jalandhara bandha strengthens the heart muscles.

What do you mean by yogic mudras? What are the different mudras? Please tell the techniques for practice and enumerate their benefits also.

Mudra means a psychic attitude. The spiritual meaning is to unite oneself with the inner being. The following mudras are of fundamental importance:

1. Shambhavi Mudra or Bhrumadhya Drishti

Bhru means 'eyebrow', *madhya* means 'centre' and *drishti* means 'sight, gaze'.

Sit in any suitable asana, spine erect.
Look straight forward at one point, then look up as high as possible without moving the head and concentrate with open eyes on the point between the two eyebrows.

As its chief benefit, the pineal gland is revitalized.

2. Khechari Mudra

Khe means 'in the sky', and *chari* means 'one who moves'.

This name is given because it produces a state of mind in which the astral body is detached from the physical body. Then the consciousness dwells in the *akasha*, the space between the astral and physical bodies. This practice should be done only in close relationship between the guru and chela. When the tongue reaches the upper passage of the nose, a sweet liquid is tasted. He who masters this technique is able to practise kumbhaka as long as he wishes. Yogis who get themselves buried alive for days and weeks practise khechari.

Khechari revitalizes the nectar glands, which are related to vishuddhi chakra.

If khechari is done during physical action, a bitter secretion may be tasted in the upper passage of the nose. This can be harmful.

3. Kaki Mudra

Kaki means 'like a crow'.

Sit in siddhasana, padmasana or vajrasana.

Make a tube with your lips, look at the tip of the nose, inhale through the mouth, and exhale through the nose.

4. Maha Bheda Mudra

Maha means 'great' and *bheda* means 'piercing, penetrating'.

Sit in padmasana, vajrasana or paschimottanasana.

Inhale through the left nostril, then exhale through the mouth and retain the breath outside.

Practise jalandhara, uddiyana and moola bandhas, repeating mentally "mooladhara, manipura, vishuddhi; mooladhara, manipura, vishuddhi" and so on.

Then first release moola, uddiyana and finally jalandhara bandhas. Inhale through both nostrils.

5. Tadan Mudra

Tadan means 'to beat'.

Sit in padmasana with internal breath retention and beat the buttocks on the floor, raising and dropping the body using the arms and hands.

6. Akashi Mudra

Akasha means 'sky, space'.

Sit in one of the meditative poses.

Fold the tongue against the palate.

Practise ujjayi and shambhavi.

Do not do this mudra if the mind is wandering.

This mudra is very important to prepare for a trance state of mind.

7. Bhujangani Mudra

Bhujanga means 'cobra'.

Sit in padmasana or vajrasana, swallow air in through the mouth and belch it out again.

One can keep the air in the stomach for hours, enabling one to float without sinking.

This mudra tones the stomach and eliminates wind. It may be done after shankhaprakshalana for increased benefits.

8. Ashwini Mudra

Ashwini means 'horse'.

Sit in any meditative asana.

Breathe normally.

Contract and relax the sphincter muscles. Concentrate on mooladhara chakra.

9. Tadagi Mudra

Tadagi means 'water pond'.

Sit in paschimottanasana, with the feet somewhat apart, holding the big toes.

Inhale while expanding the abdominal muscles.

Retain breath and hold this position for five seconds, then relax and exhale.

10. Maha Mudra

Maha means 'great'.

Sit in paschimottanasana, inhale and practise moola bandha, akashi mudra and shambhavi mudra.

11. Yoni Mudra or Shanmukhi Mudra

Yoni means 'womb', *shan* means 'six' and *mukhi* means 'face'.

Sit in padmasana or vajrasana.

Inhale and plug the ears with the thumbs, eyes with the index fingers, nostrils with the middle fingers, and place the third and fourth fingers above and below the lips.

Retain breath.

This mudra stimulates hearing of the anahata sounds, which emanate from bindu. It is beneficial for those who suffer from vertigo, eye, nose and brain infections.

12. Pashinee Mudra

Pashinee means 'tight entrance'.

Practise halasana.

Bend the knees, bring them close to the shoulders, and wrap both arms around the legs and head.

13. Agochari Mudra

Agochari means 'invisible'.

Sit straight in any asana and gaze at the tip of the nose, holding the breath.

14. Bhoochari Mudra

Bhoo means 'earth' and *chari* means 'to move'.

Sit in padmasana, preferably facing a blank wall.

Hold the hand flat in front of the nose, palm down.

Take it away and remain gazing at the invisible point of the place of the fourth finger.

15. Gaja Karani Mudra

Gaja means 'elephant' and *karani* means 'action'.

Sit in padmasana.

Practise nauli.

Draw in water through the rectum, retain and then expel it.

This washes the colon and can be done instead of shankhaprakshalana. Basti kriya is the same. Naturopaths use this practice with cold water.

It cures fistula, eruptions due to heat in the rectum and local infections caused by venereal diseases.

16. Manduki Mudra

Manduki means 'frog'.

Sit in vajrasana. Spread the knees as far as possible and practise agochari mudra.

17. Vajroli Mudra

Vajra is the name of a nadi. Sit in any comfortable meditation posture. Inhale, hold the breath inside and draw the urethra upward. Exhale, releasing the contraction.

As a rule, only a simplified form of vajroli is taught, as the complete mudra requires a difficult technique and instruments such as rubber and silver catheters.

18. Sahajoli and Amaroli Mudra

These are similar practices for females.

PRANAYAMA

What is pranayama and what is its purpose?

Prana is the vital or life force, or vital breath; *ayama* means lengthening, exercise and control of the length. Thus *pranayama* means certain breathing exercises by which we can control the flow of the life force in our body.

What are the different varieties of pranayama? What are their techniques for practice and what are the benefits?

There are important pranayama, as follows:

1. Nadi Shodhana Pranayama

Nadi means psychic passage or channel and *shodhana* is a process of purification or throwing out of toxins and harmful elements.

Sit erect in a comfortable steady posture preferably facing east or north.

Stage 1: Inhale and exhale through the free flowing nostril keeping the other nostril closed. Do this 5 times.

Now close the first nostril and inhale and exhale through the other.

Do this also 5 times. The right nostril is closed by the thumb, the left nostril by the fourth finger.

Keep the breath normal and comfortable.

Practise this for fifteen days, increasing the number of rounds by 5 every third day, thus reaching twenty-five rounds through each nostril in fifteen days.

Stage 2: Keep the thumb over the right nostril, fourth finger over the left. Now inhale through the left nostril keeping the other closed. Then exhale through the right nostril keeping the left closed. Then inhale through the right nostril and exhale through the left.

This makes one round. Inhalation should be through the nostril by which you have done the exhalation.

Do 5 rounds for the first three days, and increase by 5 rounds every third day.

Practise this stage also for fifteen days, completing 25 rounds.

Stage 3: The methods are the same as in the second stage except that after inhalation one does a comfortable retention, *kumbhaka*, or more precisely, *antar kumbhaka*, internal retention of the breath.

Stage 4: In this stage the inhalation, retention and exhalation should be practised in the proportion 1:2:2.

When this becomes comfortably easy, then increase the ratio to 1:4:2.

After practising this for a sufficiently long time, again increase the ratio to 1:6:4.

When this also becomes absolutely comfortable, then start practising the ratio 1:8:6.

Only after gaining success should you proceed to the fifth stage.

Stage 5: Now you have to add outer retention, *bahir kumbhaka*, retention after exhalation also.

The respective proportion for inhalation, inner retention, exhalation and outer retention should be gradually and comfortably increased like this: 1:2:2:2; 1:4:2:2; 1:6:4:4 and 1:8:6:6.

For measuring the proportion of units, different methods can be used, e.g. counting by numbers. Some prefer to count as one hundred and one, one hundred and two, and so on, as with a little practice each count will work out to exactly one second. After ten seconds begin again with one hundred and one, one hundred and two, and so on.

The most important benefits of nadi shodhana pranayama, the so-called king of pranayama, are: it is good for abnormalities of the lungs, removes depressing tendencies of the mind, cures vertigo, develops concentration, is a good preparation for higher yogic practices, removes dullness and gives tranquillity to restless persons.

Precautions to be observed are: practise in a well-ventilated room; take a short rest, if required, after finishing a complete round; finish pranayama with a deep inhalation; add outer retention only after attaining perfection in inner retention. Advanced pranayama should be started only in spring (March in India); do not begin in summer, autumn or extremely cold winter; diet should be properly balanced.

2. Bhastrika Pranayama

Bhastrika means 'bellows'. In this pranayama the lungs are exercised like the bellows of a blacksmith.

Facing north or east, sit erect in a steady asana.

Start inhaling and exhaling through the free-flowing nostril, keeping the other one closed.

Do 20 rounds with the left nostril, *chandra nadi*, and 20 rounds with the right nostril, *surya nadi*.

This will make one complete round.

In the beginning, do only 3 rounds.

Final stage of bhastrika: Take rapid respirations through both nostrils together.

The chest should not move, only the abdomen should expand and contract.

Do 20 rounds.

Then exhale deeply, practise jalandhara, moola and uddiyana bandhas and release them in reverse order.

Then inhale.

Benefits: Purifies the lungs by throwing out bad gases, carbon dioxide, cures pleurisy; and when practised gradually and carefully it cures tuberculosis.

3. Surya Bheda Pranayama

Surya means 'sun' or pingala nadi; *bheda* means 'to pierce, to control'. Surya bheda activates the pingala nadi.

Sit in a meditative asana.

Take a deep inhalation through the right nostril and practise jalandhara and moola bandhas.

Press the knees down with the palms and raise the shoulders.

After a comfortable time release both bandhas and then exhale slowly through the right nostril.

This is one round.

Practise 3 rounds.

Benefits: This pranayama activates the pingala nadi and thus digestion, longevity and strength are increased. It activates the solar energy of manipura chakra and brings it to sahasrara; it cures leprosy, venereal infections and chronic indigestion.

4. Bhramari Pranayama

In this pranayama a sound like that of a humming bee is produced, so it is known as *bhramari* or humming of bees.

Sit in an erect and comfortable asana.

Inhale deeply through both nostrils.

Do jalandhara and moola bandha for a while and release.

Plug both ears with the index fingers and exhale through the nostrils, making a humming sound.

Do a minimum of 3 rounds.

Benefits: It relieves mental tension and high blood pressure due to mental agitation. It is very good for singers because it soothes the throat.

5. Moorchha Pranayama

Due to long inner retention of the breath, carbon is increased in the lungs and generates a condition of inertia, resulting in a kind of fainting sensation. Thus it is called *moorchha* or 'fainting'.

Sit in an erect meditative posture.

Inhale through both nostrils, gradually bending the head backward, looking towards the sky and fixing both eyes between the eyebrows in shambhavi mudra.

Press the knees down with the palms.

Retain the breath comfortably.

Then exhale with closed eyes and gradually lower the head to the normal position.

Practise 3 times or until a sensation of fainting is felt.

Benefits: It induces a state of introversion. It is a very powerful means for sense withdrawal and helps in making meditation a success.

6. Sheetali Pranayama

Sheetali means 'cooler'. By this pranayama a cooling effect is experienced in the whole body.

Sit in an erect meditative posture.

Put out the tongue and fold the sides like a tube.

Inhale slowly and deeply.

Practise a short retention in jalandhara and then exhale through the nose.

Benefits: Sheetali purifies the blood and removes high blood pressure. It gives mental and muscular rest and eliminates the feeling of thirst.

7. Sheetkari Pranayama

It is of the same nature as the above pranayama.

Sit in an erect meditative posture.

Fold the tongue back and up to the upper palate. Clench the teeth and separate the lips widely.

Inhale through the teeth.

Retain the breath for a few seconds with jalandhara bandha. Close the lips and breathe out through the nostrils.

Benefits: As for sheetali pranayama.

8. Ujjayi Pranayama

Ujjayi is a kind of deep breathing after contracting the glottis in the throat.

Fold the tongue against the upper palate; this will produce saliva which in turn will irrigate the glottis.

Breathe creating a soft and gentle snoring sound.

Benefits: It has a serene effect on the nervous system, increases the intake of oxygen and thus induces freshness. Insomnia is removed by practising ujjayi, without khechari, in shavasana.

9. Kapalbhati Pranayama

Kapal means 'frontal region of the brain' and *bhati* means 'bellowing'. It is classified as one of the six kriyas of hatha yoga.

Sit in a steady asana.

Perform a series of fast breaths with emphasis on exhalation; inhalation should be spontaneous.

After some rounds, exhale and practise jalandhara, moola and uddiyana bandhas, then release the bandhas one by one and inhale. One round should consist of 30 to 100 breaths at a time.

Benefits: It stimulates and purifies the frontal area of the brain, removes cerebral thrombosis and is a preparation for meditation.

10. Plavini

Plava means 'to flow' and *plavini* means 'something which enables one to float on a river'.

Swallow the air in small instalments through the throat. It means to drink the air into the stomach just like drinking water. Then push it out through the mouth.

Benefits: Plavini cures stiff stomach walls. One who has wind in the stomach should practise 5 to 6 rounds.

11. Shakti Chalini Pranayama

Shakti is the spiritual, psychic or pranic force; *chalini* means 'to move, to conduct'. Therefore, shakti chalini is a practice by which the psychic or pranic force is rotated and controlled.

Sit in a steady posture.

Inhale and practise jalandhara and moola bandhas.

Now rotate your mind from ajna chakra to mooladhara and back, through the spinal cord.

Circulate the mind 4 to 10 rounds during one internal retention. Release moola and then jalandhara bandhas.

Exhale.

Benefits: It is a powerful exercise for sex sublimation. It increases vitality and sharpens the memory.

12. Chaturtha Pranayama

It is an independent pranayama, separate from the three varieties of higher esoteric pranayamas like the fusion of (a) prana into apana; (b) apana into prana; and (c) prana into prana. As it is kept in serial order after the aforesaid three pranayamas, it is termed *chaturtha*, fourth.

It is a very simple pranayama, which comes automatically due to perfect relaxation and steadiness.

In this state of breathing, the distinction of the breaking points between inhalation, inner retention, exhalation and outer retention, ceases to exist.

The breath becomes very subtle and fine.

Sit in a meditative pose.

Practise some of the above-mentioned pranayamas.
Make the inhalation, exhalation, inner and outer retentions of equal length.
Try to become more and more relaxed; keep on dissolving the efforts of breathing and let it become automatic.
Eventually you will achieve the state of chaturtha pranayama and then the higher field of yogic practices can be opened to you.

Points to note

1. Pranayama should be learnt under advice from an expert yogi. Simple pranayama can, of course, be started independently.
2. See that you don't have constipation; if it is there; remove it by asana and special diet.
3. Don't practise pranayama on a river bank, sea shore, under hot sun or in an open place where the wind is blowing.
4. Keep the chest and head covered with clothes.
5. Increase the variety and quantity of pranayama very slowly and gradually.

AJAPA JAPA

Can you please explain the meaning of ajapa japa, explain its technique and enumerate its benefits?

A means 'no', and *japa* means 'continuous repetition of the same thing'. Thus, *ajapa* literally means rotation of consciousness or japa without any sound or without any effort for repetition of a mantra. It is the spontaneous rotation of consciousness with the help of mantra. Ajapa is a powerful technique for sense withdrawal and can induce concentration and deep meditation. Even samadhi can be attained by the process of ajapa japa.

Technique

Ajapa japa is divided into six different stages and its technique is described below.

Stage 1: Sit in a steady, meditative posture. Breathe in ujjayi pranayama by contracting the glottis.

Try to feel as if you are breathing from the navel, through a psychic passage, up to the throat.

Then chant *Aum* while descending your consciousness from the throat to the navel in the same psychic passage.

In this way, chant *Aum* 3, 5, 11 or 13 times.

Stage 2: Fold your tongue back, touching the upper palate in khechari mudra.

While breathing in ujjayi with khechari rotate your consciousness from the navel to the throat and back.

With inhalation imagine your consciousness ascending from the navel to the throat, and while exhaling imagine your consciousness descending from the throat to the navel.

This makes one round.

Practise 49 rounds.

Stage 3: While breathing in, listen to the sound *So* with ascending consciousness from the navel to the throat.

While breathing out listen to the natural sound *Ham* and at the same time descend the consciousness in the psychic passage from the throat to the navel.

This is one round. Practise 30 rounds with khechari and ujjayi creating a continuous awareness of *So-Ham, So-Ham*.

Stage 4: Now, with exhalation become aware of the sound *Ham*, while descending the consciousness from the throat to the navel, and become aware of the sound *So* while ascending your consciousness from the navel to the throat, in the psychic passage.

Practise 30 rounds with khechari and ujjayi, making a continuous chain of *Ham-So, Ham-So*.

Stage 5: Continue khechari mudra and breathing in ujjayi.

Now unite *So-Ham* and *Ham-So* in such a way that the whole thing becomes *So-Ham-So-Ham-So-Ham*.

Start ascending your consciousness of *So* from the navel to the throat; a moment before reaching the throat you become aware of *Ham* along with *So*, or fuse *So* into *Ham* so that it becomes *So-Ham*, then descend with *Ham* consciousness.

A moment before reaching the navel you become aware of *So* along with Ham, making it *Ham-So*.

Thus, when you continue this process of uniting *So* with *Ham* and *Ham* with *So* it will make a continuous circle of consciousness, with the vibration of *So-Ham-So-Ham*.

Practise this for about 30 rounds.

When the rotation of consciousness becomes automatic and spontaneous, one finds it difficult to count due to the absence of any dividing point.

In that case, instead of 30 rounds you can practise it up to feeling the jerk of introversion.

Stage 6: When you feel the jerk of introversion in the fifth stage of ajapa japa stop ujjayi and khechari mudra and forget the psychic passage between the navel and the throat.

Now become aware of the dark space within your whole personality and start looking into it.

Try to understand the nature, form and quality of the dark space in front of you. Watch attentively the changes going on.

You might see changing colours, forms, visions, clouds, landscapes, old memories, good or bad, darkness or formlessness.

The whole area within your perception is called chidakasha.

Chit means 'consciousness' or 'awareness'; *akasha* means 'range', 'space' or 'field'.

Take a flight into your chidakasha. Go on penetrating it and try to find out the end of it.

Go on witnessing the things coming your way.

Try to imagine yourself in the infinite darkness, fusing yourself into darkness and becoming one with it. Try to look above, below, to the right and left, in the front and back, all around you and witness the changes. Don't move either eyes or head.

Try to be a spectator of all that you see. Don't act or react to it.

Finally, the darkness will disappear and you will experience something like the dawn of day.

This is the sign of chidakasha.

At the end, after long and patient practice, when no samskaras remain and when your chitta will cease from all possibilities of modification, then you can work for samadhi.

Benefits: It gives deep relaxation and withdrawal of the senses; removes mental agitation and keeps the practitioner calm, quiet and happy; increases oxidation in the blood, thus giving vitality and freshness; helps in achieving deep meditation and even samadhi; is a powerful technique for exhausting the accumulated samskaras; decreases the rate of metabolism and therefore decreases the quantity of food and sleep required; cures many mental and physical abnormalities.

CHIDAKASHA DHARANA

What is chidakasha in greater detail, and what is meant by chidakasha dharana?

As explained in the sixth stage of ajapa japa, chidakasha means the field, area or range within the capacity of sense perception and reaction of individual awareness.

Chidakasha dharana means concentration on or watching the reactions on the plane of physical, mental and psychic existence within one's whole personality. Changes in chidakasha may be due to the inner reality and also due to the reaction of outer reality upon the inner reality. These phenomena may manifest in the form of colours, lights, forms, visions, thoughts, old memories, or sound and energy waves.

What is the technique of chidakasha dharana and what are its physiological, psychological and spiritual reactions?
Chidakasha dharana comprises five stages.

Technique

Stage 1: Sit in a comfortable meditative posture like padmasana, siddhasana or sukhasana.
Close your eyes and look into the dark field of space in front of you.
Watch it carefully as a witness.
Do not try to interpret or analyze it in any manner.

Stage 2: Now you will see some changes in the dark area, like the emergence of different colours, golden light, streaks of light or mixtures of colours. Don't react to anything.

Stage 3: Make your awareness deeper and more penetrative.
Investigate and travel across the deeper layers of consciousness.
Take a deep plunge into the dark night of the soul; your consciousness will penetrate into subtler planes. Here one develops the power of telepathy and deeper realities are revealed.

Stage 4: This stage consists of an overall survey of chidakasha.
Search into all the dimensions of chidakasha, and at the same time be aware that the search is going on.
When you start your journey into different directions, your field of consciousness goes on expanding.

Stage 5: Now feel yourself within the fathomless chidakasha.
Stop the exploration and penetration, and try to establish yourself in the darkness of the inner firmament of the infinite cosmos. Try to dissolve your individual consciousness into cosmic consciousness.

Before ending, try to visualize your ishta devata, then make your mind vacant, without any thought, go into inner silence and dwell within your own self.

Benefits: By the practice of chidakasha dharana a deep relaxation on the physical, mental and psychic planes occurs. Thus it removes tensions in all spheres of consciousness. One feels tremendous freshness and strength due to extreme relaxation. Chidakasha dharana, in the beginning, is a practice of pratyahara, later culminating in concentration and deep meditation. It gives all the advantages of meditation. It also develops the faculty of telepathy and other psychic phenomena. One realizes the pure form of chitta by this practice.

YOGA NIDRA

Can you please explain yoga nidra and the underlying scientific law behind the practice?

Yoga means a state where one is in communion with the inner awareness and *nidra* means sleep. Thus, *yoga nidra* is a kind of sleep in which one is aware of all the happenings within and without. It is said to be sleepless sleep, or psychic sleep. In this practice one remains awake, attentive and aware of the instructions given by the operator, but forgets one's own body and senses. The scientific basis behind the practice of yoga nidra may be explained like this:

By different methods of rotation of consciousness and by imagination of material things, one detaches the individual awareness from the sense experiences, memories, samskaras and any kind of reaction to outer impressions. The awareness is made devoid of any mechanical reaction, but at the same time the awareness is kept attached to the operator's voice.

It is a means of pratyahara. By its practice different psychic faculties are controlled and harnessed for various occult purposes. It decreases the hours of sleep necessary by giving more rest in less time.

What are the different techniques for the practice of yoga nidra? What are the precautions to be taken and the benefits which accrue?

There are many methods of yoga nidra suitable for many types of aspirants. The following are some of the different methods.

Technique

Lie down on a blanket or rug.

Adjust your body so that you can keep still for forty-five minutes.

Make your mind ready for yoga nidra.

Draw the mind within and resolve: "Now the practice begins."

Stage 1: Rotation of consciousness around the seventy-six parts of the body.

The mind should move quickly from centre to centre in the following sequence, repeating mentally the centre named.

Right side: thumb of the right hand, second finger, third finger, fourth finger, fifth finger, palm, wrist, elbow, shoulder, armpit, waist, hip, hamstring, thigh, knee, calf, ankle, heel, sole of the right foot, big toe, second toe, third toe, fourth toe, fifth toe.

Repeat for the left side of the body.

Then the back of the body: right shoulder blade, left shoulder blade, right buttock, left buttock, the back as a whole.

The front of the body: sahasrara, forehead, right eyebrow, left eyebrow, centre of the eyebrows, right eye, left eye, nose, nose tip, right cheek, left cheek, right ear, left ear, lower lip, upper lip, both lips together, chin, throat, right chest, left chest, both together, depression of the chest, navel, abdomen, right groin, left groin. Right leg, left leg, right arm, left arm, the head, the whole body, whole body, whole body . . . (seven times).

Now let the mind rest for a while then start the second round in the same way.

Repeat 1-5 rounds according to the depth of yoga nidra attained.

In the beginning name the parts of the body in order to maintain awareness.

Later on, simply be aware of these parts without naming them mentally.

Do not change the sequence of the parts of the body, the subconscious mind gets used to the same order.

Then, go to the next stage.

Stage 2: Awaken the feeling of:

i) Heaviness in all the different parts of the body, as indicated in the first stage
ii) Lightness of the parts already named
iii) Heat in soles, palms, lips, eyes and ears
iv) Cold in soles, spinal cord, heart and sahasrara
v) Pain in your body, in any part you may wish to choose.

Stage 3 – mental awareness: Through conceptual concentration on psychic centres, psychic symbols or psychic stages, one reaches the state of dharana. Now practise the discovering of the psychic centres, *chakras*. Take your consciousness to mooladhara chakra situated at the base of the spinal cord; try to feel and visualize a red triangle, with the apex downwards, a pink serpent within with three and a half coils. Then go to swadhisthana situated at the lower end of the spine. There you get the experience and feeling of sleep.

Then go to manipura just behind the navel in the spinal cord and visualize a bright yellow lotus.

In anahata, with ten petals behind the heart in the spine, try to visualize the flame of a lamp.

Then go to vishuddhi, situated at the back of the throat. Try to experience chill and cold there.

Then go to ajna, situated behind the centre of the eyebrows in the spine with a two-petalled lotus.

In bindu visarga, situated at the back of the head, try to visualize the crescent moon of the fourth day.

Now go to sahasrara, situated at the top of the head, and try to visualize a red lotus with one thousand petals.

When you find the right place of the chakras you will have these visions and experiences.

Start from mooladhara up to sahasrara and come back to mooladhara. This is one round.

Do 9 rounds.

Go along them quickly with only momentary consciousness. Try to visualize twenty or thirty articles or scenes by imagination, naming them quickly, for example: a temple, a lamp, a tall banana tree, a moving car, clouds of different colours, a dog, a horse, the rising sun, the setting sun, a red rose, a lotus flower, bank of a river, a human skeleton, your own body lying down, a beautiful garden, and so on.

Go quickly like a flash.

Don't arrange a systematic serial order of the items. Practise 5 to 10 rounds.

Don't change the sequence once fixed.

When the mind becomes sensitive enough to visualize these things, then go to the last stage.

Stage 4: In this state of dharana in yoga nidra, think of the Supreme Self. After the study of Vedanta one can reflect on conceptions like Brahman or truth.

Now awake from yoga nidra but keep the eyes closed; sit in a meditative posture and remember the resolve or sankalpa. Choose a short and simple sentence with the aim of eradicating a certain bad habit like: "I give up smoking."

Before opening the eyes reflect on the resolve, and then get up.

Precautions: Do not practise in the open air. Keep the disturbance of flies or mosquitoes away by using a mosquito net. Keep the body without any movement. Never open your eyes during the whole practice, never keep the head towards the north and don't use a fan which makes a sound.

Benefits: Bad habits can be changed through yoga nidra; it cures many mental diseases; it is a powerful means for sense withdrawal from all bodily centres, culminating in dhyana; one can reduce sleep to an unbelievable extent and save the precious hours of life.

SHANKHAPRAKSHALANA

It is a practice by which we wash the entire alimentary canal right from the mouth to the excretory system. *Shankha* means 'conch', *prakshalana* means 'to wash completely'. In the hatha yoga of six bodily purification techniques, it comes under one of the dhautis named varisara dhauti, *vari* means 'water' and *sara* means 'essence'.

Technique

Fill a clean bucket with lukewarm water and add some salt to it. Drink two glasses of this salty water and practise the following asanas eight times each.

1. **Tadasana**: Stand erect, feet a little apart.
   Raise arms overhead, palms up, look up at the intertwined fingers, lift the heels and stretch the whole body.
2. **Tiryak Tadasana**: Stand erect, raise both arms, then bend to the right and left from the waist.
3. **Kati Chakrasana**: Stand up.
   Keep the legs two and a half feet apart. Now twist the upper body, bring the left hand to the right shoulder and the right arm around the back. Turn the head to the right and look over the right shoulder. Do the same towards the left side, changing the hands.
4. **Tiryak Bhujangasana**: Lie down on the stomach.
   Put both palms on the floor near the chest.
   Now raise your chest and head.

Keep the waist near the ground and from the left side look at the right heel, and from the right side look at the left heel, thus twisting the waist.

5. Udarakarshanasana: Squat and keep both palms on the knees throughout.

Bend the right knee to the ground and turn the trunk as far as possible to the left, looking behind the body.

Repeat in the opposite direction.

Then drink two more glasses of salty water and practise these asanas again.

Go on drinking up to six glasses and do asanas for each two glasses.

Those who feel the urge for toilet before six glasses should try to control it and hold out, but if the urge is very strong they can go.

Otherwise, go only after six glasses.

Don't strain at the toilet, let the stool come out automatically.

Then go on drinking salty water and follow the same procedure of asanas after each two glasses.

Go to the toilet whenever it becomes necessary.

You will find that your discharge gradually becomes more diluted, containing more and more water, then only yellow water will come out and finally only clear water.

This shows that your intestines are now clear.

The total number of glasses required may be from sixteen to twenty-five, sometimes more.

Then drink quickly several glasses of salty water in order to do kunjal kriya and vomit the water out from the stomach voluntarily. Bend from the waist and rub or press the back of the tongue with the second and third finger.

The water will come out in quick gushes.

Then practise jala neti.

Rest for forty-five minutes to one hour.

Then take khichari, prepared from rice and dal with ghee.

Take enough to fill the stomach fully and thus facilitate complete lubrication.

Don't take water, vegetables, fruit, curd, milk, or spices.

It is better to rest for the whole day.

In the evening again take khichari with ghee.

Precautions: The weather should be hot and dry and not windy.

Do not expose the body to temperatures less than that of the body. Take khichari immediately after the rest period.

Don't take water for the next four hours at least and even then it should not be below body temperature.

Take sufficient ghee to fulfil the necessity of fats and carbohydrates to neutralize the acid secretions of the intestines; ghee also lubricates the intestinal walls.

Take about two hours rest after the meal, but don't sleep.

Strictly avoid the following food for one week: milk, milk products, curd, fruit, spices, chillies, wine, etc., and smoking. Avoid meat for at least forty days.

Practise shankhaprakshalana in a group and in a happy atmosphere.

Do not attempt the practice without the guidance of a competent teacher.

This should be practised in the morning with an empty stomach. Those who are suffering from peptic ulcers, abscess in the liver or high blood pressure should not practise shankhaprakshalana. A special variety of shankhaprakshalana for diabetic patients should be practised under strict guidance.

Benefits: It can be practised twice a year on average.

This is the best practice to cleanse the whole system from mouth to rectum.

It purifies the body of impurities, alleviates abnormalities of the digestive functions and thus renews and vitalizes all functions of the body. Rishi Gheranda says in his book *Gheranda Samhita* that by shankhaprakshalana the body becomes spiritualized and divine. It cures many chronic disorders as a side effect and expels worms.

If one is constipated a week after complete shankhaprakshalana repeat the same process with six glasses of salty lukewarm water, and without any diet restrictions. This is called laghoo shankhaprakshalana.

The word hatha has its origin from two bija mantras: *ham* and *tham*. *Ham* represents the pranic or solar force in the human body, and *tham* denotes the psychic or lunar energy, or consciousness.

The purpose of hatha yoga is to establish perfect harmony between the psychic and pranic forces in the body. Thus complete equilibrium in the body and mind is achieved, resulting in higher spiritual realization.

It also aims at the perfect purification of the body by throwing out all accumulated toxins. It is a wonderful technique of making the body and mind healthy and sound, which is a compulsory condition for higher yogic practices.

SHATKARMAS

The shatkarmas are six scientific yogic techniques for the purification and removal of disorders of various organs, and the metabolism of the human body. They are powerful physiological means of purification based on the yogic studies of the human body. Those six techniques are as follows:

1. Neti

It is a technique for cleaning the nasal passages with different liquids like water or milk, a thread or rubber catheter.

Varieties of neti

1. *Jala neti* is cleaning with lukewarm salt water; for special purposes cold or plain water is also used.
2. *Sutra neti* is cleaning with a rubber catheter or special thread.
3. *Ghrita neti* is cleaning with ghee.

4. *Tael neti* is cleaning with oil.
5. *Dugdh neti* is cleaning with milk.

Benefits

It cures diseases of the eyes, nose and throat, and also vertigo; it is helpful in combating sinusitis; it awakens the sushumna nadi and activates the brain; it cures colds, sneezing, migraine, inflammation of nasal membranes, adenoids and polyps and facilitates the practice of pranayama.

2. Dhauti

A process for cleaning the alimentary canal.

Varieties

1. Vaman dhauti is cleaning the stomach by drinking water and vomiting. It is also known as kunjal or *gaja karma kriya*, the elephant action, and cures asthma and bronchial congestion.
2. Vyaghra karma dhauti is the technique of cleaning a loaded stomach by drinking lukewarm salt water and vomiting.
3. Varisara dhauti has been described as a process of shankhaprakshalana.
4. Vastra dhauti is a technique to clean the stomach with a long piece of cloth.
5. Moola shodhana dhauti is a process to cleanse the anus and discharge heat.
6. Ganesh kriya is a process to cure constipation by rubbing the anus with fine mud or silt.

3. Basti

It is a kriya by which the abdominal activities are improved and the large intestine is washed.

Varieties

1. Jala basti is practised standing in hip-deep water. Perform nauli and jalandhara bandha and by the contraction and

expansion of the rectum, water is sucked in and then expelled. Thus the large intestine is completely washed out.

2. Sthal basti is the same as jala basti but is practised without water.

Benefits

It cures spermatorrhoea and leucorrhoea. Sthal basti is very beneficial for gastritis. It is a kind of yogic enema; it cures constipation, stimulates digestion and is very useful for brahmacharya.

4. Nauli

It is a technique of churning or rolling the rectus abdomini and is divided into four stages: isolation of the rectus abdomini muscles at the centre, to the right side, to the left side, then moving the muscles from left to centre and then right and reverse, in one smooth motion. This is churning the rectus abdomini from left to right and from right to left.

Benefits

It cures various abnormalities related to the intestines, disorders of the stomach, weakness of intestinal peristalsis and loosening of intestinal flexibility. By nauli one can join apana with prana, which is one of the practices of kundalini yoga. It is also good for sexual diseases and gives vigour, strength and longevity.

Precautions

It should be learned very carefully and thoroughly under the guidance of a guru, stage by stage. Practice should be regular. Sufferers from haemorrhoids should not practise it.

5. Kapalbhati

This has already been described.

6. Trataka

This is a part of hatha yoga as well as raja yoga and is a technique of unbroken gazing. It is a powerful means to develop many psychic faculties. Trataka is done on different objects, each having different effects. Some of them are: candle flame, black spot, an idol, tip of the nose, centre of the eyebrows, shivalinga, sky or water, rising sun, moon, a crystal, and so on.

Benefits

It cures many eye diseases and awakens the power of attraction of the eyes; the mind becomes calm and introvert; pranas are harmonized; it can cure mental abnormalities and check extra emotions; helps in higher occult and tantric practices; increases willpower; brings a state of chaturtha pranayama; by the practice of trataka one can see one's samskaras and spirits of different planes.

Warning

It is advised not to practise trataka only to obtain siddhis, as it can cause harm. It should be learnt with a guru; therefore, those who are interested in trataka should search out an adept.

However, simple trataka on a candle flame, black dot, etc., for eyesight and concentration can be practised without harm.

ANTAR MOUNA

Antar means 'inner'; *mouna* means 'silence'. It is a practice of sense withdrawal or *pratyahara*, the fifth stage of raja yoga. By its practice individual awareness is cut off from the sense perceptions, the mind is drawn within and one becomes aware of inner phenomena. By the practice of antar mouna one can enter into deep meditation. The practice is divided into six stages.

Technique

Stage 1 – awareness of sense perceptions: Sit in an erect meditative posture with eyes closed.

Relax the body and mind from all tensions.

Forget all worries, engagements, worldly affairs and relationships.

Be aware of all outer happenings.

Now become aware of the breath going out and coming in; long or short breath, comfortable breath.

Breathe with relaxation, the body becoming lighter and lighter. Then become aware of the outer surroundings. Listen to the sounds such as birds, wind, people walking, cars, somebody talking or the typewriter noise. Be aware of all sounds coming within the range of your perception. Relaxation and alertness will become deeper and deeper. Then enter into the second stage.

Stage 2 – awareness or visualization of spontaneous thought processes: Now you will notice that many thoughts are coming automatically, like a flow.

Be an impartial spectator.

Your consciousness will enter into deeper layers.

Thoughts will first arise from the conscious level, then later they will start coming from the subconscious plane.

Old memories, past events, unfulfilled desires, many things will come before you, like a motion picture or theatrical show. The only thing you have to do is be a witness to them.

Don't make any effort. Neither react nor choose any thought.

After sufficient witnessing go to the third stage.

Stage 3 – to pose and dispose of the thoughts at will: This stage is meant to get control over the thoughts and their automatic flow.

You have to create a new thought and mental image at will; after observing for some time, you cancel it and replace it by some new thought.

For example, you think of a garden, visualize it, move in it, see its beauty and then replace the whole scene by a library hall with people reading books and newspapers.

Then replace this by a flower, such as a rose.

Watch it, then replace it with a church scene.

Bring different things or scenes and go on replacing one with the other.

Try to visualize as clearly as you do when you see with eyes open.

Don't lose command or control over the thoughts.

Then go to the next stage.

Stage 4 – awareness of spontaneous thoughts and disposal at will: In the third stage, occurrence and disposal of thoughts were at will.

In this stage, occurrence will be spontaneous and disposal at will.

Suppose you see a dog walking in the street.

Go on looking at it and watch the changes, then suddenly remove that scene from your mental screen by willpower.

Leave your awareness free.

See what comes.

Suppose you see a pandit doing the worship of goddess Kali in a temple.

Watch him, then suddenly remove the whole scene and wait for a new thought or vision.

This is the process to follow in this stage.

Then go to the fifth stage.

Stage 5 – freeness of thoughts: Become a spectator of your thought process.

Let it move in complete freedom.

Now you are in a deep state of your consciousness.

The contents of the unconscious layers of consciousness will begin to manifest.

Watch all the reactions going on within your own consciousness.

Be awake, alert, attentive.

Avoid sleep or a slip of attention; be a witness to the scenes, thoughts, visions, whatever they may be.
Then, when you feel sleepy, you transcend the fifth stage and enter into the sixth and last stage of antar mouna.

Stage 6 – awareness of the sleep state of consciousness: Now watch the sleeping tendency of your awareness.
Try to understand its nature, reactions and feelings.
Whatever is happening, watch it.
See how sleep awareness is coming over your consciousness.
Continue this for a long time; don't miss your awareness.
This is the state where a psychic symbol is necessary to avoid going into a state of unconsciousness.
Psychic symbols are determined by the guru.
One should keep this symbol clearly visible to avoid the grip of sleep and forgetfulness.
This completes antar mouna.
It will help to reveal and manifest many dormant and deep layers of your consciousness and psychic personality.

NADA YOGA

Nada means 'flow of consciousness', or 'the automatic sound going on within one's own self'. It is a process of penetrating more and more deeply into the nature of one's own reality.

Purpose

Nada yoga is one of the practices of laya yoga. It aims to reach the subtlest state of awareness with the help of sound. As the consciousness goes deeper and deeper one begins to hear inaudible sounds. One can attain sense withdrawal, concentration and deep meditation by the nada yoga practice.

Baikhari is that sound which is produced by the striking or friction of two things. Speech or the sound of music is called baikhari.

Madhyama is a more subtle sound than baikhari; it is like a whisper.

Pashyanti is a kind of mental sound. It has no concern with the sound producing organs such as tongue or throat. It is like a sound heard in a dream. It is more subtle than madhyama.

Para is a quality of the psyche or soul. It is a sound without any vibration or a sound of infinite wavelength. It can be heard only in *samadhi*, deep meditation, or in a deep state of nada yoga.

Technique

Nada yoga should be practised in the calm hours of the night between midnight and two o'clock.

First practise moola bandha, vajroli and yoga mudra, then bhramari pranayama.

Sit over a high and round pillow, similar to riding a horse, placing both soles on the ground and elbows resting on the knees.

Now close both ears with the index fingers and concentrate on bindu, trying to catch any internal sound there.

You may hear the roaring of sea waves, a bell ringing, the sound of a flute or birds chirping.

Make your mind one-pointed and concentrate on the clearest sound.

It will become clearer and clearer.

You will hear a new sound emerging behind it.

Leave the first and follow the second sound.

When it becomes clear you may find another sound behind it, then leave the second sound and follow the third.

In this way you continue your practice.

Day by day you will hear and develop different sounds in your mind.

You have to go deeper and deeper.

In this way you will come across the subtle nadas pertaining to your annamaya, pranamaya, manomaya, vijnanamaya and anandamaya koshas.

The deeper the penetration of your awareness, the more subtle the manifestation of nada.

The first two koshas comprise your gross body, the third and fourth the subtle body and the fifth kosha is the causal body.

By the practice of nada yoga you can penetrate into the subtler layers of your own consciousness and experience the mysteries of your own innermost existence.

Important considerations

1. The diet of a nada yogi should be light and easily digestible.
2. Food causing hypertension and high blood pressure should be avoided.
3. Pranayama practice will help in the manifestation of nada.
4. If one hears any disturbing nada in the ordinary working state, stop the practice of nada yoga for some time.
5. Practise higher nada yoga under the guidance of a nada yogi.

Hari Om Tat Sat